JOHN UPDIKE
REMEMBERED

JOHN UPDIKE REMEMBERED

Friends, Family and Colleagues Reflect on the Writer and the Man

Edited by Jack A. De Bellis

McFarland & Company, Inc., Publishers
Jefferson, North Carolina

LIBRARY OF CONGRESS CATALOGUING-IN-PUBLICATION DATA

Names: De Bellis, Jack A., editor.
Title: John Updike remembered : friends, family and colleagues reflect on the writer and the man / edited by Jack A. De Bellis.
Description: Jefferson, North Carolina : McFarland & Company, Inc., Publishers, 2017. | Includes bibliographical references and index.
Identifiers: LCCN 2017042268 | ISBN 9781476667065 (softcover : acid free paper) ∞
Subjects: LCSH: Updike, John—Criticism and interpretation. | Novelists, American—20th century—Biography. | Updike, John—Appreciation.
Classification: LCC PS3571.P4 Z7435 2017 | DDC 813/.54—dc23
LC record available at https://lccn.loc.gov/2017042268

BRITISH LIBRARY CATALOGUING DATA ARE AVAILABLE

ISBN (print) 978-1-4766-6706-5
ISBN (ebook) 978-1-4766-3018-2

© 2017 Jack A. De Bellis. All rights reserved

No part of this book may be reproduced or transmitted in any form or by any means, electronic or mechanical, including photocopying or recording, or by any information storage and retrieval system, without permission in writing from the publisher.

Front cover image of John Updike © 2017 Photofest

Printed in the United States of America

McFarland & Company, Inc., Publishers
  Box 611, Jefferson, North Carolina 28640
    www.mcfarlandpub.com

For Patty, and for all those who were
touched by the work of John Updike.

"This great American presence—a presence that
is now an absence of the same dimensions."
—Martin Amis, "John Updike." *The Times* 24 Oct. 2009.

Table of Contents

Preface   1

Introduction   3

Part I—Shillington and Plowville, 1932–50: Interviews with Updike's Classmates from Kindergarten through High School   9

  1. Ann M. Weik (Cassar)   10
  2. Jim Trexler   15
  3. Gerry Potts   16
  4. The Rev. Dr. Robert I. Rhoads, Sr.   18
  5. Shirley F. Smith (Berger)   24
  6. Joan P. Venne (Youngerman)   28
  7. Jackie J. Hirneisen (Kendall)   33
  8. Richard W. Manderbach   35
  9. Barry R. Nelson   37
 10. Emerson W. Gundy   39
 11. Harlan L. Boyer   42
 12. The Rev. Victor Kroninger   48
 13. Jack E. Guerin   49
 14. Barbara L. Hartz (Behney)   53
 15. Tony VanLiew   56
 16. Joan Borner (Conrad)   61
 17. Nancy A. March (LeVan)   64
 18. Myrtle Council   66
 19. Benarda A. Palm   69

Part II—Harvard and New York, 1950–57: Writers Recall the Early Years — 73

   20. John Hubbard: "Updike at the Harvard *Lampoon*" — 74

   21. Austin Briggs: "John Updike's First Fan Letter" — 76

   22. Jeffrey Ludwig: "Roommates and Rivals: John Updike and Christopher Lasch at Harvard" — 79

   23. Mary P. Weatherall: "John at Harvard" — 83

Part III—Ipswich, Massachusetts, 1957–75: Looking Back and Moving Forward — 87

   24. Nicholas Delbanco: "R.I.P." — 88

   25. Catherine Hiller: "Groping for the Truth" — 91

Part IV—Beverly Farms: 1976–2009: Writers, Fans, Friends and Family Reflect and Reminisce — 95

   26. John Barth: "Remembering John Updike" — 97

   27. Stephen Bergman [Samuel Shem]: "My Dear Friend John Updike" — 98

   28. William H. Pritchard: "John Updike" — 101

   29. Jack De Bellis: "Updike in Sync" — 104

   30. Burl N. Corbett: "The Centaur's Son" — 107

   31. Jay Parini: "Updike and the Numinous" — 112

   32. Claude Clayton Smith: "Touching Genius: John Updike's Odd Obsession" — 114

   33. Nicholson Baker: From *U & I* — 118

   34. Nicholson Baker: "The Nod" — 120

   35. Lini S. Kadaba: "Who Was John Updike?—Ask His Driver" — 121

   36. Harry Charles Buck Niehoff: "John Updike: Gentleman" — 127

   37. Roxana Robinson: "John Updike" — 129

   38. James Schiff: "Updike as Correspondent, Literary Performer, and Composer of Sentences" — 131

   39. Stephanie Vanderslice: "My John Updike" — 137

   40. Terry Gross: "The Problem I Had in Common with John Updike" — 138

   41. James Plath: "Fringe Benefit" — 139

42. Adam Begley: "Updike's Dangerous Charm"	145
43. Lynne Davis: "My Night with John Updike"	147
44. Avis Grey Hewitt: "Knowing John Updike"	149
45. Donald J. Greiner: "Creating John Updike"	151
46. Robert M. Luscher: "John Updike: Short Fiction, Long Impression"	156
47. D. Quentin Miller: "All the Clever Young Men"	161
48. Richard A. Davison: "Brief Encounters with Updike (2002–2008)"	167
49. Robert Wilson: "Updike at Rest"	170
50. Joyce Carol Oates: "Remembering John Updike"	171
Part V—Family Remembrances	**173**
51. Elizabeth Updike Cobblah: "Remembering Daddy"	173
52. David H. Updike: "A Toast to the Visible World: Remembering John Updike"	175
53. Miranda Updike Freyleue: "Reflections on My Father"	177
54. Updike Family Panel in Reading, Pennsylvania	178
Appendix: A Chronology of John Updike's Life and Works	189
Chapter Notes	195
An Updike Bibliography	205
General Bibliography	207
Index	209

Acknowledgments

I wish to thank the following Updike classmates for allowing me to publish their interviews: Barbara L. Hartz (Behney), Shirley Berger, Harlan Boyer, Ann Weik Cassar, Joan Borner (Conrad), Myrtle Council, Jack Guerin, Emerson Gundy, Jackie Hirneisen Kendall, Victor Kroninger, Nancy March (LeVan), Dick Manderbach, Barry Nelson, Benarda A. Palm, Gerry Potts, Bobby Rhoads, James Trexler, D. Anthony VanLiew, and Joan Youngerman. Grateful thanks to Updike's first wife, Mary Weatherall, and their children, Liz Cobblah, David Updike, Miranda Updike, and Michael Updike for allowing me to use their "Updike Family Panel in Pennsylvania."

I gratefully acknowledge these publishers for allowing me permission to use the following:

Alvernia Magazine. Lini S. Kadaba. "Want to Know Updike? Ask His Driver." *Alvernia* Winter, 2010: 28–31.

American Scholar. Robert Wilson, "Updike at Rest." Vol. 78, No. 2, Spg. 2009. Copyright © by Robert Wilson. Permission of Robert Wilson.

The John Updike Review. Fall 2012: 79-[92]. I would like to thank editor Professor James Schiff, for permission to use "Updike Family Panel in Pennsylvania," originally given at the John Updike conference in October 2010, then published in the *Review.*

"The Nod" is reprinted with the permission of Simon & Schuster, Inc. from *The Way the World Works* by Nicholson Baker. Copyright © 2012 by Nicholson Baker. All rights reserved.

Pages 160–68 from *U & I* (New York: 1991) by Nicholson Baker are reprinted with the kind permission from Penguin Random House.

My deepest thanks to Updike scholars James Plath for devising this project and supporting it through several years; David Silcox who arranged the many meetings with Shillington High School classmates; Adam Begley who was instrumental in helping me contact Updike's Harvard friends; and Jackson Bryer for pointing me to McFarland.

Mary Weatherall generously answered my many queries and, with her husband Bob, kindly provided a lovely walking tour of Ipswich one cool fall day.

Thanks to Burl N. Corbett who wrote his remembrance under very challenging circumstances.

I am grateful to Nicholson Baker and Joyce Carol Oates for various accommodations.

Warm thanks to the Lehigh University computer technicians who gave me important assistance.

I am appreciative of Ann Cassar, Updike's classmate and my loyal and brilliant indexer.

And once again I am indebted to my wife, Patty, who has aided me with her eagle eye, her limitless cheer, and her abundant love.

Preface

> "On June 2, 1885, several men were in the Plowville Tavern ... when an approaching storm caused a team of horses tethered in the yard to grow restless. Two men went to the open door of the tavern to check on them. At that instant, a bolt of lightning struck, killing the men instantly and knocking another man to the floor. The man, temporarily stunned but otherwise unhurt, realized that he had been spared by a miracle and began seriously to re-think his life, consider his mortality, and decide to marry the long-waiting girlfriend."—Burl N. Corbett, "Lightning Bolt Led to Author Updike." *Country Shoppers News* 3 Feb. 1987: 35

The girlfriend, Katherine Kramer, became Mrs. John Hoyer and gave birth in 1903 to Linda Grace, who married Wesley Updike, and then on March 18, 1932, gave birth to her only child, John. John Hoyer recorded in his diary that day: "Partly cloudy and pretty cold. Wesley came at 6 o'clock in the morning. Wesley went to the hospital a few times. Male child born to Linda." What other modern author has had his life depend upon a clap of thunder and a flash of lightning?

When I helped to launch the John Updike Society five months after Updike's death in 2009, the Society's president, James Plath, suggested I compile a book of reminiscences. This struck me as an important tribute. I could bring to light many aspects of the multi-layered author.[1] This book would have been impossible during Updike's lifetime because his friends and commentators knew that Updike did not relish speaking about personal matters; they complied with his tacit wish. So, previously published remembrances are scarce.

Updike encouraged writers to address his work but discouraged them writing about his life.[2] He deemed my *John Updike Encyclopedia* "harmless,"[3] apparently meaning that it avoided making connections between his work and his life.[4] No doubt Updike bristled at such inquiry. This meant I would need to find persons to interview or who would be willing to write original essays. Since many of Updike's friends and acquaintances were near his own age, I acted quickly, and in the summer, 2009, I found and interviewed several of his high school classmates in Updike's hometown, Shillington, Pennsylvania.

Several of these interviews appear in Part I: Shillington and Plowville, 1932–1950. Meanwhile, I appealed to Updike's family, college friends, New York associates, writers, scholars, and casual acquaintances.

The enthusiastic support of Updike's first wife Mary and her children, Elizabeth, David, Michael, and Miranda, was matched by writers Austin Briggs and John Barth, scholars William Pritchard, interviewer Terry Gross, biographer Adam Begley, and budding writer Burl N. Corbett. As some of Updike's friends passed on during the seven years I worked on this project, I realized how lucky I had been to have connected with waning oral history. These fifty-plus contributors comprise a mosaic portrait of John Updike, with each tessera, so to speak, an individual remembrance, but all collectively contributing to an unforgettable portrait.

For example, William Pritchard sifts through his Updike correspondence to present Updike as charming yet avuncular. Nicholson Baker notes his astonishing memory. Ann Goldstein reveals his punctilious revising. James Plath describes how Updike played Cupid for him. Terry Gross notes Updike's sharing with her one of his own blemishes. In his remembrance Donald Greiner explores the last line of *The Afterlife*, "Nobody belongs to us, except in memory," to conclude that we each create our own Updike. *John Updike Remembered* may help you to create your Updike and counter the sense of loss at his passing by participating in the communal affection that lives in so many memories. These few remembrances create an extraordinary man whose prismatic life threw discrete rays of light upon so many.

Unless otherwise noted, comments in brackets are those of the editor. The remembrances are arranged chronologically but not necessarily by the date of publication.

Introduction

Allow me to introduce my subject with a few personal reflections. My first encounter with John Updike's work occurred in 1960. A friend gave me *Rabbit, Run* and I reviewed it for my radio program on KPFK, the Los Angeles PBS station. And while teaching at UCLA I used it in my modern fiction course. Later at Lehigh University, Updike became essential in virtually every course I taught from freshman composition to graduate seminars. As he published I included his work in my courses.

But, nearly twenty years would pass before I developed sufficient courage to write to him and ask permission to use several of his poems for a "Visual Poetry" exhibit I curated. Updike was the first to reply and with his approval. I was flattered that he continued corresponding with me, but I was astonished that he sent me his personal documents to help with my research. He even wrote introductions to two of my books.[1]

Like so many others, I was stunned at John Updike's death on January 27, 2009. It seemed intolerable that a man so visible and whose writing was so dependably a part of my life should suddenly vanish. I would no longer be able to read his stories, poems and reviews in *The New Yorker*, or anticipate new novels.[2] Nor would I chuckle at his distinctive wit as he read at nearby colleges or venues where he received awards. He would no longer be a televised presence in my home on C-Span or PBS. Letters and postcards laden with his pointed remarks couched in his patented charm would cease. Updike had been one of the most accessible writer-celebrities who achieved both popular and critical acclaim throughout a long and varied career. To me he seemed as reliable as the sunrise. I felt his passing to be a personal deprivation.

When Updike died he left behind at least sixty books, hundreds of drawings, dozens of recorded interviews, and crowds of people who had indelible memories of him, from elementary school classmates to academics to fellow writers and enthusiastic readers. Besides being dispossessed of his writing and his presence, persons interested in Updike had been deprived of firsthand accounts by those who touched his life.[3] Some of those individuals now provide recollections in *John Updike Remembered* that show Updike as a classmate, artist, friend, and family man.

To provide a context for these remembrances, allow me to review Updike's life. In retrospect, he seems to have progressed directly from his early years to his position as one of the world's leading writers. Updike was born in West Reading, Pennsylvania, March 18, 1932, to Linda Hoyer Updike and Wesley Updike. His mother was a disciplined writer who chronicled in two story collections her conviction that her son was quite remarkable.[4] Her perseverance and passion for writing demonstrated to him that he could become a writer too even as he licked the letters on his alphabet blocks. Wesley Updike taught mathematics at Shillington High School and he was remembered as a concerned and unconventional teacher. He cared about the welfare of his students.

Although Updike's family lived close to the poverty line, his parents provided "Chonny" with lessons in piano, tap dancing, and art. Growing up in a suburb of Reading during the Depression with loving, hard-working parents, Updike's early years were happy and stable. His first grade teachers predicted he would be successful at whatever he undertook. His friends called him a genius. At Shillington High School he mastered everything from science to literature, wrote voluminously, and became the senior class president. He graduated magna cum laude in 1950.

Yet he was no book worm. During classes he was an inventive prankster, and after school he led a lively "gang" that acknowledged him as a leader. Some were even willing to play dangerous games while he gave them thrilling car rides. Updike said that Shillington was his "being" his "idea," and he returned there time after time to re-absorb the texture of the town and the singularity of its people. Deep into his life he recorded the town and its people in his fiction, poetry and essays.[5]

Linda Updike surely stoked his talent into a hard flame, but as essential to Updike's literary maturity was his family's relocation in 1945 to the farm in Plowville, eleven miles from Shillington. On the farm Updike felt isolated from his friends, but ironically, the separation sharpened his focus on reading, writing, and drawing. By graduation in 1950, Updike had published in his school paper, *Chatterbox*, hundreds of cartoons and poems. He festooned nearly every page of his year book, *Hi-Life*, with art work, and he probably wrote most of the captions beneath photos of the graduates.[6] Despite his prophetic caption beneath his senior photo, "the sage of Plowville hopes to write for a living,"[7] he aspired to become a cartoonist for Walt Disney.[8]

This plan led him to choose Harvard, his first of six decisive decisions. He reasoned that at Harvard he could draw for the famous *Lampoon*. Not only did he work for it but he quickly became its most visible artist. With his left hand, so to speak, he continued to write light verse and fiction. Then came his second major decision. Between his sophomore and junior years, Updike married his Radcliff sweetheart, Mary Pennington. As an only child, Updike had envied large families; in less than six years they would have two boys and two girls.⁹ His third major decision quickly followed. While he was studying art in Oxford, pursuant to his career in drawing, he became a writer for *The New Yorker*. As his work had flooded *Chatterbox*, then the Harvard *Lampoon*, reportage, stories, and poems filled the pages of *The New Yorker*.¹⁰ However, in less than two years he realized that New York threatened his fledgling art. Quoting Hemingway he said that the New York writing community consisted of "tapeworms devouring tapeworms."¹¹ So he left New York and moved to Ipswich, Massachusetts, intending to write short fiction without New York's distractions. This was his fourth major decision in five years. Disappointing as his New York experience must have been, he learned something of immense importance: his career lay in writing, not drawing.

Updike had moved from Shillington to Plowville to Harvard to Oxford to New York and to Ipswich, and each move was daring and important for his maturation as a writer. He hadn't abandoned New York. Short flights from Boston to New York could put him in touch with his editors, William Shawn, William Maxwell, and Judith Jones. But the move to Ipswich was a serious gamble based on the assumption that he could support his wife and four children by publishing six short stories a year. He did far more, as the following sketch of his writing career and the accompanying chronology of his life will show.

In 1958 Updike gathered his *New Yorker* verse into *The Carpentered Hen*, the first of his sixty books. As a poet, Updike steadily turned from writing witty verse to personal and philosophical poetry in *Midpoint* (1969), where his familiarity with scientific subjects revealed an informed wonder at nature. He went on to publish several volumes of poetry, comprising light verse and serious poems side by side, even in his last work, *Endpoint*.

Though known to most readers only as a writer of fiction and poetry, Updike also published book reviews starting in 1960 when he told *New Yorker* editor William Shawn that he thought he could improve on the state of reviewing. His reviews sparkled with zest, erudition, and constructive criticism and were featured in his abundant books of essays and criticism. Those volumes also contain critical studies of major American writers like Herman Melville, travel pieces and personal remarks on poker and cars. As he had shown in his days as a *New Yorker* "casuals" writer, Updike was adept at any assignment. He alone of his contemporaries could arguably be called "America's Man of Letters," in William Pritchard's phrase.

Shrewdly realizing that an autobiographical coming-of-age novel would be too conventional for a first novel—he had discarded three such works—Updike's *Poorhouse Fair* focused on the problems of the elderly, using his grandfather as his central character. Then he wrote *Rabbit, Run*, arguably his best novel.¹²

Updike decided to make his first novels different from one another. He set *The Poorhouse Fair* in a future American dystopia. *Rabbit, Run* was written in the present tense. *The Centaur* sandwiched myth and surrealism. So Updike explored point of view, structure, myth, and history, seeking from the start to expand the novel's boundaries. This quest would always characterize his writing.

In his essay "The Dogwood Tree" (1962) Updike had identified three "great secret things": sex, religion, and art. His notorious novel *Couples* (1968) explored all three. Updike's hero Piet Hanema, a talented carpenter, seeks in sex a palliative for anxieties formerly assuaged by religion. *Couples* offered sex as a "new religion" for two reasons. Like religion, sex promises companionship in facing death; and sex permits you to experience transcendence. Piet also used an artistic perspective to frame a spiritual dimension to his life. Updike had earlier dramatized the difficulty of transcendence in *Rabbit, Run*, *The Centaur* and several stories.

Until his father died in 1972, Updike regularly took his wife and four children for summer vacations to the Plowville farm, of course visiting Shillington. The visits kept alive Updike's memories of the area he loved, honing his verisimilitude. At times he wrote his old friends to ask for precise details that would vivify his Pennsylvania memories. He used them in what he called his "Pennsylvania thing," particularly in his "Rabbit" novels (*Rabbit, Run; Rabbit Redux; Rabbit Is Rich; Rabbit at Rest*; and the sequel *Rabbit Remembered*.) Within thirteen years these books won him two Pulitzers and other prizes.

In 1975 Updike embarked on the first of a trilogy of "*Scarlet Letter*" novels, *A Month of Sundays* (1975), *Roger's Version* (1986), and *S.* (1990). They treat respectively art, religion, and sex. *A Month of Sundays* examined Minister Tom Marshfield (*The Scarlet Letter*'s the Rev. Arthur Dimmesdale) who is forcibly rusticated for seducing the women he counsels. By writing a mandatory journal and a sermon every Sunday, Marshfield eventually restores himself to love and faith. *Roger's Version* scrutinized a theologian, Roger Lambert (*The Scarlet Letter*'s Roger Chillingworth) who ostensibly supports a computer virtuoso, Dale Kohler (*The Scarlet Letter*'s Dimmesdale), who intends to force God to reveal Himself through the computer. In *S.*, Sarah Worth (*The Scarlet Letter*'s, Hester Prynne), seeks spirituality at an ashram but discovers her guru is a fake. The end of each novel shows that the search for transcendence is problematic.

Updike wished to explore the knotty problem of evil that religion must confront; he undertook to face the issue directly by using witches in two novels, *The Witches of Eastwick* (1984) and *The Widows of Eastwick* (2008). The former novel shows how empowering women can lead to tragedy. Alexandra Spofford, Sukie Rougemont, and Jane Smart are modern women who use their powers to advance their careers as sculptor, writer, and cellist. Though they can create storms and seduce men, their attraction to the devilish Darryl Van Horne causes a rival to die of cancer. For *The Witches of Eastwick* and other explorations of evil, Updike was given the Edmund Campion award by the Jesuit magazine *America*.

By 1989 Updike had become, with Saul Bellow, Norman Mailer, Joyce Carol Oates, Philip Roth, and Kurt Vonnegut one of the most prominent American writers, but unlike them Updike refused prospective biographers. To thwart them, he produced six memoirs and issued them as *Self-Consciousness*. It had been germinating since Updike published "A Soft Spring Night in Shillington" (*The New Yorker*, 1984). Other memoirs followed: "At War with My Skin" (1985), "Getting the Words Out" (1986). For the book Updike added: "A Letter to My Grandsons," "On Not Being a Dove," and "On Being a Self Forever." These reminiscences record Updike's physical ailments (bad teeth, stuttering, asthma, and psoriasis), being bullied, and his support of President Johnson and the Viet Nam War. He researched his family in "A Letter to My Grandsons" dedicated to his two inter-racial grandchildren.[13]

The many-faceted concerns of Updike's writing reveal an author who explored worlds beyond his comfort zone and who tested the waters of innovative fictional techniques. Consider his comical view of his imaginary third-world country Kush in *The Coup* (1968), or the adventures of writer Henry Bech (*Bech: A Book*, 1970, *Bech Is Back*, 1982, and *Bech at Bay*, 1998.) These show the playful side of Updike not always apparent in his realistic fiction. Updike was once asked if he considered himself a post-modernist. He replied, "In which work?" In fact, he seems to have undertaken *Memories of the Ford Administration* (1992) in order to see what could be done with post-modern devices, such as corrupt texts, an absent presence, and intertextuality. In *Roger's Version* he explored the twilight region between fantasy and realism while considering the possibilities of literary pornography. In addition, Updike wrote *Gertrude and Claudius* (2000), a prequel to *Hamlet*, modeled on three different texts, and produced an epistolary novel, *S*. Updike tried other audacious paths, blending the Tristan and Isolde legends to magic realism in *Brazil* (1984). And he produced a *Bildungsroman*[14] (*In the Beauty of the Lilies*, 1996) and a thriller (*Terrorist* 2006). He capped his career with a kind of wicked travel book (*The Widows of Eastwick*, 2008). At his death Updike was working on "The Last Epistle," a novel about St. Paul. Updike relished the opportunities to expand the novel's potential.

Earlier we noted that Updike made six major decisions in his life. The fifth and most painful decision came in the mid–1970s, when he divorced his wife of twenty-three years, remarried, and moved to a bastion in Beverly Farms. Updike chronicled the dissolution and finish to his marriage in several stories (*Too Far to Go,* 1979). Yet, unlike the rowdy Norman Mailer, the scene-maker

John Cheever, or the unstable John Foster Wallace, Updike had led a very stable life. While faithfully writing at least three pages a day every day, he played poker every Wednesday night for forty years, and golfed devotedly even in winter.

He always enjoyed his role as a roving literary luminary, lecturing at colleges and libraries, chatting at book signings, giving readings around the country and around the world. Those who saw and heard him found Updike charming, witty, and captivating as well as supremely articulate. He gave hundreds of interviews, blurbed books of countless authors, and cheerfully signed hundreds of his books at readings or by mail.

Like Henry James he found time to write thousands of cards and letters, usually returning his messages the same day they were received. Updike travelled throughout Africa, Australia, South America, United Kingdom, Europe, the Middle East, and the USSR. He has been translated into two dozen languages, from Chinese to Serbo-Croatian. He once remarked that his ideal reader was a boy in a library in "a vague spot a little to the east of Kansas."[15] Now that reader is everywhere in the world.

Updike's legacy is undoubtedly the Rabbit Angstrom tetralogy with the short novel *Rabbit Remembered*. He spent forty years producing this study of an average American's life, and he universalized it through a lyric style, the adoption of the free indirect point of view, and a precise and unsentimentalized sense of place. With the "Rabbit" saga, Updike blended traditional and unconventional forms in order to, as he said, "give the mundane its radiant due." Who could be more mundane than an ex-athlete, and who more radiant in Updike's vision of him? No wonder that Rabbit Angstrom is thought to be the equal to Huckleberry Finn and Holden Caulfield. Through Harry "Rabbit" Angstrom, Updike revealed what Randall Jarrell called, praising Whitman, "the tears of things and the joy of things, and of the reality beneath either tears or joy."[16]

PART I: SHILLINGTON AND PLOWVILLE, 1932–50

Interviews with Updike's Classmates from Kindergarten through High School

In 1926, when Linda Grace Hoyer married AT&T lineman Wesley Updike, the newly-weds came to live with her parents, John and Katherine Hoyer, in Shillington. Linda Updike's World War II defense work made it possible for her to spear-head an effort to re-purchase the family farm in Plowville where she had been born. So, on Halloween, 1945, the Updikes and Hoyers moved to Plowville. Though Updike, like his father, never enjoyed farm life and disliked the severed connection to Shillington where his friends lived, the move had its bright side. The relocation was fortunate and formative for Updike, for now he spent more time reading, writing and drawing,[1] especially in the summer. As a result Updike published over 300 of his works in *Chatterbox*, the school newspaper. During his senior year he is said to have written the captions for the seniors in the yearbook, *Hi-Life*.[2]

Though he lived in Shillington only until he was thirteen, Updike later came to describe it as the locus of his "being," and he returned often not only to visit family and friends but to re-energize what he called his "idea."[3] Since Updike asserted that Plowville was his talent's "incubator," Shillington, then, must have been his place of gestation. In Shillington he read Big Little Books; in Plowville he read T. S. Eliot, James Joyce and other writers in preparation for Harvard. In Shillington he created unassuming drawings; in Plowville he wrote prose and poetry. In Shillington he ogled the Philadelphia *Evening Bulletin*'s cartoons; in Plowville *The New Yorker*'s band of artists became his mentors. Companions in Shillington became lasting friends in Plowville and models for his writing. Throughout his life Updike plumbed the depths of those he declared on his deathbed were

> a sufficiency of human types: beauty, bully, hanger-on, natural,

twin, and fatso—all a writer needs,
all there in Shillington....[4]

The following interviews reveal how Updike's friends could retrieve images long dormant and turn memories into tributes. If for Updike they were all a writer needed to kindle the flame of his creativity, Updike was sufficient for them to fan the coals of memory.

1. Ann M. Weik (Cassar)

Ann M. Weik (Cassar). Amulet 3, 4; Band 2, 3, 4; Chatterbox 1, 2, Associate Editor 3, Chief Editor 4; Class Play 3; Orchestra 1, 2, 3, 4; Torch 1, 2; Y-Teens 2, 3, 4. The only letters lower than A on Ann's report card are those in her name ... explosions in chemistry lab.... We don't know whether to call this versatile miss a female Faraday, a petite Piatigorsky, or a small-town Swope."—Shillington High School Year Book, *Hi-Life*

Ann Cassar (born 1932) was a co-valedictorian with John Updike at the 1950 Shillington High School commencement. She graduated from Albright College[5] magna cum laude in 1954 majoring in chemistry, minoring in math. She was immediately employed by Atlas Powder Co. (now Astra-Zeneca), in Wilmington, Delaware. After several years at the technical library indexing lab reports and answering reference questions, she started free-lance writing of indexes for major publishers in the U.S. and India. This work continues to the present day. This interview was conducted in the summer of 2009.

Ann, what can you tell me about Updike's maternal grandparents?

I don't clearly remember Mr. Hoyer. Mrs. Hoyer was quiet, at least around us [kids]. She was probably responsible for the backyard garden at the Philadelphia Avenue house and the vegetables and fruits grown on the Plowville property. They had plenty of yard space compared with our small yard. Once, when our family was visiting at the Shillington house, someone served cherry brandy to the adults. Perhaps it was homemade?

The large strawberry patch on the Plowville farm was Linda's pride and joy. She was well known for the delicious fresh berries and sold them for many years. My parents always visited during strawberry season and bought a few quarts. My cousin, Warren Ritter (my father's sister's son), remembers going there to pick berries when he was 8 years old... Linda mentioned that this was "pea month." I interpreted that to mean that they ate only peas for a whole month. They were anticipating cabbage month later. As delicious as homegrown peas are, I was concerned that they were so poor with such an unbalanced diet. As a gardener myself I now understand that we overindulge in the seasonal vegetables when they are available, but don't ignore the meat and potatoes.

Tell me about John's parents.
    Linda Updike was a delightful woman, and she and my mother got along very well together. Both appreciated literature and languages. Our family, being on the order of 5 ft. tall, perceived the Updikes, including Linda as being quite tall. My mother told me one time that Linda was distressed about John's relationship with an older Japanese woman in New York City after his divorce from Mary. Wonder who that was/is? My parents and the Updikes went places together many times as a foursome. My father and Wesley shared an interest in fishing and enjoyed each other's humor. They traveled together to Philadelphia to the University of Pennsylvania on Saturdays to take graduate courses; my father's involved school administration subjects. Don't know what Wesley studied.

People have told me much about Wesley Updike. What do you recall of John's father?
    Wesley Updike was our math teacher for 7th and 8th grades. I wonder if he also taught some of the math for the older business and shop students. This was arithmetic. We had algebra in 9th and 10th grades, with plane geometry in 11th. In 12th grade there was a half-year of trigonometry and a half-year of solid geometry. Miss Margaret Stamm taught algebra, and Mr. Freed the 11th and 12th grade maths. Miss Stamm's parents, brother and sister, lived on the other side of Philadelphia Avenue, a bit beyond the Updikes. It was then the last house in civilization on that street.
    The school students from K through 8 were from the town of Shillington. There were two classes in each grade, probably 25 to 30 [students] in each. They were formed according to academic ability, the better students in the A section and the less able in the B section. The elementary school, still standing on Lancaster Avenue but remodeled into offices, had kindergarten in the basement (it had windows, however) with the lavatories, grades 1 through 3 on the first floor, and grades 4 through 6 on the second floor. Mr. Dickinson was a 6th grade teacher as well as the principal. He was the only male teacher in the elementary school, and we were somewhat intimidated by him. Allen Richards, unfortunately known as Junior Richards, was a double teacher's brat because his mother Ruth taught the 5th grade and handled the chorus in the elementary school, while Allen's father, also Allen, taught social studies in the high school and was a sports coach. In the high school grades 9 through 12 also included students from the outlying countryside, such as Adamstown, Mohnton, Cumru Township, and Brecknock Township.

Wesley [Updike] had some sayings that have remained with me all these years. There were the "21 Forms of Escapism," which were written on the blackboard, usually not in entirety, but those appropriate for the current situation. They were mostly behavioral sins. He said many times that there's good in EVERYONE, even Charlie McComsey. Charlie was kept back a year, and we inherited him from the previous class; he was a big boy, liked the girls, and was not well behaved. In high school he was on Wes's swim team. Last year my sister sent me Charlie's obituary, which proved Wes was right; [Charlie had] many years of success in the educational field, including Supervising Principal of a large district, exemplary family, deacon of his Lutheran, I think, church, and community volunteerism. I personally have applied Wes's faith in his fellow humans to my own life. It works. One way Mr. Updike dealt with student misbehavior was to open the window, even in dead of winter, stick his head out, and close the window on his neck. Just remained there for a while. School windows in those days were huge, double-hung, and you could actually open them. The radiators were always churning out heat, and no one worried about saving energy. I'm sure there were more wise sayings, but at the time who would think to store them in memory for your [*John Updike Remembered*] project? We learned lots of math during these classes, obviously, because we had a good foundation for subsequent courses. I was a math minor in college.

Please describe John. What was he like physically?

Again, the perception of tall comes to mind when describing the physical features of an Updike. Also, not exactly handsome in the popular notion, because of the craggy features. Perhaps John resembled his father more than his mother, but you can also see maternal influences in his appearance. Emotionally, I would say, thoughtful, quiet, and studious, in the early years. More gregarious in the teen years and afterwards. Intellectually it was obvious from the beginning that John was unusual. My mother said more than once, "Johnny will be either a master criminal, or be an outstanding success in some other field."

Was Updike in any of your classes?

According to the yearbook [*Hi-Life*], he was on the debating team, not active in sports [but was active in] Honor Society, yearbook staff, and *Chatterbox*. (I just looked at the *Chatterbox* picture and saw my sister, Jean, in the last row on the right; she's also on the Junior High orchestra playing viola in the front row center).

You will note that John is not involved in any musical organizations. In 1st grade the traveling music teacher came to our room and divided children into several categories according to her evaluation of their singing voices. Bluebirds and robins were the good guys; John was a crow, also Barbara Hartz who had a lower voice. If that doesn't discourage one from future musical endeavors, I don't know what does. I wonder if John and Mozart[6] have met as yet. Our town had a piano teacher, Miss Wilma Yoder, who lived on Philadelphia Avenue across the street from the Updike's before moving, in a few years, to March Street. John took piano for a year or so until it was decided by mutual consent there was no hope for progress in this area of the arts. In the beginning Miss Yoder would walk to the student's house for a lesson, which was $1. She was a delightful person, and I studied with her from the 3rd grade through 12th. John's reading as a child is well documented. I remember one instance when four of us gathered at Fred Muth's[7] house (John, Larry Essick, and I) to look at the collection of Big Little Books and comics. They had small pages; perhaps 3 inches square, but maybe 2 inches thick. Fred and John remained very close over the years. Fred died a few years ago.

Would you characterize your friendship with Updike as close?
Close to John? Probably not very close compared with his senior high friends. As I explained earlier, my social life was closely supervised and involved music and studies, not running with the crowd. Certainly not allowed to go with any student drivers (my father also taught driving at one point). However, after I got involved in indexing, and we talked at the class reunions, we had much more in common. He understood the value of indexes, being a frequent user of them in his research. His memory was fantastic, both for personal happenings and factual details. Five or 10 years between reunions, and he would remember what we talked about before.

What was the earliest publication of Updike's that you read?
There was an elementary school newspaper, *The Little Shilling*, of which I was editor in 6th grade, and he also wrote for it.

Did you read John's novels, poetry, reviews?
I feel terrible. I haven't read many of the novels. *The Centaur, The Poorhouse Fair*, and *Of the Farm* were delightful because I was reading about Wesley Updike, the poorhouse, which we could walk to and watch the farming operations, and the farm, which was familiar. I look at most of his writing, especially these three books, for familiar places and people and probably miss some of the literary depth of it. I like *The Witches of Eastwick* and identified with Jane playing the cello. When *Couples* came out, it had negative publicity in the Pennsylvania Dutch community about the great amount of sex in it. This is embarrassing to us on the surface, although most families had no trouble producing 12 children with one mother back in the early days. Most of all, I like the short stories. John's word selection, everyone knows, is unparalleled, and you want to appreciate every phrase and sentence. So it's slow

reading. You feel guilty not holding up each bit for admiration. Somehow I feel intellectually inadequate to partake of such perfection. The short stories are a peek into John's life as a young person, at college, in England, and as a family man. I started the Rabbits but didn't like the character, so didn't want to spend time with this person. John's death will prompt me and many others to continue to investigate further reading ventures.

Did you correspond with Updike or see him later?

Only when he returned for reunions. And a few postcards exchanged. When I informed him that my mother had died (can it be twenty-four years already?), he mailed me a copy of *A Soft Spring* [*Night*] *in Shillington,* which was so appropriate for the situation.

How did Updike respond to other people?

John seemed to carry on his father's appreciation for people of all kinds. No snobbishness or uppity attitude there. No celebrity persona. Interest in people's lives. Not talking about himself. Time to talk to everyone individually at class reunions. Of course, when people are treated like this, they can't help but enjoy the interaction. Can't say anyone disliked him.

Can you describe how he felt about his classmates?

He was elected president of our class for life.... It was obvious that he cared for our group all these years. Never missed a get-together. You probably know why our class has such weird class colors: Aqua and white. It was a reaction to the common ordinary blue and white, red and gray, etc. A bit of rebellion toward the school advisors and administration. They couldn't really say much. As a result, Joan [Venne] Youngerman has had to search out party favors and prizes in these colors for all the reunions. Not always easy to locate because the rest of the world was still on the primary color scheme. At the first reunion she brought her whole supply of aqua kitchen gadgets, shampoo, lotion, you name it, stored [them] in her cellar and passed the items around to those present.

Did you ever meet Updike's wives?

I never met Mary Pennington. Only heard third-handed from my mother who learned from Linda that she was mighty busy marching in protests. Martha has attended all the reunions in later years. She is charming, pleasant, interested in what people have to say. Being a book editor, [she] also appreciated indexes, and is particularly interested in medical projects I do. Seems like a good pick.... Never met any of the children, but delighted to read in recent news articles that they are all artistic in their own ways. It must be impossible to follow in such footsteps, so variations of the theme are a good idea for the second generation.

2. Jim Trexler

> James M. Trexler. "Band 1, 2, 3, 4; Class Play 3, 4; Homeroom President 1; Orchestra 1, 2, 3, 4; Swimming 1, 2, 3, 4. *The Fords really roll when Jim's driving dialect jokes ... just naturally full of mischief ... 'Tex' suited Trex to a T ... The Big Boy and his tuba gave the band an extra something."* —Shillington High School Year Book, *Hi-Life*

Jim Trexler (born 1932) graduated from Shillington High School in Updike's class, and then went to Colorado to work as a truck driver, loading railcars. Returning to Shillington in December 1951, he enlisted in the Air Force and spent three years in London, accumulating 43 credits at the University of Maryland Overseas Program. Afterwards, he studied at Cambridge University, then at Albright College in Reading. James Trexler was the sales manager for thirty-five years of Heizmann Tool Makers, later Columbian Cutlery, Inc. This interview was conducted on June 11, 2009.

When did you first meet Updike?

It was kindergarten. His mother invited me [to their home] ... on two occasions so he would have a playmate during the summer.

So you played roofball too?

Yes, and during the war we saved paper and tin cans. I became a Four Star General, because I had a paper route and customers would save papers and cans for me.

What was he like in high school?

He did cartoons for *Chatterbox*. The guy with the long chin in one cartoon is me I am sure.

I see you were on the swim team, so you must have had Updike's dad as a coach.

Well, that's an interesting story. Wes Updike hated the farm and would do anything not to go back to the farm. One day he said he would sponsor a swim team if we wanted one, and we swam in the Reading pool, and that kept him away from the farm.

Did you ever get out to the farm?

They had parties for kids, sometimes as many as 15, 20, 25.

Did you read John's books?

I have read all of them, except for *Buchanan Dying*. But the early ones, I can sit and relate and know that this is so and so and this is so and so and that's fun reading. He remembered all of that. His descriptive powers are absolutely beyond imagination.

Did he mention anyone you know?
I'm in page 157 of *Five Boyhoods*, so this guy called me "page 157." In *Self-Consciousness* he said that I told him that the sailors would hang the Japs by their heels down behind the ship with their heads going into the propellers. It was my 15 minutes of fame. Another time he got lost trying to find the Crab Barn where we had our reunion, so I got him to follow me.

What were the reunions like?
I was the MC. We'd have a couple of drinks and a lot of dirty jokes that offended some of the girls. I was a pretty good joke teller. With me, Eddie Pienta and Charlie McComsey, it was kind of like a three way diatribe going on there. I could tell Pennsylvania Dutch jokes. John wrote me that he liked them. When he stood in front of the group, he'd crack his hands [knuckles] the whole time.

John wrote some pretty funny light verse.
I know.

Did you know Linda Updike?
She was a disappointed authorist, if that's a proper term. She went to Ursinus with one of my aunts. I knew her from a little kid. I couldn't have been more than five or six. She was refined.

Would he have gotten his refinement from her?
He could be as refined as anybody, or as raucous. He was really a regular guy except he was god-damned smart. Everything came easy to him. Everybody liked him.

3. Gerry Potts

Gerry Potts (born 1930) graduated from Shillington High School in 1948, then attended Albright College. Afterward he did a stint in the army during the Korean War. When Shillington High School was being converted into Governor Mifflin High, Gerry Potts rescued chalk and the chalk trough, from the homeroom of Wesley Updike. Gerry Potts has been a member of Shillington Borough Council and the Governor Mifflin School Board for twenty-four years. He passed on in 2016. This interview was conducted on June 7, 2009.

3. Gerry Potts

So, Gerry, you were in the class of '48, two years ahead of John?
  Yup.

Where did you live in relation to John Updike?
  I lived at 41 Philip Avenue; right across the street was Franklin Street. Up Franklin in the first block was the ice house Flikinger's, and my grandfather used to run it. We'd watch him saw the ice. I helped him; carried a fifty pound piece of ice into somebody's refrigerator. The gutter water was cold and we'd put our feet in it.

What were some typical things you and John did together?
  We used to go to the playground, maybe a block or two from his house, and we were always down there playing box hockey or roofball.

Box hockey?
  Well, it's a box where there's a ball and then you hit it and you gotta go through the hole at each end and you put the ball at the top and then you, "one, two three" and you hit it. You try to gain an advantage, so there's a box at one side and a box on the other. And the swings were there. Every morning we had to say the Pledge of Allegiance to the Flag.

There were a lot of girls on the block. Were they part of your gang?
  Sort of. One day John came down because he liked our place and he liked my younger sister. Well, one day she's standing in the kitchen naked and my mom is washing her off. John looked in the door and saw her.

So he was about nine or ten at the time.
  Yeah. I used to call him Uppy, maybe I was the only one.

Later on he was interested in Peggy Lutz. Any reason they didn't hit it off?
  He was, in comparison to her, weird, kinda. But she was lovely, outgoing and everybody loved her. And I guess he didn't want to get that carried away.

Did John change after he moved to the farm in Plowville?
  I guess a little smarter, little wiser.

How did he get to be class president?
  I guess because of all his connections, putting articles in *Chatterbox*. People knew who he was, he sort of said, "Here I am."

Did you read many of his books?
  Yeah, a great deal of them, maybe half of them. I enjoyed them, really. I always read them a little slower, so I could totally comprehend what exactly he is trying to tell us. He would send me autographed books. I have tons of cards and letters from him.

What was he like when he returned to the area for reunions or talks?
  We got him to come back to Governor Mifflin High School, the old

Shillington High that was torn down. I sat in that room, he's standing at the podium, and I almost was thinking that he had his shoes off. He was in his stocking feet.

Do you know that much of his work is now taught in colleges.
   Why not? I remember for my class reunion, I put together a 20 line poem. I sent him a copy and John wrote back and said, "Oh, man, that was fantastic." From Updike? I used to tell him, you know the only reason why you are famous is because you hung out with me. He didn't quite agree.

Did anyone in Shillington ever think of putting up a plaque for Updike?
   I know, when you get to be that damn famous. It's kind of a no-brainer.

Did you and John ever talk about basketball?
   Yeah, at the end of my grandmother's yard at 112 Philadelphia Ave. we had a backboard up there, and we'd sit and talk about basketball all the time.

Would that have been the place where the kids are playing basketball at the start of the movie Rabbit, Run?
   Probably. But his mother just didn't want him to have any parts of it at all.

What was his dad, Wesley Updike, like?
   In his math class he'd threaten to jump out the window if he got a stupid answer. And we're on the second floor of the high school. When they were gonna tear Shillington high School down, I snuck into the building, got into Wesley's room, and I tore one of the chalk troughs off the wall and hauled it home. I cut a piece, sanded it down, refinished it, and then I sent it to John.
   His father was one of the best teachers I ever had. When you got done at the end of the year you knew what the hell was going on, and why you were there.

Sounds like you liked the father as much as you liked John.
   I am really thrilled that I grew up with him.

4. The Rev. Dr. Robert I. Rhoads, Sr.

The Rev. Robert Rhoads (born 1932) was a classmate and roofball buddy of Updike's from the lower grades to their graduation in 1950. He became a minister, and after serving as assistant Pastor, he succeeded his father as Pastor at Immanuel United Church of Christ, Shillington, 1969. He was an army chaplain in Colorado and a hospital chaplain in Philadelphia. The Reverend Rhoads retired in 1995. This interview was conducted in the summer of 2009.

What do you recall about Updike in the lower grades?
   Well, when we were kids we played a lot of roofball. Here's a picture. I am about to hit the ball. There is John. Ok. There I am again at the foot of the line. That's John. Gerry Potts was there too.

Who took the pictures?
   Thelma Kutch Lewis[8] took the pictures. I have all the letters from her to me. She showed me a letter from John where he said, "I'm sorry Bobby Rhoads needs a walker." ... My mother for some reason always sent John a Christmas card or whatever. She was at Phoebe Berks [in assisted living] and for many years he would write her. I'd go up and she'd say I got another card. I'd say where it is and she'd say I threw it away, and I'd say Mom, how could you do that? His signatures! Those letters are worth money. Here's a good one to her from John, "I'm glad you are aiming for 100. Don't stop there. Best wishes, John Updike." He always sent cards with rabbits on them.

Those rabbit cards, I understand, were his mother's, and he took them after she died.
   Did you ever know where Rabbit's name came from?

I've heard that there was a fellow named Richard Heister [pronounced "Heester."] Because he was on the track team they called him "Rabbit." Is that right?
   Exactly right. No one ever said anything, and John picked him because he was the "Hiester Bunny." Did you know that? Heister was Rabbit Angstrom, not Bob Arndt[9] who was a clarinet player in the band with me, a year ahead of me. Never smoked or drank, that's why it couldn't be Gerry Potts.

Did you know Bob Arndt very well.
   He played football. He was a very ordinary guy. He was fun. Just a good guy. I had nothing but good feelings for him. Here's another card from John. I signed something Yogi Bobbie, and he said, "You preferred Bobbie to booby"—that was John. Here's more: "Your parents couldn't have been sweeter at that unexpected encounter. I actually was delighted to discover your dad was still alive. Shillington people I discovered long ago—and keep discovering—are pretty good sports. I had some more nostalgic experiences. Mary Ann [Stanley] Moyer helped me walk through the old house in Shillington. First [time] I'd been inside since we left it, Halloween night, 1945. Barry Nelson led Mary Ann and me through Shillington High School, which was about to be torn down. The creak of the wood was familiar and the lockers and the tall windows. I'll send your parents a copy of the book."

You know which one?

I think that must have been *Self-Consciousness*. So that was 1986, then. In '89 he gave me a copy of *Self-Consciousness*. In the book he talks about going up the hill to the cemetery and his mother was "carrying him in her womb or in her arms." Nobody knew that he was thinking of fictionalizing people in *Self-Consciousness*. He does mention some people by name like Jim Trexler. Here's another one from John: "My mother used to tap out her short stories and send them off to the *Saturday Evening Post*. That was a long time ago." ... He said, "Of my baptism I have no memory. Pappy [Clint] Shilling[10] would wear all his medals and walk down the street. Clint would walk his big dog down Phila. Ave. They were making room at Mifflin center and digging out to make grounds there and he was laughing because the guy in the tractor was not let's say our skin color. And he was laughing because that was where the pauper's burial ground was, right there at the end of Phila. Avenue. He knew they were going to dig up some bodies, probably blacks. It was across from the Poorhouse, where a parking lot is now. Well, he was a character, Clint Shilling."

The town is Plowville, but they call it Plow Church. Why is that?

That's a good question. I think Plow is the name of the family. That's where the funerals were. I was at both funerals of his parents and John was in the first row. Don't know who the minister was and he was so nervous with John Updike in the front row that he forgot the creed. This poor guy. I did not know that John wanted his ashes spread there.

That was David and Liz's idea. He was constantly reviving and renewing his experiences. It's wonderful.

He'd make mistakes on his postcards. March 13, 1964: "Dear Bobby, Impertinent greeting to a clergyman. I can't see the type, but it means a great deal to hear an old Stone [Shillington?] voice. I did read the review in the church mag and it was better and more informed than secular magazines. Now I am at the UCC but at heart I'm a Lutheran, very best regards."

Drawing of himself.

Not initialed but something he would do.... I remember most of all that as you know he stammered and I knew that he stuttered and years later he was interviewed and I thought oh, my gosh, he had worked it out, he said how hard it was since he was always thinking ahead of his words. It was so hard hearing him talk.... John was just a wonderful guy to know, his smile, his laugh, no matter what you said to him. Last time I saw him he was walking down Lancaster street and he said, "Wow Bobby, what a car." It was just an old Taurus, but that's John always complimenting first. "There's a German crew here, and maybe you can help me out. Isn't there a German restaurant around here?" I said, John, go back to the light, one more block, first left and down the road, The Hoffenstock ... my last conversation. Always smiling.

So there was nobody who would bully or disrespect him?
No, I really would have no knowledge of anyone bullying him. More stories of his father. Once the football coach said to me, "Go play with the girls" and other demeaning things and at the time it would hurt me terribly. Mr. Updike was compensating for what coach was doing. I had the last word. I buried him. Prayer can be very ironic.

Go play with the worms! He and his father got along very well.
He did not like calling his father Uppy. John was very upset that they wouldn't respect him.

The faculty didn't respect him?
I think they did. It was the kids.

The Centaur *shows Wesley had problems with Principal C. J. Hemmig.*[11] *Was this the case?*
The bad guy was C.J. He was always over at the Overpark club. C.J. would go over there and play cards. Harry Stevens the bartender told me C.J. would cheat at cards and Wes or someone knew this and John's whole book was against him. *The Centaur* is my favorite of all his books.

It's so funny and so poignant... Who did John date?
A very bright girl, Nancy Wolf. Her father was my chaplain at Camp David, New Rochelle, New York. I was married and lived at West Lawn, first year in chaplaincy. I was invited by the head chaplain and he was Major Wolf at the time and he asked, "Where you from?" "Shillington," I said. "So am I!" ...

What was John's mother like?
Last time I saw Linda was at the Windmill restaurant, and she was in the lot when I pulled in and she said, "Oh, my, the food is still plentiful." Now who but Linda would use a word like "plentiful?" She was in many ways scholarly, etc., above the people in town, but not I guess overly welcoming ... but she and my mother were very good friends because my mother was a teacher and always spoke to her with respect. Not too many people knew her, but those two got along very well. We visited John and Mary in Ipswich. My uncle Ed wanted to know about him. My parents would go to visit and when it was nap time Updike went to bed and called down, "Must I sleep in this big bed by myself?" Someone visited him and the mail came and he went over and started to read his mail.

What classes did John take?
   Frau Lewis during the war taught German, though most schools did away with it. She taught the army method, putting a record on and we had to repeat it. "Where is the streetcar stop?" "Across the street on the corner."

Which Updike books did you read?
   Terrorist. I did not like that. You could see what was coming.

What were your favorites?
   Self-Consciousness.

Any of the "Rabbit" books?
   I was so sorry he killed him. I knew where Rabbit was going. I just knew those places.

Month of Sundays?
   Oh yes, I read that in Germany when we were on a tour. That was very, very interesting. The theology. He had to write that sermon. Got a kick out of that.

John even mentions his father-in-law's Unitarian views. How do you account for his becoming an Episcopalian?
   His wife maybe. Congregationalist would be more John. Might have heard some darn good sermons, scholarly. Probably why he would choose that.

He wrote some sermons for St. John's.
   What a mind, unbelievable. Loved his final chapter in *My Father's Tears*. I was reading this morning about Peggy [Lutz]. John loved her. Gave up on her because she chose a guy in the Navy named Jady Roberts.[12]

Did John ever date her?
   I think he tried. Peggy was a very nice girl.

John tells about Peggy playfully slapping other boys, so to catch her eye he grabbed her hair, and she really slapped him.
   I don't know what Peggy thought of John. She was a pretty girl. I'm sure she liked him. All the classmates did…

He had that gift so early.
   And his sense of humor too. "Pigeon Feathers" was my favorite. He was David. God who made the pigeon feathers surely will take care of me. I used it in sermons several times. So many of my friends never read a book by John. I would say about *The Centaur*, you got to read this. They'd say, "Who reads that? I don't read such stuff."

Do you think Shillington High School was a place where they would seek out books?

Well, Miss Showalter was one of the greatest influences of my life. She was wonderful. Introduced me to all the great writers. She'd say, "Robert you know what you read," [Quotes the "Tomorrow" soliloquy from Shakespeare's *Macbeth*] "Now why did you like that?" "I don't know. It all fits together." "You go on with this. Don't ever stop." She was a big influence on John too and Miss Estelle Pennypacker[13] too.

What about his friends. Gerry Potts, for instance?

Gerry had an influence on the Rabbit books in many ways. He was a good athlete and John always wanted to be an athlete. He had an appreciation for that.

But what about those nefarious things in Rabbit, Run. *Do you think they were from John's life too?*

No, nothing like John. They had a carnival next to his house off 2nd Street. My parents never wanted me to go there. Skip McCoy and I and John played the wheel. He had .50 and he kept putting it down and losing. The wheel would stop and John didn't make it, and the guy that was in charge gave him his money back and said, "Don't you ever come here again!" He was helping John to form a better character.

This was during the war and Updike's family was poor, so where did he get the money?

I think from his grandfather. Boy, he wanted to play that wheel and the guy chewed him out. Had to be before the war.

How did the war affect Shillington?

We turned in papers, bottles.... My father later on was the first on Civil Defense. I would walk around 2nd street and by the Porgy. On Philadelphia Avenue, the pigpen and the "porkers" were burned when in 1938 the poorhouse burned and my father showed me from the front room. The horses and cows were buried right in the woods. "Porgy" because of the pig sty on Phil Avenue.

John ever go to the poorhouse fair?

Sure he did. He was attracted to this. They had a band. Very important to him was how they treated the poor people.

The sympathy and the empathy he shows those poor people! How could he have gotten all those details about them? Maybe his grandparents knew some people there.

The fairs were a big affair. I went only once, and I got a paddling because my father did not want me to cross Philadelphia Avenue.

Updike was accepted, even though he was plagued by personal problems, wasn't he?

He was.... His psoriasis, he'd let his hair come down to cover it. With his stuttering we'd just wait. Kindest thing you could do. He looked forward to just being with the guys whether it was merry-go-round or roofball.

Were the kids in Updike's class as poor as he?

All in the same boat.... But Fred's father was a lawyer.

Did you ever go to the movies with John?

He was a nut on movies. We'd take pieces of paper and make noise, we'd throw them like brrrrr firefly coming down. Then to Ibach's and the milkshakes were out of this world.

5. Shirley F. Smith (Berger)

>Shirley F. Smith (Berger). "Cheerleading 2, 3, 4; Class Play 4; Hockey 2, 3, 4; Homeroom Secretary 1; Volleyball 2, 3, 4. *Proven—Good things come in small packages.... Shirl seems enthusiastic about everything ... hard-hitting hockeyette ... wowed 'em as Tootie[14] in the senior class play.... Kenhorst may well be proud of this home grown product.*"—Shillington High School Year Book, *Hi-Life*

Shirley Berger (born 1932) was in Wesley Updike's Homeroom at Shillington High School for four years, then worked for Dr. Ernie Rothermel, the Updike's family dentist and model for a character in *The Centaur*. She played cards with Updike who signed his name in her yearbook, "Uppy." Shirley Berger worked twenty years at the Reading Hospital School of Nursing. In 1950 her husband played second base for the St. Louis Cardinals, managed by Berks County native, George "Whitey" Kurowski. This interview was conducted in the summer of 2009.

What was it like working on Hi-Life with John?

All I did was the typing.... I lived in Kenhorst and had to come here in 9th. I had no classes with John but I was in his homeroom for years and Mr. Updike was our teacher, a good wonderful soul. John was, I guess, embarrassed by him, but he never had an unkind word about anybody. We had a cutup, a thorn in Wesley's side, Charlie McComsey, who became a teacher. Oh, Mr. Updike used to go wild, but he'd said, "But how about his physique?

Boy, would I like to be built like him." Oh, he had a good word for anyone. My step-sister had college prep and Mr. Updike loved her because she was smart and ... she would say, he should be a professor in college because he just doesn't understand that what to him and John was so simple the rest of us just couldn't get.... John could have been anything—he was so smart. If he had gone into NASA, he'd be up there with the Wernher von Brauns[15] and whoever. In medical research he probably would have come up with the Salk polio thing. He was talented on the yearbook; he did drawings, caricatures, he was an artist.... I was so flighty then, I don't know why they bothered with me. I didn't know it then, but he was like a sponge, just soaked up life. Just didn't miss a thing, what he saw already went over our heads whether it was nature or people or what.

Was he a genius?
Oh, he was. Not just intelligent but music, art, writing.

Why was he embarrassed by his father's name "Updike"?
I didn't think the name was funny or Mr. Updike was a joke. He was sort of an odd looking man. He reminded me in his body like Abe Lincoln.... One time he was jumping up and down on the desk and Mr. Hemmig came in ... and Wes was jumping up and down. And a thing concerning decimals. [Once he] opened the window and threw it [a snowball] at the board. He was a lovely man. I was never aware of John's psoriasis but John always did wear long-sleeved shirts. He was a really terrific person.

Was Updike interested in any girls in particular?
John loved Jackie and Peggy all through school. They were like idols... I didn't think of John as a date. But they did pick me up two or three times a week and it was always at Fred's and we'd go with Forry and we'd play pinochle. I'd bid 30 and make 20. That was my most.... John was great to be with because he spoke the way he writes. And he'd observe and then make with [a joke?] his wonderful wit and he would say these things the rest of us would totally miss. And he had these twinkly eyes and wonderful smile.

Why did he say Peggy was "too much girl for me"?
Well, his opinion of himself [was low] with psoriasis and stuttering. His stuttering never dawned on me that it was bad. Anyway, she was too glamorous, our May Queen. Same for Jackie.

Was it a class thing?
I think her father owned an apartment ... on Philly Ave.

Did he date only Nancy Wolf in his senior year?
Might have taken her to the prom. I don't know.

Know why they broke up?

It was the mother. She did not like Shillington or the Shillington people, so she stepped in with her own plans. He mentions in one book, a mother says "you going to see hot pants again?" And I'm thinking ... she's talking about Nancy.

Must have been Nancy. You said he could have been anything partly because his mother made him use all his abilities.

But he hated the farm. He was a kid; he wanted to be where the action was with all his friends.... We'd get in John's car and I was flighty. We get in his car and play chicken. If Wes had seen what we did in that old car on the road towards Adamstown!

Did the people in Shillington feel bothered by The Centaur?

I worked for [the dentist] Dr. Ernie Rothermel. I'd gotten the shorthand award and I was supposed to work for a lawyer, but I heard he needed a girl, and I went there so they said, "You won't be using your office skills." I wasn't a hygienist. Ernie had a fit, because he [Updike] refers to Ernie as the man who couldn't cut it in medical school so went into dentistry. Ernie was furious. I really liked him, and I was never aware.

At the end of The Centaur *he shows his psoriasis to some girl.*

Wasn't me. I remember Fred's folks belonging to Bower's Country Club. Fred invited Jackie and I and Fred and John and another couple. We're down there swimming, and I never realized his skin was different from anyone else's, and he was in a bathing suit. I never noticed it. I thought, where the heck was I when I read about his sensitivity to it.

Did John ever say who was who in Couples?

John told me a few things in the twentieth reunion. They had this key-switching thing and that's how he ended up with his second wife, got this from Joan Venne. They had this unwritten rule was you could sleep with anybody but the unpardonable thing was to get a divorce and marry.

John said he was seeing someone else before Martha.

Yes, it was a girl from Japan.

Then she might have been Foxy [Foxy Whitman from Couples*]?*

Right. She was classy... She kept telling John she was doing him a favor by not coming to reunions.... One time he said to somebody that Martha said, "I can't believe you want to go back to those class reunions. What could you possibly have in common with them?" Well, he made a lot of money writing about them.... When he came to the class reunions he was John. He never became a snob.... I had [seen] something about him on TV, and he wrote back, "Wasn't that exciting watching me put up screens?" I have two or three letters from him. I really like him. I thought his dad was almost a saint. He was wonderful company.

Ever read Linda's stories?
  No, she left a bad taste in my mouth because she thought the people were snobby and above her. I loved the town, the school. I was a cheerleader and I'd stay with Joan or Jackie. I wouldn't go home afterwards. And the town was so pristine. The corn fields, the mall, the trolley car and the old ball field. That was great. Fields that didn't have anything in them but weeping cherries.

Is it possible that she didn't hate Shillington as much as she loved the farm.
  Yes, I shouldn't be judging her. I apologize. But she just didn't like us. John was fantastic. [The] way he describes basketball or baseball not just description but empathy.

He wrote about baseball when he went up to Boston to see a woman though he was married, and she wasn't home.
  I can't imagine John doing such stuff. This one [Martha] he must really love. Very affectionate. I read through *Endpoint* twice already. If you had known Peggy when I did… She was like I wanted to be. She wasn't drop dead gorgeous, but green eyes and a few freckles and was peppy and [the] soul of life. Her father was tough on her. Peggy had to lie and say she was going with me and my parents to the Shore, but we got on the bus, and she was going to spend the weekend with Jady and I'd be with Ron and she with Jady. But it got screwed up and I got back and no Peggy.… Another time Jady hid behind the furnace in the basement when they saw Bill [Lutz] coming. I was allowed to smoke. An aunt even gave me a lighter at graduation.… And Peggy would go up in the bathroom and smoke. Eventually somebody saw all the cigarettes on the roof next door. I could see why John thought Peggy was the nuts.

Can you compare Peggy to Nancy Wolf?
  Peggy was very vivacious. Nancy was matronly, the type I thought Mrs. Updike would like.

When did John start smoking?
  Oh, in Stephen's you couldn't see him for the smoke.… I always called him Uppy. We all did.

Anyone call him Ostrich?
  Is that that Eddie Pritchard thing?

Yeah, he was a bully to little Updike.

6. Joan P. Venne (Youngerman)

Joan P. Venne (Youngerman). "Band 1, 2, 3, 4; Class Play 3; Hi-Life 3, 4; Homeroom Secretary 1, 2; Student Council 1; Y-Teens 2, 3, 4. *Joanie.... As head majorette, she had the whole band in back of her ... a gracious hostess.... The Venne homestead never wanted for visitors.... Stardust.... Oh, those New York Yankees! ... one in whom you can confide.*"—Shillington High School Year Book, *Hi-Life*

Joan Venne Youngerman (born 1932) met John Updike in the 4th grade and instantly became a close friend. Joan was seated next to John in school. They played games at the playground together, and he was a member of her "Second Street Gang." Joan became a chief purchasing agent for Pomeroy Department store in Reading where Updike's mother had worked. She and Updike exchanged correspondence until his death. This interview was conducted in the summer of 2009.

I think you said that John based his story "Friends from Philadelphia" on an actual experience involving you. Can you explain that?

Yes, John's parents had friends in Philadelphia. They came to Updike's house [in Plowville] in spring of '50, it was a Saturday evening. We were in our senior year. His parents sent John into town in the old Plymouth to get a bottle of wine. We had just turned eighteen that spring, but we were not able to buy wine, so we asked my father to get the wine for us. An evening I remember so well. My father was a Buick dealer so we had a Buick. Didn't seem fair that Wesley Updike was so educated and had only a Plymouth. My mother was a little miffed at this story and said, "Sounds like sitting around drinking coffee and smoking cigarettes." She smoked Herbert Tarrytons, and John even got the brand right.

So he immortalized you, while playing a bit of a joke on your father. Were there other jokes in his stories?

Not sure, but there's a funny one about a book signing. This is a book he signed to my son, Mark Youngerman. Updike wrote, "For Mark Venne, my only Shillington fan [of the Boston Red Sox] many thanks. Nice of you to set up that little party by your mother's pool." He wrote me, "Lovely to be there with you and Mark. I have this terrible suspicion that I signed Mark's book to 'Mark Venne.'" So he just wrote Youngerman in there. But then he did a funny thing again, on his most recent one, I think it was *Terrorist*, he said, "I did my usual goof, signed it to Mark Venne." So he sent a copy from

England. He autographed the book right. But he and Mark were such good friends, because they were both Ted Williams fans.[16]

How did Updike get along with other kids?
Everybody liked him. Somebody said, "He's so amazing, John's a genius."

Updike had a stuttering problem, a skin condition, and very high intelligence, so what made him popular?
Well, one thing was that when he borrowed his father's car he'd give us all rides at lunch break. He would scare us to death by taking his hands off the wheel and the first person who grabbed it was chicken. I gave in and from the back seat grabbed the wheel. It was just a dumb thing to do.

John did everything in that old Plymouth except sell vegetables. His parents had a vegetable garden and his father would drive from Plowville to Shillington to sell produce. This embarrassed John, so we'd sit around—Barbara Hartz Behney, John and I—and we'd play three-handed pinochle, but smart as he was, he always forgot the kitty and if you buck on your first play you've lost the bid.

This was during the Second World War?
Yes. Jim Trexler and Jackie Hirneisen Kendall were pictured by the local paper on a pile of tin cans. She was new and pretty and everybody liked her. John would get a wagon and we'd go up and down the street collecting cans of fat that people would keep for drippings. Maybe the following week we'd do rubber.

I only got to Shillington in August or July 1941, and of course we were in the war shortly after that so for 4th, 5th, and 6th grades we did this kind of thing. We even made a kind of army; we called ourselves "Junior Commandoes." Nancy March started it all. I was the Colonel. We had caps with initials sewn on, Mary Orff's mother was very active in hospital auxiliary, so once a week we marched from school to the Orff home across from the high school at 225 Lancaster Avenue. In their pine-paneled basement we did bandages, her mother would bring all the things there and we would wrap them. During the war everyone helped. My mother had a victory garden; my father was an airplane spotter. We also bought savings stamps. I hate to say this, but it was such an exciting time. John wrote we were children of the "Turgid Thirties."

What was John like in school?
I was running for student council in eighth grade, each of the four homerooms had to have a representative, and I asked John if he would be our (Shirley Smith, Joan George, and Peggy Lutz) campaign manager. He wrote a song "George and Lutz, Jackie and Venne." Joanie and Peggy won. Shirley ran against Barry Nelson and he won. I was running against Donald Schwartz

and he was a big flirt and he won. John almost didn't get to be President of our senior class, because Richard Barthold and Peter Novak were popular too, and in the eleventh grade—I can remember I was in study hall when this teacher reminded us—we were told, "The person you elect this year will be the president of your class for all time." And for John then it was a landslide. Barry Nelson would have been an excellent president too, but the fact that John was our president always brought a crowd.

Senior year John got the father's part in the play.[17] I wanted to be the mother. Mr. Gelnett wrote a song "Me and my Shadow" for the play. John wrote poetry and did cartoons for *Chatterbox* and did poems and drawings for *Hi-Life* [The Shillington High School yearbook]. He also wrote most of the captions with me one Saturday. Under his own picture he put the caption, "Sage of Plowville."

What did you do for fun?

I was at the playground with John about 1945. We played roofball and made lanyards. He'd sit on the curb at the ice plant making moss out of the gutter water and weeds, and sometimes he'd throw the moss at us and we'd have a fight.

In our senior year we went into the seediest bowling alleys, then we'd play Canasta[18] till 2–3 o'clock in the morning. John would go off in a corner and play chess. At my senior birthday party John came, and one of my friends invited my old boyfriend, so John and Peggy acted as if they were me and Gary, and everybody applauded. He was very funny.

How did you and John get along with the teachers?

Mr. Updike was my teacher for algebra and I hated it. He used to say, "This girl is on top of Fool's Hill. We do not know yet what path she's going to take." Showalter's the one that taught me the Palmer method in the 1st grade. I had a nice handwriting but it wasn't Palmer method and she'd come along and Fred Muth would nudge me, and I'd get knocked. I never made a B till I ran into all that competition and also because I had so much fun.

We had a substitute teacher, Janice DeLong's sister, Jane, and because she was a substitute we pranked her. John would say, OK, everybody, chairs to the back of the room today," when she would substitute, or, "Hey, she's coming again today, upside down chairs."

Did he try such stuff on the regular teachers?

One time he took off this big yellow shoe—I always teased him about the color—put it on the window during Mrs. Showalter's English class. She had no sense of humor. We called her "The Gritzer." Anyway, she doesn't see this, she's up in front and I saw him do this, and Fred Muth—the other brilliant man in the class—had a pencil and we had metal desks, so Fred starts tapping slowly and not even I knew who it was until later. So Updike puts his shoe up there, passes it around the class first. Then in comes the supervising principal to observe and never noticed the shoe. As he was leaving someone in the back row passed it back. Showalter never knew about the shoe or who tapped the pencil.

Do you think John got away with it because his father was so popular a teacher?

No. It wasn't a question that John's father was a teacher that he got away with such stuff; that was ridiculous. We all knew that he already knew everything there was to know. John would write a note and pass it to me and I would just crack up. I couldn't hold a pencil. We had a teacher with a lisp, Russell Kistler,[19] and every time he said something with a lisp John would make some small sound only I could hear, and I'd say, "Please don't do this, we have a test today." No one could ever copy from John. Who could read his handwriting?

People were surprised when the Updikes moved to Plowville. Do you know how that happened?

That was Linda's idea. Wesley was smart enough to know he would lose if he argued with her.

Did you visit John when he moved to Plowville?

One time I went down to Plowville, first time I was in her living room, one of those places I wanted to go and stay forever. The color, yellow, the lighting was good, and all those books and comfortable furniture. She was very pleased with that. I was in the 7th grade play [Agatha Christie's *And Then There Were None*], and later Mrs. Updike said to me, "Joan, you have the best stage presence in the whole school." I fell in love with her.

Another time Linda Updike asked if I would pray for John when he was in Russia because he was having a bad time, and she thought it wasn't just a cold. She seemed to think it was more serious.

Linda and Wesley were at Walden's book store at the mall, and I was in charge of promotion at Lit Brothers, and Mr. Updike said, "Joan Venne," and Linda's sitting at the table signing books [*Enchantment*]. It was so nice to see them. The two of them were just sitting at a long table at the very entrance.

Did you know she was a writer at the time?

I knew she typed a lot. I knew she wanted to be a writer. She dressed John well for school. He wore mustard colored shoes just to devil me. She liked me because I wasn't good looking so I was no threat.

What threats did other girls pose?

In high school John was laid back, wasn't romantic. He only dated one girl ever, Nancy [Wolf]. Until he met Nancy he traveled with us. He took Joan

Zug to the senior prom at the Reading Country Club. But he hadn't broken up with Nancy by then. What scared me was he later wrote in [my copy of] *Villages*,[20] "A real villager!" No doubt he was kidding.

You were a Catholic and a Republican, but John's parents were Lutheran Democrats. Did this ever cause friction between you?

I was a Catholic and asked if I could read the Bible in school. I did such a good job that I did it periodically. But later I changed to Lutheran like John. As for politics, I never considered being anything else but Republican, since I like tradition and convention. I've always been conservative. I showed my Dad FDR's face on *Time*, and, oh, he was so mad. Peggy Lutz told me, "We're so glad you got here, because before you came Jimmy Trexler and I were the only Republicans." John and I just never discussed either religion or politics.

Any idea why he changed his religion to Unitarian, then Episcopalian?

His father-in-law was a Unitarian minister, I think, so he wanted to please his wife. I think he was looking for material.

What was John like at reunions?

Well, John asked me to make sure Mr. Francis Gelnett, a teacher of commercial subjects, got invited, and so I arranged to have Mr. Gelnett brought down from Harrisburg for a reunion. We sent the limo service to fetch him.

For a class reunion, he came into Pomeroy's with Joan Zug to have lunch with us and also have some free advertising, and of course we laughed the entire time. I said, "I don't want to read a warped version of this," and he said, "It will be warped." As he walked back to my office, I passed a friend who said "My God that's John Updike." I said "Now before you go promise me that you won't have a book signing at Boscov's."[21]

For the 1970 reunion Mary wasn't with him at Bower's Country Club. It was the twentieth reunion. We were dancing and he said, "Aren't you sorry you were so mean to me in school?"

John referred once to being in a Shillington parade. Do you remember this?

In the mid-70's John was in a parade.[22] When I saw the parade coming, I ran down the street to catch up. Jim Gallen was driving him and John was in the back seat, and as soon as he sees me he wants to chat, and I'm running alongside the convertible. And he shouts, "I'm living with a middle aged woman," laughs and says, "Hey, of course I'm middle-aged too." This was around the time of his divorce.

Could you see the divorce coming?

He got closest to telling me he was not at fault. I never thought he left Mary for Martha. Living in Georgetown with an Asian woman. He met the Asian woman while writing *Couples*.

My aunt Betty Troy wrote a gossip column for a Reading paper. She told me that no one would read Updike after The Centaur *appeared. I've never been able to verify that.*

John told me he only named people who were no longer living. John used all the names, but he never used them in ways that could be identified.

7. Jackie J. Hirneisen (Kendall)

Jacqueline J. Hirneisen (Kendall). "Amulet 3, Secretary 4; Chatterbox 4; Cheerleading 2, 3, 4; Class Secretary 1; Class Play 3, 4; Court 3, 4; Hi-Life 4; Hockey 2, 3,4; Homeroom Secretary 1, Vice-President 2, 3; Torch 1, 2, 3; Y-Teens 2, 3, 4. *Jackie runs the gamut of adjectives from attractive to zealous ... combines intellectual acuteness and athletic prowess ... took leading roles in both class plays ... the blondest streak in school... Shillington High's gift to the business world."* —Shillington High School Year Book, *Hi-Life*

Jackie Hirneisen (born 1932) joined Updike in the 5th grade when she moved to Shillington in 1943. Updike wrote affectionate poems to her that year. She had the leading role in *Meet Me in Saint Louis*. She was Updike's classmate through her senior year. Her husband, Carl Kendall, knew Updike as a child since he was three years older than she. This interview was conducted in the summer of 2009.

Did you know anyone in your class that Updike used in his fiction?
He wrote about me in "The Alligators."[23] I am the heroine.

Oh, you're the girl the 5th grade hates, though they eventually love her?
Yeah. That was I would say about 79 percent true, about 30 percent embroidered. He said I was the one he wrote about. Carl saw it on the internet and bought me a copy.[24] As soon as the book came Carl looked inside and he said, "This is not John's signature." So Carl sent the book to John and John wrote back and said, "Yes, Carl, a deception has been perpetrated." So here he put "not mine," then he signed his name and put "mine." What are the odds that Carl would have known [Updike's signature] well enough to know that it was a fraud.

Do you have any of his school papers, The Little Shilling *or* Chatterbox?
Here's an original *Little Shilling*. He drew the cover, 1944. Signed it "JHU."

Oh, here's a copy of *A Soft Spring Night in Shillington*. This is the first edition that Updike gave to us. It had some mistakes.

Several people noted his mistakes. Betty Adams told him that Carl Adams wasn't the Chief of police, but her father, Clifford was.

And he corrected all those things. Oh, and he sent a card telling Carl of the torrid romance we had in 5th grade and how everybody thought I'd be off to Hollywood as soon as I graduated.

Did you live near Updike?

I grew up on Summit Avenue next to the Shracks, both Shillington High teachers. She taught English. She told me his genius was recognized in 1st grade.

How did you see him?

I adored John, but I knew him as a person. I read some of his works. I found some of them difficult to get through. Now, I read this last piece, *Endpoint*. In recent years he seemed rather preoccupied with death.

What were his parents like?

[Carl Kendall weighs in] His mother was a recluse, but I had his father, Wesley, for two years of algebra, and he was a social person. He would walk all over Shillington and he would never walk by and say, "Hi." He'd always stop and talk to you. He'd always compliment you on something.

And he loved the street cleaners. He used to hangout down at Morgan Stern, at the used car lot; they had a little building there, an office. He loved Becker's garage, just sat down there and played checkers. They tore that down and made a Turkey Hill.

So you didn't know John's mother well?

JACKIE: In May 2007, John wrote to me about her, and he said, about an interview in 1982, that he was amazed to see her so funny and honest, and she was so forthright about describing how she and Wesley were confused about how to make a living. He also said she was very poised during TV interviews. She also noted John was closer to Wesley than to her, which he didn't like seeing in print.

You've kept a great deal of his early material?

JACKIE: There I am in the 5th grade [shows a poem]; he scribbled this just on a piece of paper and pencil. And just handed it [to me], and why at that age would I have thought to keep it?

You guessed he'd be special.

JACKIE: We all did, we all did. We all knew that because he just was so different. I met him on Pine Street and he had this big brown paper bag and he was bouncing the whole bag down the street. Here it turned out he had purchased a basketball and he was bouncing this big bag. That was the first summer after we had graduated, first year after Harvard. He looked terrible, as he always did. Wrinkly sweater, and wrinkly pants and never tied his shoes so his sneakers had the laces tucked in. Anyway, he said let's go down to Whitner's Tea Room for lunch and I am thinking it over, because I am embarrassed. But it was wonderful because the conversation was so stimulating and so fascinating, so fun.

8. Richard W. Manderbach

Richard W. Manderbach. "Class Play 3; Homeroom Secretary 2, 3. *Mandy follows up his jokes with a sober stare ... usually in a Plymouth ... curliest hair this side of a wire-haired terrier ... expansive smile ... extensive sideburns... Rex hopes to become a mechanical engineer."*—Shillington High School Year Book, *Hi-Life*

Richard Manderbach (born 1932) nicknamed "Mandy," moved to Shillington from Reading when he was twelve in 1945 and became Updike's classmate from 7th grade through 1950. After graduating, he spent four years at Wyomissing Polytech Institute. He served a year in Korea with the Army, graduating on his return from Penn State University. Manderbach worked at Western Electric in Allentown, Pennsylvania, and was a volunteer 3rd grade teacher's aid for 15 years. He is married and has three sons. This interview was conducted in the summer of 2009.

You grew up in Shillington?
    We moved to Shillington from Reading when I was 12. I went to Shillington High School.

Let's see, you arrived in the 7th grade, and John left for the farm in the 8th grade. You didn't have much chance to see him, then?
    No. John was only in Shillington on certain occasions, and the rest of us lived very close. I went around with Bill Forry, Marlon Frankhauser, and Fred Muth who had a car. We were called "The Hamsters."

Did "The Hamsters" gather at Stephen's Luncheonette, as John and Fred did?
    I didn't spend a lot of time there but John did because he had to wait for his father to get a ride home. One time the guys played a trick on his father. They took the [distributor] cap off his Buick so the car wouldn't start.

Did they do this prank because they didn't like John?

Oh, no. He was a friendly guy and very talented. You might say he was a goof. When we had to recite some poem for English Lit., he would get up and would really struggle, he was a stutterer. He never did get through the damn poem. The teacher let him get away with it but he was putting it on of course. I mean when he wanted to say something he would say it.

So John would do little jokes in class just to goof off?

Oh, yea, he was a clown. The neatest thing he did was, John would take a whole sheet of paper and would draw a little cartoon and write a little poem and send it to someone in the class.

I guess some of those appeared in Chatterbox *where he had a fake feud with Fred Muth.*

Yeah, I learned to play football with Fred and John in Fred's back yard.

What was it like at Shillington High when you were there?

I was in *Meet Me in Saint Louis*. John didn't write that. He was writing poetry.

Did you read his last volume of poetry?

I haven't read all of his stuff. My wife has read more than I have.

Did you learn much from Updike's father?

Oh, sure, sure. He spent half the class just sitting there talking about boys' and girls' business, you know. He was a great philosopher. I was pretty good in math. I remember telling him, "Well, this is the way I figure it out," and he would say, "Hey, that's good." He called it "Manderbach Math." John was also very much interested in my girlfriend from Hyde Park. He wrote "The Happiest I've Been" about a New Year's Eve party at my house. Bill [Forry] was going to take him to Chicago because John had met this girl and was in college[25] and he was going to go out to see her.

Who was the girl who falls asleep on his shoulder in the story?

That was my former girlfriend. Actually, Fred [Muth] latched on to her for a while, and Bill married a friend of hers.

In the story they drive in a blizzard. That sounds pretty dangerous after being at a party all night.

I don't know if John was drinking. Bill liked his Scotch, so he let John drive almost all the way out because he had too much to drink.

So this party was while he was at Harvard. Did you ever see him after he was married?

One time [in 1955] we went to New England and we stopped to see John. After we were there a short time, he went out and got the paper or the mail or something, and he came back in and sat by himself in the corner reading the paper or his mail. Like when Fred and John would when they were at a party.

9. Barry R. Nelson

Barry R. Nelson. *"Baseball 3; Basketball 2, 3, 4; Chatterbox 4; Class Treasurer 3; Football 1, 2, 3, 4; Hi-Life 4; Olympus 3, 4; Student Council 2, 3, 4; Torch 2. Busy—that's Barry ... this three-fold sport star finds time to serve the school in a dozen sundry ways ... pleasing personality could tame a tiger ... full of humor ... future M.D. ... has what it takes, plus."*—Shillington High School Year Book, *Hi-Life*

Barry Nelson (born 1932) joined Shillington High School in the 9th grade and met Updike while working on *Chatterbox*. A star athlete Barry Nelson was honored as an "Olympian." He wrote essays identifying Shillington places and people in Updike works and produced a program showing how Updike used those.[26] Of Updike, Nelson remarked, "He put Shillington on the map."[27] Nelson taught journalism at Governor Mifflin High School and became the school's principal. This interview was conducted in May 2009.

How did you meet John Updike?
I lived in Adamstown and when you reached the 8th grade you went to Shillington High, since it was the closest high school, so I met John [in 1945]. I was in his homeroom and had his Dad for a teacher.

What was Updike like?
Skinny kid, tall, angular, he was in the First Section—the smartest kids—and I was in the Second Section, so I was very seldom with him in class. John wrote all the plays and skits and everything else. Usually we all had parts in them. I remember, once he made up his mind about something, that was it. When the class was arguing about where they wanted to go on their senior class trip, and the guy who ran the meetings broke down and cried, John took over as president.

Were you in any of the same clubs or teams?
First year may have been inter-mural basketball and John played on the home room team.

Was he any good?
He was not a good basketball player but he was pretty good [at shooting],

he could put them in. Probably played forward or center. We played "Horse," and I taught him how to shoot over his back. I showed him a hook shot and he got to be pretty good at that. He played baseball in gym class. Had trouble hitting the ball, catching it, fielding it. He just didn't have native ability.

Did you share other extra-curricular activities?

We were really close friends. The last year in high school, particularly the last half, we spent a lot of time together, going to lunch, taking rides. We were both on *Hi-Life*, John was art editor and I was sports editor. I'd go up to the typing room and John would be in there at the mimeograph scratching his drawings and writings, scratching the "O"s out. Misspelled word on a mimeo for him was like a tragedy. A lot of times he'd drive out to Plowville to pick up something and I'd go with him. I also drove him to Reading, to the Bague Bindery where he had his *New Yorkers* and his *Chatterboxes* bound. Updike wrote a story called "Ace in the Hole."

Did it have any relevance to his basketball playing? ["Ace" was an ex-basketball star.]

John was always poking fun at athletes. He wasn't that athletic. But he was a great supporter of athletics, though he could poke fun at them too, like in the drawings for *Chatterbox*.

Did other students like his drawings?

He was a pretty good cartoonist. We had some good cartoonists but nothing like John. Soon as you saw it you knew it was his.

How did John respond to living in the country, in Plowville?

Used to complain about living so far out in the country and not having great facilities there. He stuck close to Stephen's luncheonette where he'd eat hamburgers and smoke Kools because that way nobody would bum them off him. Kids would take aspirins and 7-Up. But I never tried it, neither did John.

Was John closer to his mother or father?

She was a strange person, very quiet; you never really saw her much. I kinda think he was closer to his father since they went back and forth to school every day. His mother wanted him to be smart, go to Harvard, make something of himself. His father did too but didn't worry about it.

Are any of his fictional characters traceable to a real person? ... What about Penny in The Centaur. *Was she based on a girl he knew?*

Maybe, but he couldn't have shown his psoriasis to her. In our gym that would have been impossible. There would have been no place to go under the grandstand.

How did other kids see him?

There were about six kids in our class had straight A's, and he was one of them. It was pretty difficult to get an "A." I don't think he had to struggle much. He was funny, and could break up the class, but they couldn't very well punish the class for laughing at John's stuff. His father was funny, so like father like son. We had elections for student council, people running used to perform on the stage. Each week at assembly a different home room would perform. He appeared in plays, wrote plays. He was a good actor. He liked to write them and direct them.

Did he campaign for senior class president?
He was so well liked he didn't need to, but I beat John out, quite handily, but I was president of student council, and Principal Luther Weik said I couldn't hold both offices.

The photos in the year book seem to show that he doesn't give a damn.
He probably didn't. Must have had lots of laughs at the foibles he saw.

What kind of fun did he have?
We used to have car games when he would drive. Four guys would be in the car and they'd open doors and change seats, since the back doors opened the other way and they'd step onto the running board. It was something to do.

Who did he date?
Nancy Wolf. She was his secret love. The kids knew but John later told me in a letter, "Don't mention Nancy."

Who were his most inspirational teachers?
Thelma Lewis certainly influenced his writing because she was advisor to *Chatterbox* [and] *Hi-Life*.

Even as a teenager Updike seems to have religious problems. Did he tell you about this?
That was too deep for us. We'd tell him, "Well, John, you die, you go to heaven."

10. Emerson W. Gundy

Emerson W. Gundy. "Class Play 4; Football 2, 3; Hi-Y 2, 3; Track 3. *A prominent Morgantown roader… Emerson and his Ford are just about inseparable … dead eye with a shotgun … basketball and nighttime ice skating on Green Hills Lake … held down Fred's lines in senior class play.*"—Shillington High School Year Book, *Hi-Life*

Emerson Gundy (born 1932) is John Updike's second cousin, his grandmother being the sister of Linda Hoyer Updike's mother. In 1945, as the Updike family moved from Shillington to Plowville, Emerson's family moved nearby. From September 1945 to February 1947, Wesley Updike drove Emerson and John to and from Shillington High School. Emerson Gundy visited the Updikes at Harvard while in the army. He married in 1956, and founded American Telecommunications Diversified. In 1990, Updike was delighted to sell him the Plowville farm. This interview was conducted in the summer of 2009.

Tell me about your family connection to John Updike.

John's mother Linda was a first cousin of my mother. Both graduated from Kutztown Normal School, so they were very close. She ... was nearly ninety [when she died], same as John's mother.

You lived outside Shillington in Mohnton, so when did you come to Shillington?

Ninth grade [about 1946]. I came from a one-room school house, one room, eight grades.

What was your impression of John when you first met him?

Well, I rode with John back and forth for two years when he lived here. When he rode with his dad they'd pick me up down by Route 10. I wasn't yet sixteen and I didn't travel in his group. I was in the sports group and we were average students, and of course John was the brain of the class. I used to have to sit in the back of the old '34 Buick and do my homework. His dad [Wesley Updike] never stopped at the stop sign at the intersection, and it used to scare the daylights out of me. He was not a happy fellow in the car.... If it was raining the night before, the next morning they'd come to pick me up and the windshield wipers would still be running on a dry windshield, and we'd drive all the way to Shillington without turning off the wipers.

That sounds pretty odd.

When I rode with John I'd hitch-hike home after track or football practice. My dad redid a '39 Ford for me and I got my license when I was four days past sixteen, first kid to have a car.

Did you ever ride when John drove?

No, never, and I never saw him drive in high school. I never traveled with John or Fred Muth or any of his group. I was a farm boy.

What was he like in class?

I had a couple of classes with John. I remember one time; I think in Mrs. Shrack's English class, we did a fake legal case. I was representing the defense for some criminal and John destroyed me. But Mrs. Shrack gave me good marks because I'd talk about theater—I was in Summer Stock.

Where did you do Summer Stock?

At Green Hills Lake[28] I worked as a stage hand and played bit parts. One show was *Dracula*. We had to do a lot of howling in the lampshades as wolves.

Were you in the plays Updike wrote?

I was in the junior or maybe senior class play and had a pretty good lead in that. I think we played *Meet Me in St. Louis*.[29] I remember I learned the waltz clog.

About your high school experience, did you read Chatterbox?

We all read it and it was fun. He was so far ahead of everybody half the people couldn't even comprehend what he was saying.

How often did you see John after graduation?

He visited here almost every June for the last 20 years. He loved my wife Marlene more than he loved me, I'm sure of it. She'd always give him homemade strawberry jam. She always had cookies for him. And candy. He ate constantly the two or three hours he was here. One time we sent the jam to him and he was so elated that he sent fifteen notes. But John and I became really good friends more so after I bought the property. He would always say, "if only mother could see it now what you have done to this property." It was pretty bad when I bought it.

Was John still tied to the farm?

He always said, "I didn't like the farm when I lived here. This is your place. I don't want the name Updike used on that farm anymore." John said he didn't want notoriety in Shillington. "I don't want people to even know I am here."

So he never enjoyed living here?

Well, he did say that he never went outside for four years, but later John said, "I wish I had gone outside and paid more attention. I don't know what the trees are." He didn't even know the old tree back there of the house was an oak.

His mother certainly knew about trees and flowers, but not his dad Wesley, I think.

Wesley used to stop at our house all the time and get money for gas. I'd give him a dollar and he'd always come back the next day and pay it back.

I think John wanted his mother to move to Ipswich after his father died. She wouldn't go.

I wouldn't leave the farm either. But he wanted to clean up the farm. The brush was horrendous. But she would never ever want to take a bush out or cut a tree because then she wouldn't have the birds. After cutting the brush he would say, "Oh my, mother can now see the birds." She had chores for him whenever he came back. No wonder he didn't come home often. Once a year for a week or two he came back with the kids. They used to sleep in the barn. Martha didn't come at all. She said that was her gift to the mother, "Let her have him by herself."

So Linda kept up the farm into her 80s?

She didn't really. Before we could move in, I did repairs for four or five months. Then I bulldozed down brush, trees you wouldn't believe. Then I stored three tractors in the barn but pigeons came in and crapped on the tracs. I kept shooting them in the barn with .22 spread shot.

Would it be common for a fifteen- to sixteen-year-old boy to shoot those pigeons?

You can't shoot in a barn with low volume spread shot. You will shoot holes right through the roof. And she was a bird lover. She also had forty cats that ate all the birds. When she passed away the neighbors shot cats for about two-three months. They shot about thirty-five. Updike came back when the Germans made a film about him for TV. Well, I'll tell ya, I learned a lot about John that I didn't know by just listening to his interview.

11. Harlan L. Boyer

Harlan L. Boyer. "Class Play 3, 4; Football 1, 2, 3, 4; Hi-Y 3, 4; Homeroom President 3; Track 1, 2, 3, 4. *Scotty.... Cars are his main interest, and he is happiest when driving one ... black Pontiac... Grandpa Prophater of senior class play ... lover of good food and Dixieland jazz ... a future jeweler who will study at trade school."*—Shillington High School Year Book, *Hi-Life*

Harlan Boyer was born in 1932 in West Reading Hospital only two hours before John Updike. During the war he made brass scale model versions of Japanese and German warships; some are in the Smithsonian. After piloting planes for the Navy, 1953–55, he earned an M.A. from Millersville State College and remained there for twenty-three years supervising Special Education. Manderbach built a plane in his garage in 1980, and later farmed his two acres. He appears in Updike's poem, "Upon Becoming a Senior Citizen." This interview was conducted in the summer of 2009.

When did you first meet John Updike?

In the nursery at Reading hospital. I'm two hours older than John. I used to kid him about respecting his elders. We went to Kindergarten together right up through the grades. Chronologically, when John and I were somewhere around ten or twelve, that's when we were closest of friends, we'd ride our bikes across King's Boulevard to the Poorhouse wall.[30] John always brought along his lunch, always peanut butter and jelly. He was making lunch for both of us and he had one of these old bread toasters you'd flip out and you'd snap 'em shut. John put the peanut butter on the bread then put it in there. I'm sure he did it just to get a rise out of me.

Do you remember John in kindergarten at all?
   Can't think of any occurrences, we were just all together. Banging on sticks for the rhythm band, marching around. When we got to 7th grade we parted company, not friendship, but I was a mediocre athlete and John was uncoordinated. He was a man of letters, the school newspaper and so forth.... Emerson Gundy and I were in a different group, and John's clique were in the school plays, and one night—that was 1950, his senior year—after rehearsal ... John and his cohorts hatched the idea to go to Larue's [hardware store] and buy ... something like paint and whitewash the Ephrata school. We were playing Ephrata [football] the next day. He got something more durable, the paint didn't wash off readily. They painted Ephrata's buildings. Next morning, Principal Weik ... came down hard on John and Fred and the play cast. That was something between whitewash and paint and they had a hell of a time getting it off. They had to have it professionally removed. This was the scandal of the year. Getting back to my chronology ... in his senior year, the two cliques, the Athletes and the Artsies ... became distinct. I didn't socialize with him, but John appreciated and valued his friends. John was a clown and he was a gregarious, fun-loving boy. He'd do things just to get a laugh. At lunchtime he'd pile as many in his father's car and they'd come back kinda shaken. I remember them coming back from those jaunts and they'd say I'm not going to go through that again!

Who were his best friends?
   Fred Muth was his best friend—he was such a nice guy, and became a lawyer, but unlucky with his wives. He did my divorce. When I sold the business he did that too. When I transferred my house to my son, Fred did that too. He did my mother's estate. Extremely reasonable. And my pre-nuptial agreement. He passed away year and a half ago. Surprised he lived as long as he did. His feet were always getting infections. He shuffled. To add insult to injury when his father passed away he didn't leave anything to Fred. The crosses that we bear!

Other friends?
   Bill Forry, Joan Venne, Mary Ann, [Joan] George. That's the group he used to hang out with at Stephen's Luncheonette. They used to get a booth back there, and they'd be raising Cain. He did smoke.

Did either of John's parents smoke?
I don't think so. His grandfather tended the chickens but the coop is gone and he was from a farm. It was a two story chicken house.

Did Updike's interest in psychology appeal to you as a counselor?
I never liked John's work. OK? I found them difficult, ponderous. Difficult to keep continuity, a thought. He was always breaking away and winding me down these alleys.

Barry Nelson said the same.
Here's a question I have to ask you: Who was Rabbit? I asked John at a class reunion and asked him, was Rabbit a composite of Rabbit Hiester, class of '47 or '48, and Gerry Potts. John said, no, Rabbit Hiester is where I got the name and Heister was a very good athlete, but that's all. I said Rabbit sounded like Gerry Potts. No, he said, Gerry wasn't involved. John's dad and my dad used to take tickets at the games and for so doing they were allowed two free tickets to all the games in the valley. He got in free. So John's father had an interest in athletics and he especially liked the basketball players. So Rabbit is the guy who's still living in Canada.... What was his name?

Bob Arndt.
Right. I asked John, "How did you know about Bob Arndt," and he said "I just used him as a model of the athlete, super basketball player," So I asked, "What about all this stuff that happened to him?" He said, "I just made this up." That came right from his mouth.... So it wasn't Gerry who was Rabbit.

I saw a card John wrote Gerry saying "No, it was Bob Arndt, not you."
So by taking the gate receipts, that allowed Wes Updike to have season tickets and that allowed John to go with his father and follow Arndt. So his father's interest led to the creation of John's most famous character.

So it might have been wish fulfillment on John's part.
John himself was very uncoordinated. Never made the teams. Maybe that shifted his interest over to the literary thing. Also, John was not a handsome man. Full of acne. Stuttered seriously. But that was John and we accepted it.

Did he stutter more around girls or guys?
He was just a serious stutterer. To add a little credence to that the first class reunion I attended ... and here's John and he's talking so slowly and deliberately sort of in a sophisticated manner, and I thought he doesn't stutter and he had the aura of royalty around him, and I began thinking he worked with a professional speech therapist, but somehow he found out if he slowed down, see, he used to talk a mile a minute but his speech manner became slower and with a sophisticated manner. But it wasn't John. Probably had everything to do with slowing it down and maybe he could get rid of it.

First time I ever heard him was on PBS in the 60's and I was amazed he spoke so beautifully.
That would be something to pursue, how he got rid of the stutter.

Did his psoriasis show up then?
Yes, and he was always pockmarked.

He had all these negative things but he was able to magnetize people!
He worked at it, always the focal point of clowning around. Orally he was always kind of the particular head of the conversation; he always had something to say. And he was funny. He was comical. Started off after graduating to be a cartoonist and that didn't surprise me at all.

So how young was he when you saw his drawings?
Probably in junior high school. Even then he rubbed elbows with upperclassmen who put out *Chatterbox;* but John was the equal of all of them.

Was he doing drawings in Little Shilling?
That's right. It was called *The Little Shilling.*

His Chatterbox *cartoons were already great. Where'd he learn it?*
Just came from John.

Carlton Boyer [Art teacher at Shillington High School] said, "The best student I ever had was John Updike, and he could have had a career as a cartoonist if he wanted it."
That's right. Carlton's related to me.

Ever see Updike socially, at dances, maybe?
He was coordinated enough for that. But basketball demands major coordination and John wasn't good at it.

Was Barry Nelson on any of the teams?
We played football together. He was quarterback. I played guard at 137 pounds. Played unbalanced line, so we pulled the guard on the weak side, and he would lead the interference, and that was me.

Did John ever brag about his mother?
He would say she was upstairs in her studio which I think was her bedroom. Only thing I knew of the upstairs was hearing her typewriter. I don't remember ever talking to her. His father was the exact opposite. In *The Centaur* everything that happened there was true, like smashing the car's grill. I was there when one of the kids smashed his grill when he was coming out of an alley from State Street. The road's crowned, so when he pushed the kid across the hump, the Buick went down in the dip and the grill went down too under the bumper of the kid's car. That Buick had a smashed grill for as long as I knew him. Picking up the hitchhiker also actually happened. John told me

about it later.... If you're going to do a case study, Wes was a better character than John. He'd lay down on the floor in front of the class and say, "Go on walk all over me." He'd sling open a window and put half his body out and say, "I'm going to jump."

He must have shocked them into thinking he really was going to jump.

I remember Mr. Updike smacking Charlie McComsey [Classmate who had a habit of mischief] He sat in front of me in the very first desk. Wes was explaining how to do a problem and Charlie is talking to me and Wes comes and bam! hits him on the side of the head. Another time, somebody in the back of the room was making noise, so Wes picked up an eraser and lined it the length of the room at this kid, and he missed him.

In a funny way?

No, Wes had a low tolerance. He went after the kid.

Wesley wasn't disciplined?

You deserved what you got. We had a penmanship teacher. Mrs. Showalter, and she had a ruler. If you didn't have your hand just right while doing those push-pulls she'd rap your knuckles with a ruler.

Different from Caldwell in The Centaur. *There he takes all this abuse and doesn't do anything about it.*

Yeah, Wes's opposite. One time Wes locked himself in the closet and the kids didn't know where he was and he yelled, "Hey get me out of the closet." But the real Wes was the kind-heartedest. I never heard him say a mean thing about anyone and I knew him so many years. He'd go out of his way to tell you what a neat guy you were.

He put everyone first.

And it's obvious that's how he felt. I was working at a jewelry store one Saturday morning, and Wes came in, and he was in the Lion's club with my dad and they yakked there for a while and after a while my dad said, "Wes, can I do anything for you," and Wes said, "No, I'm just making the rounds." He'd talk to all the business men, talk to the guys at La Rue's hardware store. Last time I saw him he was walking along Route 10 ... and I said, "Wes can I give you a lift." "No," he said. "I was just going down to talk for the afternoon."

Did he neglect his son?

He was more of a role model. I think he pulled John more than he pushed. John was closer to his father in his sociability than his mother. That last time I saw her Barry Nelson had a little program for John after he won one of his Pulitzer prizes here at Governor Mifflin, and I took my mom, and my mom and I sat there and witnessed the program and when we stood up there was

Linda sitting five or six rows behind us and I think my Mom went over and talked to her, and I think if she hadn't of done that Linda would have ignored us. She made no effort to flag us down or even wave.

She seemed to feel she was socially above others?
　She never associated with people.

Did she ever come to the school plays?
　I was in the plays, so I don't know that.

What was John's romantic life like?
　I think his romantic life is the catalyst for a lot of John's writings. He would like to have seen himself in a more sociable setting than he was in life. So books like *Couples*—I used to think to myself, I think this is John's wishes. He did have an underclass girlfriend, Nancy. I can't remember her last name.

Wolf.
　She lived down on Brobst the northwest corner across from what used to be that store with the funny entrance… Brobst and Walnut.

Thelma Lewis said Wes always feared he'd write about that romance. But John saw potential there.
　I didn't know her. Jackie [Jackie Hirneisen] and Peggy Lutz were good looking girls, very vivacious and outgoing and kind of a cheerleader-type girl.

In Updike's story "Flight" a mother forcibly breaks up a romance because she's afraid her son will get stuck in Shillington. Could that have happened?
　Yes. Linda was very controlling. I really don't know how he and Nancy parted. I was in college, then I went away to the Korean War. I didn't get back till the reunion in '55…. If you had something you wanted to talk to John about you couldn't get close to him. He was a celebrity and everyone wanted to talk to him. I never wrote to him. He was a member of a different clique. We were very good friends, but we just didn't associate with each other. I remember his rattletrap of a bicycle, a girl's bike and his wheels were going like this as I rode behind him. He liked to go fast.

How did he respond to moving to Plowville?
　He felt he was out there in no man's land.

What did you like the most about Updike's writing?
　He remembered even the cracks in the pavement in *A Soft Spring Night in Shillington* [the first chapter of Updike's *Self-Consciousness*]. He doesn't miss much.

Did you read much of Updike?
　I wouldn't read John Updike for pleasure. People who appreciate the way he put together the English language said he would put it together the

way an artist puts together a landscape, but to me it was plodding. I'd have to read some passages more than once to see if I got the gist.

You're not alone, because I taught lots of Updike's books and some students had difficulty.

It was like reading a technical manual. How do I put this bicycle together? Not reading for enjoyment. As fellow students we didn't pick up on that too well. We accepted him the way he was. We didn't idolize him. He was John. We knew he was bright, clever, but he was always bright. He was always clever; we just accepted it. We always thought he'd do what he did.

12. The Rev. Victor Kroninger

The Rev. Victor Kroninger (born 1932) attended first to twelfth grades with Updike then graduated from Muhlenberg College and the Lutheran Theological Seminary (Philadelphia). During his thirty-eight year ministry, he served four parishes. A challenge was his tenure as President of the Reading Area Council of Churches. In retirement he received the American Motorcycling Associations Most Valuable Person award for taking almost 200 seniors for rides. The Reverend Kroninger rode his Indian motorcycle for the 12th Annual "Bike for Hunger."[31] His Family Band (Psalm 150) led worship (Catholic, Protestant, Orthodox Jewish) in over 300 churches in four states. His father baptized John Updike. This interview was conducted in the summer of 2009.

Tell me about life in Shillington and the Updikes.

Wesley was an usher at Grace Lutheran when they lived in Shillington. Back in those days women breast-fed in the back pews. I recall all around me nursing babies and Wesley would wink to me and then he'd pass the plate.

The wink suggests he liked kids.

Oh, yes. He was wonderful.

He was a colorful teacher, I've heard.

I had him for math in 7th and 8th grades. When he was on stage everyone would cheer. He said once, "If you boys are smart, you'll marry a homely girl like mine, and you'll have no trouble keeping her." On the day John was baptized we went to the Updike home for dinner and Wes got orders to clean out the poopy diaper, and I was 1½ years.

Did your father's sermon style differ from yours?

It was longer. Sang hymns in German. Sermon was in hochdeutsch. Otherwise in Pennsylvania German. Amish would come on their bikes; painted the chrome black.

Was his portrait of a Lutheran minister in Rabbit, Run *authentic?*

Yes, I feel so…. His mind would wander during the long sermons. He was never too serious. He loved the movies.

Did you go swimming nearby?

I lived on Broad St. and we'd ride our bicycles to the edge of the field and the tree is still there by the dam and we crawled through the bushes and cut the vine off with our knives and swung naked about fifteen feet in the water and dropped naked in the deep water. John said, "Your dad's the holy man, so I guess we can risk it." … We would check to see if there were any girls around, and a woman showed up with a dog on occasion and we had to wait to strip before she was out of the field of view.

What about his parents?

I think his mother spoiled him. Didn't want him to get his hands dirty…. She would even mow the cemetery lot. John wrote back for the picture I took of Linda, "Thank you for the photo of my mother on the tractor."

I take it that Wes was religious?

Wes [once] said, "Victor, listen carefully." He pointed a finger in my face … "You preach like John writes." That gave me courage, so I thought, "I'm going to stick to it and raise hell." I sent John some sermons.

Did you visit the poorhouse?

Visited with my dad. That's when they had 15–20 people in the wards. They would die and no air conditioning just a huge fan. The stench was awful, terrible. I could cry [about] what they went through there.

13. Jack E. Guerin

Jack E. Guerin. "Class Play 3, 4; Hi-Life 4; Hi-Y 3, Secretary 4; Homeroom President 1, Treasurer 2; Secretary 3; Student Council 1, 3. *Jack is the energetic, irrepressible redhead always involved in activity—good or bad … old Stephen's grad… American Casualty's favorite son … smooth dancer, competent thespian, future dentist … a young man with personality plus."—* Shillington High School Year Book, *Hi-Life*

Jack Guerin was Updike's close friend, along with Fred Muth. He worked as a buyer for Met-Ed and in public relations for the Three-Mile Island installation. He later went into business building home swimming pools. He passed on in 2015. This interview was conducted in the summer of 2009.

JG: You have to remember at my advanced age what I remember might not be accurate.

He was not just a gifted author he was so brilliant in many facets, scientific, mathematics, the arts. He was all-around genius.

I came upon his science papers. Remarkable.

He was brilliant. His father, Wes, was a math teacher, and sometimes in the algebra class John would tell him, "There's an easier way to do that."

Any stories about Wes?

Once he said, "There's too much sex in this class. Will Peggy Lutz and Jack Guerin please leave." John was a complex person. I visited him in Oxford while in the service, and Mary had a baby they kept in a dresser drawer.[32]

John's son David has a book out now, Old Girlfriends.

Does he write like his father?

Similar nostalgic style.

John had a severe stuttering problem. He certainly got over it. I was amazed when I saw him on TV or in person. His psoriasis affected him personally. John was an attention-getter.

You must have played chicken with him. Ever grab the wheel?

No I couldn't do that one of the girls had to, Joan George, Mary Ann Stanley, Joan Zug. We went places mainly in a group. I came to Shillington in the 5th grade. Once he moved to Plowville things changed. I always admired him. Easy to see he had great intellect. I think his writing is just marvelous, the precision with which he used words. I have *Widows of Eastwick* on recorded books, since I have macular degeneration.

I'm sorry to hear that. You knew of his cartooning?

Yes, and John wrote a poem seniors took offence to and wrote an apology in which first letters down spelled "Seniors Stink."[33]

Who'd he date?

Nancy Wolf. She was very nice, very unlike John. He was volatile, she was calm. Last time I saw him was at a reunion. Smoked like a fiend at Stephen's.

Wonder why he gave it up?

Don't know.

Died suddenly of lung cancer.

Yes. He captured the flavor and feeling of the whole town in a piece he wrote, "A Soft Spring Night in Shillington."

What were his parents like?

We were going to play poker at the farm, and all of a sudden a mangy dog came in that had caught a skunk and smelled to high heaven. Linda said, "Now don't give the dog a complex. Be nice to him." John moved him away from us.

Who else did you play cards with?

Mahlon Frankhauser, Donald Schwartz.

He wrote a story about playing poker. I heard something about striptease poker, but it never got embarrassing. Did you form any opinion about Linda?

She was the force behind John at an early age. I don't think his father wanted to move to Plowville. I was at Pomeroy's working at Christmas selling tie bars and cufflinks and Wes said, "Oh my God, Jack. You have so much responsibility."

Probably one of the things that made people like him so much. Must have been tough on John stuck out in Plowville and depending on his father to get him in and out of town.

John would often go home with me on the school bus. I lived in Kenhorst at the time. Then his father would pick him up. One time my mother had just wallpapered the living room, and John looked at the wallpaper—it was green and yellow flocking. He just thought it was obnoxious. So he wrote a story for *The New Yorker* about how much he hated it. My mother wasn't pleased.

What sort of things passed the time for you?

I played chess with Fred Muth but not John. If it weren't for John, Fred would have been the most intelligent in the class. Fred and I were very good friends 5th through 7th grade. Very studious.

He was quiet and so was Nancy Wolf. Wonder if that attracted him to her? He also liked crazy people.

Like me. John was voted the most likely to succeed. I was voted the friendliest.

In one of his last poems he said, "Maybe we have Heaven at the start"?

Yeah, I think he's right.

He did remember his classmates.

In *Couples* one of the last names he used is Guerin. I was not too thrilled that he used Roger Guerin. I mentioned it to John that it wasn't too flattering to my wife or me. He said, "It's just a name. I always liked your name!" Baloney. There was no falling out over that.

After high school I didn't know his friends, wrote him a short note about *S*. I thought it was one of his best written books, not one of his most popular. He certainly captured a woman's point of view. He just wrote a note thanking me for my letter. I never asked him to sign books. I thought it was embarrassing, with people in line. I thought he should have been enjoying himself, so never asked him to sign books.

Was there ever a falling out with anyone?

No, I really can't recall anyone who disliked him. He could be annoying. He could be cynical. But he wrote incisive, brilliant criticism of Nabokov. But reading a recipe is a chore from my macular degeneration, words spread apart. His children's books are beautiful. I used to read those to my kids. My kids are avid readers.

Just like Updike going to the Reading Library.

Updike's not easy reading. I'm a very rapid reader, but with an Updike novel you can't be, you have to pour over words so much it isn't easy.

He's the kind of writer who makes you want to go back and reread him. In your English classes with Showalter or Schrack do you remember memorizing?

Not really. I remember reading nearly all of Dickens. If my father gave me a gift it was going to be a book. John borrowed a book by Alexander Dumas from my father he never returned. If you went to the farm you'd see books, magazines, newspapers piled all over the house.

He read newspapers to his grandfather. Did you ever read any of Linda's things?

Yeah, a short story in *The New Yorker* one time. Sounds cruel, but I don't think she'd be recognized if it weren't for John. Maybe I'm not qualified to say that. I think she had a dominant personality. She wanted things done her way. I wonder what she thought of John's racier works?

Did you notice anyone else who turns up in his books as a thinly-modeled character?

Principal Hemmig turned up in *The Centaur* when he wandered in the girl's locker room. Whoops, didn't know anybody was in there.

Did Linda have cause to think Shillington had done things to her?

Nothing I could see, but she may have looked at all of us as a distraction from what he should be doing. And maybe what she should be doing too.

He had such an amazing dedication.

At a reunion, I said, Well, I'm still working. He said, "So am I! What are you going to do when you stop?" I said, "Die!" He said, "You got it." John liked basketball. Had he played basketball seriously, it would have been a loss for the country.

When you worked on Hi-Life *with John, did he do the captions under the photos, or were they done by the group?*
You'd go to the person and say, do you mind. John wrote something ugly on my book. "To Jack who's living proof that ignorance is bliss." He thought it was funny.

I see what you mean now; he could be a little sharp. What sort of things did you do at the playground?
Roofball. Silly game. Strenuous. Played for hours. Peggy Lutz one of the best ones.

14. Barbara L. Hartz (Behney)

Barbara L. Hartz (Behney). "Basketball 2, 3; Hockey 3, 4; Track 3; Volleyball 2, 3. *Hartzie is another of our athletic females … stars especially in hockey and basketball … hearty, good-natured laugh … might like to further develop her talent at art school … a grand kid and swell sport.*"—Shillington High School Year Book, *Hi-Life*

Barbara Hartz lived at 107 Philadelphia Avenue, a few doors from Updike. Both of her uncles were coaches. Barbara Hartz was engaged to the athlete who gave "Rabbit" Angstrom his nickname, Richard "Rabbit" Hiester, of the Shillington High School class of 1947. Barbara Hartz's uncle rented Stephen's Sweet Shop. Later she ran a stained glass company, and she sent a stained glass panda to President Richard Nixon on his successful negotiations with China in 1972. This interview was conducted in the summer of 2009.

You want to know all about John. He lived at 117 Philadelphia Avenue, and I lived at 107, so that says a lot. In lower grades, there was John nearby. And of course in those days you didn't have a bus taking you to school. And so we all walked together. We would cross the street because the ice house was on the corner, and Mr. Shilling, an artist, lived right across the street with his dogs.

Mr. Shilling took John under his wing. I remember going into Mr. Shilling's "barn" where he had three great big oils. So we would walk along by the ice house, and the water ran down Philadelphia Avenue and was a bit slimy. Now, I was very athletic. John wasn't exactly an athlete, and he always came in these grandmother-knitted sweaters. He walked on the curb and there was a time or two when we'd sort of push John, and he'd slip and get wet and he'd come back in another sweater, one was a brown one, and the next one was a beautiful grey with a beautiful stitching.

One time on Halloween his mother, a creative person, had a circus I remember I hung my legs on the tree, a great big mighty oak in the back yard and she was so glad. She gave me a small box with a porcelain doll in it, and that was my prize for hanging on the tree. It wasn't a birthday party; she just said, "Why don't we do this?" Spontaneous.

We grew up in John's dining room. Big stained glass shades on the lamp, and I remember hitting my head on it, and in another room were John's early grade things. His mother bound everything. You always felt welcomed. And John would say, Barbara let's read Big Little Books, so we'd pick one and I'd get a chapter done while he consumed a whole book.

What were the books like?

They had stories and pictures. John read the newspaper to his grandfather every day, and he had a phenomenal memory.

So for recreation he read either Big Little Books or the newspaper?

Yes. We were so fortunate so many kids were interesting. I was a picture framer and got this poster of the Poorhouse. I took art with Mr. Boyer.

So you had art class with John, then.

Yes. He was such a good artist. He did a cartoon and sent it to *Saturday Evening Post*. I have it framed and mounted.

Do you think he wanted to be an artist?

Well, his name card has a caricature of him. We had a group that we called "Our Gang" and he did caricatures of them for *Chatterbox*.

Who was in it?

Mahlon Frankhauser, Richard and Bobby Daubert, Jackie Hirneisen, Mary Ann Stanley, and Jackie Le Van.

Did John date Jackie Hirneisen?

Everyone says that, but I'm not sure. There was Jouette Eifert too. John admired Peggy because she was good looking, out-going. I always said I was a tomboy and very athletic, so how did I ever get into that group? I guess because I was co-captain of all the teams. After playing Ephrata, a number of kids went to Ephrata and whitewashed the buildings. When I saw all this stuff going on I went back and sat in the car.

Was John there?

I don't think John really went along, because they went in different cars. By then [1946] I was living on Waverly Street, and John had moved too. He never complained about living in Plowville.

Was he fun to be with?

Oh, yes. He wrote on my book, "To one of my old girlfriends." Up at Joan's they decided to play spin the bottle, and naturally I got John, and I said, "Pop it to me." He wrote something and insinuated that this girl at a sleep-over would hurtle the furniture. This was in a *New Yorker* thing.

What was his mother like?

Mrs. Updike was such a lovely person. I hadn't seen her in years and we were having taxes done by a fellow in Plowville, so I went to see her. I knocked at the screen door and their dog came, then Mrs. Updike. She hadn't seen me in years—this must have been about 1980. She comes to the door and says, "Barbara!" That made such an impression that she recognized me. Mrs. Updike was the kind of person who was interested in you. As a child when I went there she was always very kind. Of course Mr. Updike was fun. I had him for algebra. My brother got great marks and Mr. Updike said to me, "How can you be so dumb." He'd go to the window and shout out. In the far back alley there was the school bell, and I was a runner, so when the first bell rang Mr. Updike was coming out of the Athletic Club.

John was fascinated by Stephen's Luncheonette. My uncle, Clare Hartz, owned it and Stephen rented it. He lived above it. There was a dumbwaiter, and we would go up and down. Sometimes we would cut classes and go to Stephen's where we drank "Triple around the Fountain," with everything from the fountain—coke, syrup, cherry. One of the most sickening things you could drink.

Did you see John after you graduated?

I went to a book signing at Franklin and Marshall College[34] and overheard women talking in line, and I became very aware that they had read everything John wrote. Mary Ann Moyer was there and something was said about religion, and I said, "Oh, no, John was not like that." Then right about that time, I was up in the line and John saw me, and he said, "Barbara what are you doing there? You could have sent a message back and not stood in line." I said, "Oh, no I couldn't do that, John." My daughter has the book he signed, and she reads everything by John, and she has a wonderful collection and the kind of memory like John has. I sent him several books to sign for my daughter. She was so thrilled.

Was he good at sports?

I can remember John coming out but not much. He had a medical thing, the psoriasis, stuttering. When he comes back [for reunions], you find him stuttering around us, and yet when I saw him on television, I thought "He's not stuttering at all!" He did one thing that was really nice, one of our classmates and I could hear Joan Venne [Youngerman] saying maybe he'd want to be interviewed, and John said, "I won't be interviewed when I'm in with my class." That made good sense to all of us. He was just John Updike to me, the person I knew all my life.

Did any of you recognize yourself in Updike's characters?
John always said he never used names of real people, but I was engaged to "Rabbit"—"Rabbit" Hiester. I know who Dick Arndt was, but positively Gerry thinks he was "Rabbit."

Getting back to art, did you ever have museum trips?
We made trips to the Reading museum, but not to Philly.

John wrote in a recent poem that Shillington was like heaven for him. Did you feel that way?
Well, I was born on Philadelphia Avenue, so I was in Shillington all my life.

What sports did the kids play?
We used to go to Slate Hill and played Kick the Can. Everybody played.

Some people say his mother protected him from those games and sports. Do you agree?
He wasn't really that interested, he had other things he'd rather do. But he drew pictures of athletes. He wrote that he walked with Dick [Barthold?] on crutches from Albright football stadium to Shillington. I can hardly believe that, but that's what he said.

Did you ever think he would become an important writer?
We did know John was special. Mr. Boyer certainly thought he would be an artist rather than a writer because he was very good. My daughter doesn't even want my oil painting. John's oil painting was so much better. He was so much above us.

15. Tony VanLiew

D. Anthony VanLiew. "Torch 1, 2, 3. *Tony ... rabid Dodger fanatic ... not a good man to have in a china shop... 'Bah!' Spider had plenty of headaches as ad manager ... claims his favorite dish is watermelons and fried chicken (!) ... finds television wrestling hilarious."*—Shillington High School Year Book, Hi-Life

Tony VanLiew (born 1932) first met Updike in Kindergarten. After Updike left his summer work at the *Reading Eagle*, Tony VanLiew filled the vacancy, and he later worked as copy editor. He did title searches as well, and once saved his company a great deal of money. This interview was conducted in the summer of 2009.

Can you paint a portrait of John for me?
　　John developed his goofiness, sense of humor because he was the kind of kid that would have been picked on by a bully, and he was smart enough to know that with his psoriasis and stuttering, he was a kind of kid other guys would pick on. But nobody picked on him. He was a big fan of Big Little Books, and John would ask at every reunion if I still had mine. John was a big fan of Walt Disney.

There's a picture of him sitting on the back steps of his house with a Big Little Book. Must be about six or seven.
　　Here's his 1st grade photo.

John's one of the few looking into the camera in this 1st grade photo. What were his parents like?
　　Linda was kind of an old tick. His father was a nutcase. One time he locked himself in the closet. They tell me he opened the window and jumped out.

People must have loved taking his class.
　　They did.

We heard he was a disciplinarian, but that for the most part he was easy going.
　　During the summer he worked for the borough. Somebody said he never made more than $2,000. John would tell us wild stories about how cold Plowville was. It was old-fashioned.

Was it Linda's idea to move out there?
　　Linda was the moving force behind it. She lay down the law that was it.

Ever heard whether or not Wesley wanted Linda or vice versa.
　　Personal matters I don't know about. Anybody mention about roofball. He wasn't very good at sports in junior high. Johnny kind of split off to society, girls, parties. Gang I was with played baseball, went shooting. We kinda parted company there. We had him up to play baseball. They cleared an orchard 400 feet to center. I lined one out there one day. My brother called me Duke.[35]

Ever watch Ted Williams play?
　　No. John was the Boston Red Sox fan. He used to play basketball. He'd go back there and shoot baskets. He was pretty good at that but was no real

athlete. Getting back to roofball, the old baseball field was right off Philadelphia Avenue. You hit the ball on the roof and the next person had to hit it back when it rolled off. John was very noted for playing roofball. He seemed to have an instinct for it. Linda would have objected to quite a few other sports because he might get hurt, but she never objected to this.

What did she object to?
We used to go up the hill and maybe 200 feet is woods all around. It was a great place to go up and play. I'm amazed none of us were ever bitten by a snake. We'd go around the bushes and growth where we made machine gun nests. One or two summers we'd mountain climb. We got ropes, Boy Scout knives, baseball shoes with spikes and we'd scale the damn hills. We'd chop holes in the mountain and go up. I did fall once in wintertime, I guess it was New Year's Day, taking the short way, but the steps we cut in the side weren't there, and I went down the slope saw a tree trunk, and I put my arms around it. I guess it saved me. Otherwise I don't think I'd be here talking about it.

How old were you?
Fifteen. We'd make a real Battle of the Bulge back there on that gravel pit. I think it's still there. Fourth Street, you know, where the cemeteries are. Back in there. I haven't been up there in years. On the top you had a beautiful view of the area around here. We called it the Black Forest Park because it looked like it, had pine trees and went back into a more so of a jungle.

Johnny was along a couple of times. I got near the top and he was up there and all of a sudden what I was standing on gave way, and I had my hands over the edge like this, and Johnny ran to me and pulled me up and he said, "Boy, you turned about four, six shades of green while I was pulling you up." It wasn't a straight drop, but it was 200 feet, and you pick up speed going down. At the highest point. Another time we had big globs of dirt and thought we'd put a cave in there for a machine gun nest and John went in there and clump! The mud came down and just his feet sticking out. I had to pull him out. It was very dry, not really mud.

Think he could have gotten out on his own?
I don't think so.

Did he say anything about it
He didn't say much about it. I don't think he went up there again. He was scholarly, but he was funny with it. He always found a way to break up the class. Mrs. Showalter gave us every month something new to recite. We'd all sit there and sweat. She was sitting here, and Johnny starts to unbutton his shirt while he's reciting.

Did she see it?

I don't know. She couldn't figure out why the class was laughing. Then he started on his belt. He starts with the belt and that's when the class really broke up. She caught him before he got anywhere. Whether or not he was going to drop his pants I don't know. She let him get away with it. Johnny was Johnny and they left him alone.

The section of Shillington I lived in was all boys, but his was all girls. I went in the back door of the school at lunch time, and I look up and there's Johnny's face, he's hanging upside down. He went up there and was hanging upside down and all the girls were [shocked]. And he was uncoordinated, even though basketball was his game. He played with Gerry Potts. The crowd he hung out with was always on the social pages of *Chatterbox*. Sometimes they'd jump in the car and go to Pottstown. One time they went to Philadelphia for coffee in a car owned by Dolores Frederick.

Fred Muth was his close buddy; they alternated front pages in *Chatterbox*. If you knew their personalities you knew who did the page. We'd get there about 7 in the morning to practice a play Johnny wrote. I loved it. I really did. I hated to stand up and recite, but in this play I was being some other character in a comedy part, so I could let myself go.

I was in the 7th grade play, a take-off on Agatha Christie's *And Then There Were None*, and the door wouldn't open so I went through the window. Another time I was sitting on a sofa with a girl next to me, and she started going through my pockets, so I slapped her hand and she slapped me right back. One girl was carried off on a stretcher she was supposed to be dead but her skirt blew up, and she sat up to smooth it down. One girl was named Irene Sideways. There was a lot of off-the-wall nonsense. This would have been 44–45.

So when did you first meet John?

Kindergarten up to 9th grade when all the new girls were coming in. 9th grade is when they brought in kids from all the other districts. We kind of broke apart. Found a Christmas card from John & Martha, "See you in heaven!" I thought, "Oh boy, Oh, boy." I sent him a card with the obituary of Peggy Lutz. Never got a card back and didn't know what to make of it. I was scared to death of girls, esp. Peggy. We were at a reunion and she says, "Why didn't you ever ask me for a date?" I said, "I was scared to death of you. She was dating everybody. Johnny made a hit with the girls, and nobody ever put him down. He'd be back in the corner of Stephen's smoking and sitting with three or four girls. He started to smoke around 14 or 15.

Did John date Peggy?

Oh, yeah, I'm sure. Ann Weik asked me to go with her and I guess that's the first time I dated, and I was scared. Some guys were born Lotharios like

Bill Forry. I worked as a title searcher a year and a half; could have been a permanent job. They asked me to work permanently because the boss told me "You just saved the company $200,000, finding a piece of land that nobody ever knew about.

You followed John at the Eagle *1956–57? Any idea what his job there was like?*
Before leaving he did a profile on all the people there, and they tell me the managing editor and city editor filed it away, and nobody has ever seen it since because it was derogatory. Some Saturday nights I worked the Sports section. I had a chance to go to Albright College in the public relations department for $100/week. That was ok.

What were your duties at the Eagle*?*
They hired me when I showed them short stories I'd written. They put me on obituaries. Then the Sports section. I hated basketball, and I was sent out to cover a game or I'd be fired. I hated to cover general news like school board hearings.

You must have seen a lot of Updike stories.
Not too many. I was amazed that they didn't have an obit ready on John.

Was the Eagle *indifferent to Updike's career?*
Forester[36] and he were not on good terms. Some of his stories, whew. I forced myself to read *Rabbit, Run* because I knew they [were] making a movie out of it. I read *The Centaur* and remember the two driving in a snowstorm. Johnny and I and another guy took our driving lessons together in 1949 and we drove up the Tower. He'd take us into Penn Street, and the engine stalled. I was the only one to pass because I knew to put the emergency brake on. John passed later on and flunked the first time. John had his father's '38 boxy Buick. John would go over Lancaster [Avenue], then take his hands off the wheel and see who'd grab the wheel.

Why did he take such chances?
He just enjoyed it, like hanging upside down. Made him all the more popular. Girls didn't shy away from him after that. John would be with six or seven girls.

Isn't it funny to think if you'd been born in the section of Shillington where he lived and he lived where you were, your lives would have been so different. At reunions what kind of conversations did you have?
I'd say hello and he'd ask about the Big Little Books and then he was off, one time sitting there autographing books. He'd be standoffish. 1980 we got together wasn't exactly a reunion. John didn't come and he didn't want to be in a parade.

16. Joan Borner (Conrad)

Joan Borner (Conrad) (born 1933) graduated in 1951. She lived two doors from Clint Shilling's house on Philadelphia Avenue, where John took art lessons. Shilling headed the art department of the Reading Museum, fought Pancho Villa, and published cartoons. She attended a class in art with Updike and sat with him on the train to Philadelphia when the class went to see art shows. She married Harlan Conrad and has two children, Michael and Allyson. Joan Borner worked for Bell Telephone and lived in Shillington until her passing in 2011. This interview was conducted in the summer of 2009.

Were you or your friends surprised that John became famous?
    We never thought he would become a writer because he was so much into cartoons, and in the tenth grade he began making cartoons for *Collier's* and *Saturday Evening Post*. Mr. Boyer hooked up with Wannamaker's Department Store, and once a year they'd have an art show, and John would have showings quite frequently, and we'd go down on the train. Wasn't just us two, the whole class of art students, 11th, 12th grade, went together. Boyer took each student aside and told them no hullabaloo. He was very strict. You were on your own. You cleaned up.

Was Boyer a good artist?
    Yes he was. He was known greatly for his covered bridges, and different restaurants had his paintings. One in Wyomissing. Don't know what's happened to it. He was a serious man.
    I majored in art and home economics. I intended to go to Philadelphia College of Textile Art with another girl who said, "Joan, I won't be going with you because I'm pregnant." Girls didn't go there alone then, so I didn't go. Three weeks later my neighbor told me a girl was leaving with her husband to go to Korea and I got the job as a draughtsman. All men went in the service and women replaced them.

He kept up with his art?
    He'd frequently have more than one cartoon in *Chatterbox*.

Did you do paintings?
    For a while. Landscapes. The piece that I got in Wannamaker's was a design for pedal pushers [that] were coming out, and I did the top and bottom.

Did John ever give you any drawings?
   No. He was very unusual. Sort of sloppy. Always had a shirt tail hanging out. Hair always a scraggily mess, and we used to time and time again buy him combs and lay them on his desk and once a great big comb. Yet it was never in his eyes. His shirts would be buttoned wrong. His father was very neat, but they both had wild hair. A standout thing about him.

Did you know Nancy Wolf?
   Yes. She always gave us the inferior feeling. She traveled and was really educated compared to us. We always felt inferior to her. She traveled the country because her father was stationed somewhere inconvenient, so she moved in with her grandparents.

How did she make you feel inferior?
   We dressed like kids. She was very formal. She was older. Spoke kind of intelligently. Didn't associate with us much. Never rude or ugly. I was the only girl in 7th grade who was on the hockey team, and I played every game through my senior year. I lived on Greg Street, the last block in Shillington, and I had to walk to elementary school, and I ran, and that's why I could make the team.

Nancy didn't go out for sports?
   No. She was in *Chatterbox*.

Whatever happened to her?
   At a get together of Girls of '51, we keep track of who's passed or gone into a nursing home.

Was she the kind of girl John would be attracted to?
   Yes, like him very educated. We couldn't hold a conversation with Nancy. She'd have to come down. Just gave you that appearance. She was very very proper.

You probably had Wesley Updike for math?
   Yes, and he was quite a character. I was in the room the day he threatened [to jump out] from the second floor. I went up to explain the Algebra problem, because only one or two did well on the test, he opens the window and puts a leg out and threatens to jump. In the summer he'd raise strawberries and my father was always anxious to see him come, selling out of the car. He was a great socializer. I never met John's mother.

Did you read anything she wrote?
   I'm not a reader. I bought John's books but didn't read them.

Did you date John and was he a good dancer? Some say he was uncoordinated.
   He invited me to "A Tea and a Dance." They didn't drink tea, just a small

brunch then go to the auditorium and dance. He was not outstanding as a dancer. Took me to an old Shillington movie. He would walk down and pick me up, and we'd walk to the movie, but don't recall the picture. They always gave out all kinds of candy bars. Kids only went on Saturday afternoon. Mr. Joe Shivera built the new one on Lancaster Avenue, now a church, when the old one on Old Holland died.

Did you read John's contributions to Chatterbox?

Yes; he was very funny. With Boyer most of the time you could do painting or charcoals but John was doing the cartoon line. In Philly we only went to Wannamaker's not museums. Nobody ever gave Boyer a hard time. When he took you in [the] hall and talked to you he would say, "The least bit of trouble and you are out of the school." One kid he did put out of the class. Not McComsey but someone like him. McComsey, he was a wild one, oh, boy, he was wild.

So Nancy Wolf was in your class? What do you know about her?

We were in Mrs. Showalter's study hall, and back then you sat according to your name, and I was a B. One time Mr. Lewis would say give me the first two letters, I come out, "BO"; that stuck with me for years. Of course Updike was at the back of the room and he and Wolf were sitting in the far corner, and I was in the first seat. Nancy didn't like sewing and we had to do a book on the different kinds of hems, and so forth, and I must say mine were pretty good, and I even bought a note book and embroidered buttons, and she had borrowed it, and Mrs. Showalter picks this up and is bragging about this and finally Nancy said, "It's not mine." "Whose is it?" right quick she laid it down on my desk.

In Updike's last poems he talks about Shillington High School and his classmates.

His father really liked Shillington.

Do you recall any pranks John did?

Well, no. But we used to pull the comb joke. Sometimes I think he'd let his hair go so you could do that. It always looked so wild. His shirts were buttoned wrong. His big trait was the tail hanging out. But his father dressed nicely.

So you were never interested in John?

I only remember we sat together on the train that one time. Never got any vibes from him. I started going steady with Harlan and that was it for John. He was a weirdo, that's how we classified him. He was full of surprises. You never knew what he was going to do. He did a lot of strange things in art class. Most of the time he was the center of attraction.

17. Nancy A. March (LeVan)

Nancy March (LeVan). "Band 1, 2, 3, 4; Basketball 4; Chatterbox 3; Class Play 3, 4; Hi-Life 4; Hockey 3; Homeroom President 1; Secretary 4; Orchestra 1, 2, 3, 4; Volleyball 4; Y-Teens 2, 3, 4. *Nan ... never lacking a remark ... staunch member of Loyal Lovers of Loos.... Her interpretation of Mrs. Waughop's lines sparked the Senior Class Play ... witty, wise, and well-liked ... intends to work as a fashion artist."*—Shillington High School Year Book, Hi-Life

Nancy March LeVan (born 1932), who writes religious poetry, knew Updike from the 1st grade. She played the flute in a trio that included Mary Ann Schmehl Ehst (piano) and Ann Cassar (cello). Her husband, William "Bill" Le Van (born 1928), graduated from Shillington High School in 1946, obtained his degree at Albright College and went on to Dental school. This interview was conducted in the summer of 2009.

Maybe you can help fill in gaps from his earliest years. What did you know of the Updike family?
 I didn't know Linda. Wesley was my teacher and a real nutcase; off the wall.

What did he do?
 He was always making pies on the blackboard, cutting them in pieces. I never learned anything from him. Every now and then he would open the window and yell something or lean out the window and throw things out. Wesley Updike taught 9th grade Algebra. If you missed two days you were lost. Grade point was in letters. At midterm, he'd stop and pause and make a little note before handing out the grade. He got to one and said, "This fellow should be a minister," another pause. "The grades are DD, Doctor of Divinity." I wanted to disappear. Maybe I was dumb dumb. I passed with a D. Wes knew what he was talking about and just couldn't convey it. More entertaining than anything. Eventually, I graduated with double major, one was math.

I've heard that Mrs. Showalter was pretty good. What did you think?
 We called Showalter, "Eagle Beak" for her very sharp nose, very thin, very strict. Very good with her writing skills, but always pointing at you. She used the Palmer method and taught writing. Dumb dumb here is a left-hander. In one school room there were two doors she would sneak in the back and watch us writing and boom she'd hit you, if you wrote left handed, so I pretended to write with my right hand when she was there. I had a tough

time in college because it would blot when I wrote left-handed though everything might be perfect in my essay but I was too tired to rewrite. We were too poor to have a typewriter. Shillington grade school is now the doctor's office building on Lancaster.

What can you tell me John's life in school?
He was a leader of skits and plays at assemblies. "Oklahoma" or "Little Orphan Annie."

Didn't Updike write a play with Fred Muth?
I can't remember. I knew he wrote this for our 50th, "To the Juniors from the Seniors."

Oh yes, that's notorious. Nice that he signed it for you.
I never saw him in a bad mood and always had a good sense of humor.

Did you know people in his gang?
There was Peggy Lutz, Joan Venne, and Joan Zug. He drove an old car. We'd go to Stephen's almost every day after school. Kids ready to let off steam.

Can you recall any of the songs on the juke box?'
The Dorseys[37] maybe. Some rock coming in.

Did people dance at Stephen's?
It was a fountain.

I heard some kids danced on the tables.
That would have been one of my tricks. Fun place to be. Still on Lancaster across from the church. In a duplex building across from a little post office, 13 feet wide, seventy feet long.

Who else was there?
Barry Nelson. He was a heart throb.

Mentioning the church, did you get a feeling for John's religion?
I never knew where John was coming from. I was Lutheran reformed, he was Lutheran. We went to his church because it was fun, but after two years of instruction, I went back to my own church. But I've been reading things to see where he was coming from. Some of the things he'd written I would not have written as a Christian. I just didn't read a lot of his books for that reason, and others were up against the ceiling. So I really wasn't too interested in his books.

I'm sorry if I seem to be pressing you, but can you describe the parts that bothered you.
The sexual parts. And the witches of… That was a money maker. There is witchcraft and I don't think it's good to hold it up. Definitely there's witches. Why would anybody really want to write that anyway?

John used real people as models in his work. One was Nancy Wolf. Did you know her?

Nancy Wolf was a neighbor of mine. We were both in the class of 1951.

Do you know if she was going steady with John?

Yeah. She was a very sweet gal. I liked her a lot.

Did he ever do anything odd or unusual?

He was always unusual. He was a copy of his dad because he was a unique individual. He was very bashful, like his mother. He was laid back with a lot of things.

He seemed to be friendly with a lot of girls.

The girls all liked him and every time there was a picture or he was on TV the guys resented that. They never had too many nice things to say about John. The gals put their attention on him and the guys thought he was a nutcase. Any kind of book came out they had to build him up make him look wonderful. I was in art class with him and I loved those cartoons he did. For some reason I won the art award, and he won something else. We were on the *Chatterbox* together.

Did you ever read John's poetry?

I have a poetry book of his and I read some of those things but again you know they're not for me.

18. Myrtle Council

Myrtle Council (born 1923) graduated from Shillington High School in 1941. She served as President of the Pennsylvania Federation of Women's Clubs, 1984–1986. Myrtle Council worked in the fleet post office in New York City during World War II. A leader of the Shillington High School Alumni Association, she edited *Berks County Women*. She served as secretary to the guidance counselor at Shillington High School and still edits the Alumni newsletter, also called *Chatterbox*. Myrtle Council was voted to the Pennsylvania Honor Roll of Women in 1996. This interview was conducted in the summer of 2009.

Where did you live in Shillington, in relation to John?

We lived on Philadelphia Avenue, but also on Franklin Street the area across the street was a baseball diamond. That was the end of Shillington at that time. All gathered at that spot to play ball. John would come down the street and sit on the curb of Franklin Street and watch. We felt sorry for John because he was not allowed to come out and play with the neighborhood gang. I think it was too much for his mother. This was in the 30's.

So it was too rough for Linda?
No, I felt sorry for him; poor John he can't come over and play.

So he instead played with his drawing?
I think he was academic from the start. He started as an artist in 7th grade.

Yes, in A Soft Spring Night in Shillington, *he described how he used the mimeograph as a child. Did you know him after he graduated?*
Yes. We visited him in Ipswich. I had a sister there. It was a surprise to me that he had his office in the town. We had met Mary earlier in Shillington.

I had a letter from Mary the other day.
I had that feeling that she was into books and music.

So they were well suited?
Seemed so. He went right from school to *The New Yorker*. My sister-in-law Ann was his 1st grade teacher.

Some 1st grade teacher said that John was a genius.
No, she didn't say anything like that.

He had so much fun that he must have had great discipline.
Got that from his father who was fun-loving, but his mother was strait-laced. My favorite of John's books was *The Centaur*. His dad was a humble guy and an excellent teacher. He had eccentricities. We'd all talk about the crazy things he would do. When out of sorts or impatient with his students, he'd open the window and pretend he was throwing up. As kids we were taken aback by it but he made his point. He would throw chalk at the blackboard. Just his way of doing things but he also told stories that were way beyond the reasoning of high school kids. Told us different things that had a point, like "If you're going to rob something don't rob a loaf of bread rob a million bucks."

He was very inventive, would you say?
I think that's what made him an excellent teacher. One kid asked a question, and he gave him a pass to the library and said, "Here, go to the library, look it up and report."

Helps you to think what kind of father he must have been.
That's why I say John's tricks must have come from his Dad. He liked his dad a lot. With his grandparents living with them he was more grown up than others.

Did you ever hear of any difficulties between Wes and Linda?
　I think there was some dissension at times. There was a difference of personality between them. She could be on the uppity side, he was down to earth.

Ever read Linda's books?
　Yes, I read her books.

Did she use as models any one from town?
　I'm not sure. She was invited to the Women's Club, made one visit and didn't come back. She said she wasn't treated right. She was not rejected or blackballed. I told the person, "Whoever said that was lying cause that was not the case. We thought, if we didn't treat her right maybe we should have put out a red carpet and bowed down. This was in the Forties.

We heard she wouldn't participate in making bandages during the war.
　She didn't want to be part of the Shillington Women's Club.

Some have suggested she didn't want John tied down to his sweetheart.
　I don't think she had that much to be alarmed about.

John always said that his character Rabbit shows what would have happened to him if he hadn't left. What do you think?
　I think he used local people and then as a creative thinker he made his character. I think he painted with words. He had a way of describing things that after you read it you say, oh, yeah, that's true. The detail! He describes a trolley car coming down the tracks and you'd say, yeah, that's how it was. It's like he was drawing a picture.

Yes, it constantly amazes you. A piece published this month in Sewanee Review *said Updike writes language adventures. Just hitting a golf ball becomes a language adventure. Nobody ever wrote about golf that way.*
　I admired him for the words he used. He could pick out the most unusual words, or use words in a most unusual way. He was a genius in that respect.

Was he born with it?
　When he wrote for *Chatterbox* his language was already well developed.

Did you know that satirical piece he wrote for the Eagle*?*
　Don't know exactly.

The Eagle *got rid of it because John satirized people, but nobody knows. Have you kept up with Updike's writing?*
　Not really. I've collected some books and put them in the archives of the school. They're not available to the public.

I guess you read the poems in Endpoint.
　Nah, I don't think I read much of that.

19. Benarda A. Palm

> Benny Palm. "Chatterbox 4; Chorus 3; Class Play 3; Hi-Life 4; Y-Teens 2, 3, 4. Benny ... unfailingly high spirits ... loves to play, coach, and watch all manner of sports ... constant companion of Ginnie ... a conscientious worker ... vigorous laugh (some call it horsey) ... hopes to become a teacher."— Shillington High School Year Book, *Hi-Life*

Benarda Palm graduated from Kutztown University and taught second and fourth grades in Reading schools for over thirty years.

Did you read any of Updike's books?

I think Mr. Updike in his musings and his writing is a little above my level. I started the first one, and I didn't comprehend. The readability was there but where he was coming from wasn't where I was living. It's a trial. When you went to English classes in college, it was, what is the meaning of this book? But when you get Updike it's, "What's the meaning of this sentence?"

What was he like in school?

I went to Fairview school and in 9th grade to Shillington High School, so I don't remember if he was there. I was in his father's homeroom and we both were college preps and took full time art. John used to copy my Chemistry homework, and he was having a hard time getting his first cartoon accepted by *The New Yorker* magazine. Mr. Boyer would critique it and then he'd redo it. They were in *The New Yorker*, and I thought, my God, I never knew anyone who got into that magazine.[38]

Since you had Wesley Updike for a teacher, what were your thoughts about him?

I called him and John "eggheads," and he had a great sense of humor, and so did John. You had to be focused in, because a lot of times the jokes were in-jokes. One incident I found hysterical, but I didn't laugh out loud. They were talking about doing more than one thing at a time, which today we call multitasking. We went around the room asking if it could be done, and John said he could do five things, rocking in a chair, rubbing his foot on his dog's belly, reading a book, watching television, and listening to the radio. That's John Updike.

He had to because he knew so much.

He took his SAT's, and they called him wrong on one answer, and he debated with them and he was right. Now that I remember very clearly.

So, he never stopped learning?

Anything that took his fancy, he just was that kind of genius. And to me he was a genius.

Sounds like he learned how to learn. Was he restless with kids that were slower than he.

Oh, no. He was human, a regular guy, that's what I loved about him. If you didn't know the answer to a question, he'd say, "Hey you skipped no. 3." I'd say, "I didn't know the answer." He'd say, "Ok, I'll skip no. 3 too." He was almost like a farm boy.

He never dressed in fine clothes?

We weren't allowed jeans, and girls had to wear dresses and blouses. He was just a regular guy.

Who were his best friends?

I always wanted to be one of those. I don't remember them or a girlfriend. It wasn't about that then, more friendship.

Some say he dated a junior, Nancy Wolf.

I wouldn't have known her. I didn't go to proms, just one dance in high school. My one dance was 9th grade. I was having a lot of family fluctuations. The money wasn't for clothing. At the dance, we'd smoke cigarettes and go down and sit in the gym seats. I would always go down, and one boy came over, and it was Barry Nelson. I couldn't dance with him I was so embarrassed, but I did. Afterwards, I had to run to the bathroom. He was a heart throb. The girls laughed.

Why did they laugh?

Township people like me felt like outsiders. I guess they knew it. I didn't hold a grudge. It didn't add or subtract from who I was. There was a clique and you just weren't a part of it. The clique was so strong in my day in that year I didn't even try. John was valedictorian and we had 3 salutatorians, so how could I be part of that group? Dancing with Barry and having John copy my work were my stars.

Any activities you enjoyed that were your strengths?

Too many cigarettes wrecked me for singing. I tried out for every sport in 9th grade and made them in senior year. In *Chatterbox* I was girls' sports editor. I kept the last *Chatterbox* because John did cartoons of the seniors in that one. In his heart he was a cartoonist.

Did you go to Stephen's after school like John did?

No I had to go home. Made me even more of an outsider. Had to get home before dark because our house on Liggit Street had no street lights. Also, I got expelled for a while. I was accused of pulling my *Chatterbox* out of my teacher's hands.[39] He had my *Chatterbox* and was standing right in front of me, so I just eased it out. Guess it wasn't eased enough. So I wasn't a wallflower.

Do you remember the pranks some of the guys pulled?
I heard. And I wasn't one of those who did the painting at Ephrata. They were one of our big rivals. I know Joan Venne was along with Marty Stover. The kids admired that.

Did you think John was involved?
Oh, yes. That was a John joke. Updike is a name that's wonderful. But his books. I didn't quite reach the genius class.

Linda's books, though, are very approachable. Very down-to-earth. Did you read them?
She used the name Linda Hoyer because she didn't want to ride on anyone's coattails.

I asked her how she felt about John being a big success. She said, "I wish it had been me."
To me he was famous even before he graduated from Shillington High School. He was with *The New Yorker*. That *Chatterbox* has good drawings of his.

Germans love his fiction.
Maybe they understand his books better than I do.

Did you know any girls in your class with red hair and green eyes.
Mary Orff. She wasn't shy but not a bubble either. Like me, she wasn't social. You'd think us wallflowers we would be together. I was a farm girl, horses, pigs, a lot of fruit trees. I'd sell fruit from my wagon. A *nickel* for a box of cherries. It was eleven cents for a movie. At the end they gave you a candy bar. Pecan Rolls. Little ones with nougat. There was only one movie. Across from Ibach's drugstore. Three pounds of scrap iron would get you in the movies in town. Or one rubber tire. There you'd go, on the trolley with a tire. Maybe three pounds of newspapers would do it. My favorites were *The Wizard of Oz* and the one where the girl sang "Blue Bird of Happiness." That used to make me feel good inside.

Did you ever see John at the movies?
He was tall, so I might have seen him. Had a long neck. Sometimes made funny cartoons of himself so others couldn't do it. He was smart.

Did you memorize in English class?
We had a book for state of Pennsylvania. With poems you had to memorize for that year. We had to stand up, and everybody had to say the poem

of the month. "When the frost is on the pumpkin" was one.[40] I think that was 8th grade. Yeah, Shakespeare too. I couldn't understand it. The language was foreign to me.

What was John's home life like?

His parents were polar opposites, so I could imagine they would argue. And her parents were there too, so another generation added to it. But it made a good thing out of him.

Almost in spite of his family.

He had a lot of his father, and I think he rejected the tough part of his mother.

He might have seen where it got her, isolated.

Everyone liked him; nobody was "Get Updike." Nothing like that. He certainly didn't have a day when the clique didn't talk to him. If so, he would just have made it a joke.

Part II: Harvard and New York City, 1950–1957
Writers Recall the Early Years

Because Updike's mother had read in an anthology[1] that some great writers listed there had attended Harvard, she encouraged him to apply. Updike won a full scholarship and entered Harvard in 1950, majored in English, and graduated summa cum laude and Phi Beta Kappa in 1954. Updike had chosen Harvard over Cornell because he wanted to do cartoons for the Harvard *Lampoon,* and hone those skills he had learned while writing for the Shillington High School *Chatterbox.* The *Lampoon* became a vehicle for his graphic and literary talents. Though Archibald MacLeish did not admit Updike into his creative writing class, Updike, undeterred, wrote "Ace in the Hole" for Albert Guerard. The story was the germ of *Rabbit, Run* (1960), and that novel was the beginning of his "Rabbit" saga. As he said in *Odd Jobs,* Harvard gave him "the liberating notion that now I could teach myself." In short, in college Updike learned how to learn, something demonstrated in his research for many of his books.[2] Also at Harvard Updike met Radcliff student Mary Pennington; they married the summer before his senior year.[3]

After graduating, Updike studied painting at the Ruskin School of Drawing and Fine Arts in Oxford, England, on a Knox fellowship. There he met E. B. White and his wife Katharine, a fiction editor for *The New Yorker*. Updike had dreamed of working for *The New Yorker* ever since 1946 when his father's sister gave the Updikes a subscription. In a high school poem Updike appraised magazines from *Time* to *Collier's* deciding that *The New Yorker* was "beyond compare." As a teen he had amazed his friends by identifying the magazine's cartoonists even with their drawings inverted. He revered *New Yorker* writers James Thurber, Robert Benchley, Ogden Nash, and, most importantly, J. D. Salinger. So when Katharine White offered him a job on the spot, he accepted, and when the fellowship year ended the Updikes moved to New York. Updike's career direction then veered from drawing to writing.

Now, working alongside veteran writers Roger Angell and William Maxwell, Updike reported on everything from boat shows to receptions for Russian poets. Meanwhile, the magazine accepted forty-two poems and eleven short stories between 1955–57. Although in nearly two years he had risen to a point where his "casuals" (in *New Yorker* parlance) no longer required a rewrite editor, he eventually realized that such writing interfered with his creative progress. Perhaps he wanted to become a novelist and return to the three novels he had begun in high school and college. If so, the intensely competitive New York literary life was not conducive to such extended deliberation either. So, in 1957 Updike left New York for the more favorable Ipswich, Massachusetts, though he never entirely left New York or *The New Yorker*. He needed to confer with his life-long publisher Knopf, preside at the American Academy of Arts and Sciences, give readings at the "92nd St. Y," attend art exhibitions, and visit friends and relatives. As for the magazine, it would eventually publish Updike's staggering 752 poems, stories, reviews and articles.

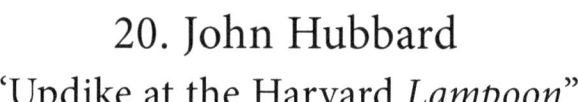

20. John Hubbard
"Updike at the Harvard *Lampoon*"

Sometime in 1951, when I was a member of the Harvard *Lampoon* staff, in the business dept., an unusual, beaky character arrived who wished to join the staff, who impressed himself on me by his appearance and voice, which showed him to be not at all a New England WASP but emanated from quite another tribe. I never learned much about that tribe but his name was Updike. Very quickly he established himself as a skilled and prolific writer of stories and poems, later on revealing his equally gifted skills as an artist.

The *Lampoon* at that time had a good number of talented men on its staff (no women), including Fred Gwynne (who later became an actor in theatre and T.V.), John Train, George Plimpton, C. B. Flood and Carey Welch (the distinguished scholar of Islamic Art). A gifted bunch. Unfortunately, due to the relatively swift turnover of undergraduates, the subsequent years were rather leaner, although Michael Arlen and Lew Gifford were also marvelous contributors but the talent thinned from then on. This was a recurrent situation with Lampy, as the years of World War II were also thin but the important thing was to ensure that the magazine appeared. As the song suggested, "in every state the *Lampoon's* late, it happens all the time." A young man called Brad Thurlow kept the magazine afloat during most of the war and Updike accomplished the same feat during his time. In some ways, it was a bit of a miracle that he was elected to membership. Although all the active members were in favor of him, there were the social members (or drones) who resisted his charms and failed to appreciate his blazing talents. That was often a hazard in a group of young men who elected certain members simply because of affection rather than an acknowledgment of their gifts. I recall that several of us had failed to appreciate the dangers around Updike's election and had to make a concerted effort to persuade the doubters.

When I realized that John had told friends that he came to Harvard principally in order to join the staff of the *Lampoon*, I recognized what had been a close shave. By that time he was renamed Upchurch and remained Upchurch for some time.

I had joined the writers on the magazine in about 1952 and, in the same year, was elected President, or Prexy, which I confess was flattering but scary, as I was aware of my limited talents (which stubbornly remained limited) but also aware of the responsibility of publishing magazines. Several issues of that period contained my work, and that of others, but chiefly the magazine became the product of Updike's imagination. I'm sure that continued during his term as Prexy but in my time he never complained of pressure or failed to deliver excellent copy. I don't recall his taking much of a role in producing the parodies that were published at intervals but he did some splendid covers and a continuous flow of cartoons (in his sure, emphatic style), plus of course articles and poems, these being my particular favorites: "recount oh Rand, recount McNally, there's been some error in your tally," etc. Updike also seemed more mature, more focused than most of us and was always a bit separate, as he lived with his future wife in Lowell House in happy cohabitation. I recall paying him a visit in my role of pleading editor and being struck by the atmosphere of serious domesticity that pervaded the rooms where he lived with Mary.

I don't believe he attended many of our regular, badly-behaved dinners but seeing him was always a pleasure. He and I attended the lectures of an English professor who specialized in the romantic poets and frequently recited their poems in a dry, pure mid-western accent which I found risible but which John hugely enjoyed, probably for mixed reasons. At some point in the early 1960's he came to London and we met at the gallery that represented me, going on to lunch. I remember him saying that the one thing he disliked about the *Lampoon* was what he thought of as its pervading homoerotic atmosphere. That surprised me but, bearing in mind what I've written about his domestic set-up, our more juvenile boys-own world could hardly be up his street.

During lunch, my wife asked him what sort of an editor I had been, to which he replied "like most of them" and left it at that. I never showed him any of my paintings and I don't think we discussed contemporary art but I doubt that it held much interest for him. Over the years, I read a good many of his essays on traditional painters but never found them interesting or penetrating. My guess is that they were a kind of light relief in the literary enterprise of a considerable talent. That is certainly one of the many attributes of visual art.

After Harvard, John Hubbard spent three years in army counter-intelligence, mainly in Japan, followed by two years of study at an NYC art school. He then worked and studied in Rome, went to London in 1960, married the next year, and settled near the channel in Dorset. He's been closely involved in the U.K. art world, having many exhibitions (modern landscape) both in the U.K. and abroad. He was awarded the Jerwood Painting Prize in 1996, published the artist's book Portrait of New Harmony *in 1988. Remaking Landscape, a biography of his work since 1957, was published in 2017 by Unicorn Publishing Group.*

21. Austin Briggs
"John Updike's First Fan Letter"

My first meeting with John Updike took place in 1950 during our freshman year at Harvard while he was engrossed in his dorm suite in Hollis. Adam Begley's biography, *Updike,* quotes me on the occasion as follows: "[John] was playing big-time gambler more than poker, a cigarette dangling from his mouth and in costume with a green eye shade and sleeve garters on his shirt." I remember as well John's intense interest when I replied to his query, that, yes, I was related to the illustrator Austin Briggs, that I was the artist's son. Illustrators and cartoonists were celebrities in those days: I recall my parents appearing in 1951 on a TV interview program broadcast from the Stork Club. John's interest, however, went far beyond that of the ordinary fan. He knew all about Dad's advertising and editorial work, and he knew that before abandoning cartooning Dad had drawn *Flash Gordon*[4] and worked on *Secret Agent X-9,* a strip created by Dashiell Hammett. John was so impressed that when he met my father for the first time, he could hardly speak, prompting Dad to ask later whether my new friend's stammer always reduced him to near silence. Overcoming his awe at a second meeting, John quizzed Dad with remarkably informed questions about the world of commercial art, but never said a word about his own long-standing ambitions to enter that world.

Although John attended the Ruskin School of Drawing and Fine Art in Oxford after Harvard, by then he had wisely decided that writing, not graphic art, would be his career. The cartoons he drew for the *Lampoon* show little talent, Dad agreed, and I daresay the same can be said of the covers and cartoons that I have heard he unsuccessfully submitted to *The New Yorker* during his Harvard years. After their return from Oxford, I do not recall seeing any paintings or drawings by John on display in the Manhattan apartments that he and Mary rented on Riverside Drive and West 13th Street, or later in their house in Ipswich. Nor can I recall any art by John, or for that matter (with the exception of some tame Audubon prints) any art of interest at all hanging in the dimly lit rooms of John and Martha's mansion in Beverly, where it seemed to me that in this—as in the decor overall—it was Martha's taste, not John's, on genteel and expensive display.[5]

As the splendid essays gathered in *Just Looking, Still Looking*, and *Always Looking* witness, John did not abandon his interest in art, of course, and from early on, before he began publishing art criticism, he became a kind of art director, overseeing the production of his books. Seeing his first book, *The Carpentered Hen*, through the press, Begley says, John "was passionate about the physical object, the item you held in your hand–the feel of it, the look of it, even the smell of it," and John wrote to his *New Yorker* editor Roger Angell in 1979 of the deep enjoyment he found in designing dust jackets for his books. Over the spring weekend in 1968 on which John received an honorary D.Litt. from Hamilton College, where I taught for fifty years, John told me of the pleasure he took in the notes on typography in Knopf's editions of books, and of his remarkable contract with Knopf that gave him control over the design of his dust jackets.

Given John's engagement in the production of his books, there is a worthwhile essay waiting to be written about his dustcovers. The obvious place to start would be "Deceptively Conceptual," his review in the October 17, 2005, *New Yorker* of Ned Drew and Paul Sternberger's *By Its Cover: Modern American Book Cover Design*. In his review, John said, "Appropriating a Blake watercolor, say, or a Dürer etching or an Ingres painting for the cover's pictorial element puts the text in excellent company without diluting its descriptive authority. Nobody confuses these artists' representations with the author's, but their validated excellence may rub off." This is coy, of course, for it was John who appropriated a detail of Blake's *Adam and Eve Sleeping* for *Couples*, Dürer's *The Four Witches* for *The Witches of Eastwick* and Ingres' *The Turkish Bath* for *Villages*.

Writing in his review as "a book producer," John spoke approvingly of the way in which digital-graphics "have the virtue of removing a contemporary illustrator from the equation." On one occasion, however, he sought out a jacket illustration by a contemporary artist—my father. When *The Poorhouse Fair* appeared in 1959, Dad wrote John to tell him how much he admired the novel and to comment on how the character John Hook reminded him of his maternal grandfather. With his warm note, Dad enclosed a crayon sketch, a back view of a standing figure that was based, he explained, on boyhood memories of grand-father David Austin Davidson. In his appreciative response, John wrote that in fact Hook was based on *his* maternal grandfather and that the drawing looked just like the grandfather John Hoyer, after whom he—John Hoyer Updike—was named. Later, when my first wife Margaret and I visited the Updikes in Ipswich in 1960 or '61, John took us downtown to see the office he had rented over a cafe on the second floor of a rundown building on Main Street. The small room was barely furnished, with the exception of the lovely surprise John had saved for us: above the army surplus desk, framed, hung my father's sketch.[6]

Over the years, my correspondence with John dwindled to the occasional postcard, but in March 1976, a letter arrived from him. What I had already heard some time ago from Kit (Christopher) Lasch, John reported the sad news that he and Mary had separated. John's purpose in writing concerned "the cherished drawing" of Hook that Dad had sent nineteen years before. John asked whether I would grant permission to use the sketch for the jacket of a new edition of *The Poorhouse Fair* he was preparing.[7] The drawing "has followed me everywhere," he said, "most recently to the apartment in Boston where I live the austere life of the separated." He expressed his hope that "this sentimental project" would give my late father "some of the small pleasure it would give me."

All in all, I never encountered much sentimentality in John in person or in print. Consider, a sentence in [a] letter asking permission to reproduce the drawing of Hook. Although separated and living in Boston, John explains, he is writing me from the Ipswich house because it is a Sunday, "my day to visit Mary, the pets, and whatever children are around." The intervention of the pets between the estranged wife and the children left behind and apparently not very interested in seeing their father seems to me to cut off the feeling implicit in the painful situation. I do recall a strong and rare note of sentimentality in John on one occasion, however. During a too brief moment alone together at our fiftieth Harvard reunion in 2004, John told me that he wasn't sure he had ever told me how much Dad's drawing, arriving so early in his career, had meant to him and still meant to him. He always thought of the gift as his first fan mail, he said, and he added—with an unfamiliar throb in his voice—it was the best he had ever received.

Sometime after earning his B.A. from Harvard and Ph.D. from Columbia, Austin Briggs (born 1932) pursued post-doctoral work in cinema history and criticism at Boston University. He has devoted most of his scholarly attention to James Joyce. Since retiring in 2007 after teaching fifty years at Hamilton College, he lives in San Miguel de Allende, Mexico, where he continues to publish on Joyce and is currently working as well on Ezra Pound's anti-Semitism and on Edith Wharton's "Love Diary."

22. Jeffrey Ludwig
"Roommates and Rivals: John Updike and Christopher Lasch at Harvard"

Roommates make such awkward farewells.[8]
—John Updike, 1969

Every once in a while circumstances conspire to thrust two young people together as freshmen roommates who will become extraordinary. In the autumn of 1950, John Updike and Christopher Lasch found one another at Harvard University's Hollis Hall. Both Lasch and Updike aspired to write fiction, and both had somewhat controlling mothers. They competed constantly, each striving to out-perform and out-write the other, swapping drafts of everything they wrote, inviting the other to criticize and scrutinize the work at hand. Lasch and Updike continually made each other better, as people but especially as writers, at a crucial moment in their formative years. Indeed, in this random pairing of roommates, alive with the petty squabbles and tender passions of teenagers, the silhouettes of their careers emerge.[9] Lasch eventually published widely, expounding most famously on a "culture of narcissism" gripping the country in the late 1970s, warning about the false promises yoked to the idea of progress, and describing the deleterious effects of elites in American life. Updike authored a wealth of fiction that chronicled the pleasures and anxieties, the limits and promise, of American middle class existence. Both authors stood apart in their generation for their uniqueness of thought, and were keenly interested in forging a better understanding of the temperament of the "American Century."

Lasch certainly picked up on the rules of the separate world dividing undergraduates right away. In his very first letter home he told his parents that "The rich boys live in Wigglesworth and Strous and are held in much contempt." The stuffy milieu of Harvard was regrouping as a still substantial enclave.[10] Updike too was struck by the insular world of Harvard, comparing his college years to the indignation of a caterpillar when struggling to become a butterfly. He recounted his freshmen year culture shock in the 1973 poem, "Apologies to Harvard" comparing the school's buttoned-up style to his youthful experiences in Pennsylvania. While the homes of his parents in nostalgic retrospect created an inspiring "hothouse world," cold Cambridge, the domain of libraries housed "the wintry smiles" of "snowmen" like Descartes, Marx, and Milton.[11]

Despite the resentment, Updike acknowledged that Cambridge was "idyllic enough"; moreover, in the same poem he admitted having "no regrets" about attending Harvard. His alma mater, he confessed, "[took] me in, raw as I was ... for one quadrennium, [a]nd spit me out, by God, a gentleman." Too, Updike never shook the fond images of the Fogg museum's glowing windows, "the snowy Yard," the "wet old magazines" smell in the *Lampoon* office (where he eventually served as editor), and various "revelations" in class. Updike felt the unique conditions of college life pushing him irresistibly, rapidly, into new friendships, a seethe of "mutual discovery."[12] College became the incubator that slowly, almost imperceptibly transformed Lasch and Updike from children to adulthood.[13]

Christopher Lasch made friends easily in college, foremost among them was another public school graduate who, like him, grew up loving to write. "My roomie's name is John Updike, and he comes from Reading, PA.," Lasch informed his parents in his first letter home. "His father is a public schoolteacher. He was accompanied by his mother and an aunt, who drove him up, and this embarrassed him somewhat, but he is a very nice guy. He wants to be either a writer or a cartoonist. His field seems to be humor writing, and he is thinking about going out for the *Lampoon*." This proved a propitious pairing, indeed.

In later years, the momentousness of rooming with Lasch compelled Updike to draft two short stories which suggested the importance of their friendship. He wrote "The Christian Roommates" for *The New Yorker* in 1964 and "One of My Generation" for the same magazine in 1969. The latter piece in particular captured the flavor of their rivalry and admiration for each other. In it Updike fondly recalled climbing the long stairs to his assigned dormitory to discover "bent-necked and narrow-shouldered" his roommate, a complete stranger inhabiting "an island of light." There, amid "the bleakest sticks of institutional furniture" sat a young man composing a poem. The Nebraska-born "Ed Popper" (Lasch) "was a disciple of Robert Lowell—the early, Boston Lowell," and who, in the "rural isolation" of his upbringing devoured every book he could get his hands on. The young Updike, who reported that his roommate's "domination of me began at once," was simultaneously awed and a little resentful. Together, in Updike's telling, they experienced how shared college explorations allowed their imaginations to grow like vines "on a sunny wall," here gliding along the "surface of a poem," there plumbing the "crannies of pun, ambiguity, and buried allusion" until new understanding revealed itself. The roommates traveled to previously uncharted literary territories; "this," according to Updike "was life lived on the nerve ends."[14] According to Updike, he and Lasch bonded over "a battery of running jokes." They kept each other awake and laughing deep into many nights "with improvised parodies," skits, and musicals, which made a mockery of their instructors and fellow students.[15]

Lasch and Updike grew so close during their freshman year that they decided to spend some of their first spring break together (a tradition they repeated). The roommates traveled together to Updike's hometown of Shillington, Pennsylvania, a place Lasch raved was "a beautiful country with broad fields and blue distant ridges." They returned to Harvard at the end of the break closer than ever.[16]

Lasch and Updike involved each other in most aspects of their writing. They read and edited assigned work, whether it was Lasch's history essays or Updike's English papers, and even opened up their private correspondence to one another. In a letter home, Lasch allowed the roommate reading over his shoulder to have his own say: "Updike is very unhappy about being left out of this letter. He states that it is all right; he really isn't that important, and after all, it is of no concern whether or not I even have a roommate."[17]

While they invariably had their share of typical college fun, writing was the tie that truly bound them together as friends. Both arrived at Harvard with designs on becoming writers, and engaged in something of a writing partnership. They often set aside entire nights and weekends to writing marathons, and each started several novel-length projects in the other's presence, trying their hands at crafting short stories, often establishing a theme for the event. On one such occasion, for instance, they locked themselves in their room to write about the old South, as depicted in the genre of Westerns.[18]

Although they often met with discouraging results from the national magazines, they continued to write despite the growing piles of rejection slips. The two kept at it as late as the spring of their junior year (their last semester together). They continued to write and shop their work, Lasch complained to his parents, "But no one is selling very fast. I really wish I knew how it could be done."[19]

A certain symbiotic relationship, one of mutual advantage, permeated the friendship between budding writers. They played off the ideas and styles of the other, and developed in the process. In a letter home to his parents, Updike contended that Lasch was pushing him to be "less glib" whereas he returned the favor by increasing the "color and verve" of Lasch's prose. While it is debatable how much glibness Updike excised from his work, Lasch's senior thesis, "Imperialism and the Independents," glowed with literary flare. For entire sections of the thesis Lasch allowed his imagination to invent and embellish entire scenes out of history, which he depicted in vivid detail. To some extent, he had Updike to thank for showing him the way.[20]

Lasch and Updike also collaborated on a number of side projects. Coupled with their impromptu nighttime musicals, they coauthored several plays, scrolls of poetry, and even a television pilot. "If only he would write a musical with me," Lasch grumbled to his parents, "We would make a great combination, with his brilliance and my capacity for drudgery." Still, some of their plays were performed in Cambridge.[21]

For all the collegiality between Lasch and Updike, and for all the fiction that piled up during their time together, the occasional stirrings of animosity also crept into their friendship. The worst, for Lasch, came when Updike was elected to Phi Beta Kappa during their junior year and he was not. "If he really is a better student than I am, then I fear for myself," Lasch complained in a letter home. "His seems a pedantic and lazy mind, and one limited to a very small area of knowledge."[22] Updike expressed his misgivings about Lasch in "The Christian Roommates," which contained a Lasch-based character, the Midwesterner "Dawson." Like Lasch, Dawson possessed "a sulky slouching bearing" and "puppyish" features, which masked a "terrible temper." The Lasch-Dawson amalgamation "was a disciple of Sherwood Anderson and Ernest Hemingway" the bearer of a "stern" and spare prose style. Disdainful of Harvard's social life, the sight of others around him having fun "spilled [Dawson] into a bad temper." Updike added to the unflattering portrait in "One of My Generation." In that story, Popper is the one whose "stuff" is noticeably lacking in perception, with prose as "compacted backward phrasing." Popper's poems, "of which I was to read many," were prime examples of "misapplied force," resembling nothing so much as "screws hammered into wood."[23]

Perhaps the greatest bone of contention between Lasch and Updike, however, came during their senior year when they were living apart for the first time. Both were nominated for Harvard's prestigious Bowdoin Prize, awarded annually to recognize the college's best senior thesis. In the end, Lasch won for his "Imperialism and the Independents," a research piece. Updike finished second in the contest with his entry, "Non-Horatian Elements in Herrick's Echoes of Horace," an analysis of the Christian side of Robert Herrick.[24] Lasch received five hundred dollars and high honors; Updike took three hundred dollars and the ignominy of having been bested by a wielder of "misapplied force."[25] Still, Lasch admitted regarding the "brilliant" Updike as the superior writer. The sinking realization "that he was a lot better at this than I was" steered Lasch away from the novelist's calling; he gave himself fully over to history. After graduation he attended Columbia University.[26] Updike went to Oxford on a fellowship. Like so many college friendships, Lasch and Updike's had a natural expiration date. They kept in touch, and, in publishing careers that spanned the rest of the twentieth century, they continued to read each other's work, much as they had when they were eighteen year old freshmen.

Jeffrey Ludwig earned his Ph.D. in history at the University of Rochester. His dissertation title was "In Search of the 'Common Life': The Intellectual Orbit of Christopher Lasch." It explored Lasch's lifelong search for intellectual communities. Investigating the common characteristics of an historical group, Jeffrey Ludwig traces in part the competitive friendship between John Updike and Christopher Lasch revealing much about Updike's intellectual development.

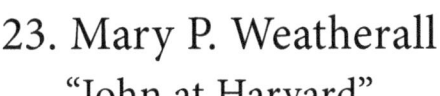

23. Mary P. Weatherall
"John at Harvard"

The first time I laid eyes on John he was rushing to a class in medieval art at the Fogg Museum just before the lights went out and the slides of Romanesque sculpture appeared. It was the fall term of 1951. I was a Radcliffe senior in Fine Arts; John was an English major, a sophomore from Pennsylvania, I soon learned, and a would-be writer, who drew cartoons for the Harvard *Lampoon*, and a late sleeper who never took a class before 10 a.m.

We soon began talking after class, either smoking on the steps of the Fogg or while walking my bicycle through the Harvard Yard to a luncheonette where we'd go for coffee. To my interested and admiring eyes he was tall, boyish, refreshingly unpreppy, an engaging conversationalist, and very amusing. He seemed to be in a state of perpetual animation. He was fond of entertaining me and whoever else was nearby, by leaping over parking meters or by dramatic stumbles and near falls all the way down the steps of Widener Library.

In January 1952, John made an unexpected visit to find me in a ward of Massachusetts General Hospital where I was being diagnosed and treated for a platelet deficiency. I had missed the Fine Arts final exam, and he had missed me and tracked me down to the hospital. I was very surprised but happy to see him, and he must have amused the whole roomful of patients. When I was well enough to leave, I felt rescued as John escorted me back to Cambridge on the subway.

With the start of the spring term we both had serious work to do: I had a thesis to write and John term papers and *Lampoon* gag sessions and deadlines. We began studying together in the Fogg Library or the Widener Reading Room and sometimes in John's small room in a fifth floor suite at Lowell House.

There he would sit under a goose-necked lamp, drawing. His desk was crowded with paper, pens, pencils, erasers, India ink, typewriter, and a smoky ash tray, with the radio often playing jazz or a Red Sox game. I sat on the bed with my books and notes trying to write my thesis on Daumier.[27] One or another of his four roommates would wander in from time to time to chat, and seemed happy enough to accept my frequent presence.

John met my roommate, Ann Rosenblum, in the penthouse apartment she and I shared on Sparks Street overlooking the tops of trees of a bird sanctuary. The place may have had a certain literary charm for him too as Robert Frost had a house around the corner and our bathroom was wallpapered with *New Yorker* covers. We sometimes cooked supper for John and Ann's future fiancé, Manfred Karnovsky,[28] a South African on the faculty at Harvard Medical School. He brought wine and flowers and a certain sophistication to these suppers. We had animated discussions about books and politics, sometimes playing word games like Botticelli or Impressions late into the evening.

By day Cambridge and Harvard Square in particular became a sort of playground for John and me. We spent time in book stores—Schoenhof's or the Mandrake, met for tea at St. Clair's. There were chamber music concerts, lectures and poetry readings to go to. I remember a reading by T. S. Eliot in Sanders Theater, after which, while the audience was still clapping, the poet sat down on a chair on stage to put on his rubbers. To us it remained an unforgettable image.

In the spring term, John and I decided to take another Fine Arts class together. This one was a first at Harvard, a hands-on drawing class, taught by Hyman Bloom,[29] a Boston artist famous for his paintings of cadavers in gemlike colors. Both of us had been drawing since childhood and thought ourselves pretty good, but neither of us quite excelled in Bloom's class, nor mastered his technique of holding the pencil upside down and with many light strokes finding the perfect line or form.

Little by little I became aware of how much John was writing. Aside from his course work, the paper on Milton or Wallace Stevens, or the fiction for the creative writing class, or the humor articles for the *Lampoon*, he was also writing a long weekly letter home to his parents and short stories and verse to be sent to *The New Yorker*.[30] Some of these he let me read. Although he was collecting rejection slips, they never discouraged either his writing or his eagerness to send the next manuscript down to the magazine. Once in a great while when the anonymous rejection included a handwritten, initialed, encouraging comment, he was elated.[31]

Meanwhile, my own writing was going slowly as I struggled to finish my thesis. John, by way of encouragement took pity on me, offering to type the final copy for me, all sixty-three pages with footnotes and plates. "Daumier's Paintings of Circus and Theater" was turned in to my anxious tutor, Mr. Solomon, professionally typed and on schedule. It was well received by the Fine Arts Department, and I was grateful to John who had rescued me again.

It had been an exhilarating spring and neither of us was looking forward to the long, hot summer apart. John returned to Pennsylvania to a job waiting for him at the *Reading Eagle*, and I after Commencement joined my parents and sister in Vermont before looking for a waitressing job in Cambridge. But our romance seemed to flourish by mail and on into the fall when we were together again in Cambridge and beginning to think about marriage.

Mary Pennington Weatherall (born, 1930) met John while a senior and he a sophomore at Harvard. They married in June 1953. She taught art during his senior year. In 1954–55 they lived in Oxford where John went to art school on a Knox Fellowship. Their family includes Elizabeth (1955), David (1957), Michael (1959), and Miranda (1960). Mary was an early first-reader of John's work. She travelled with him on cultural exchanges to Russia and to five African countries. The Updikes divorced in 1976. Mary married Robert K. Weatherall in 1982. She is a landscape painter and lives in Ipswich.

Part III: Ipswich, Massachusetts, 1957–75
Looking Back and Moving Forward

Like his decisions to go to Harvard, to marry before graduating, to attend the Ruskin School, to accept a job at *The New Yorker*, and then to abandon his dream of cartooning for Disney after joining *The New Yorker* staff, Updike undertook the move from New York to Ipswich with a clear understanding that he was protecting his writing talent. The Updikes had honeymooned in Ipswich and now settled there, perhaps because Updike saw some resemblance of the town to Shillington, and maybe because its proximity to the ocean supplied opportunities for sun-bathing in order to combat his psoriasis. More importantly, Ipswich gave the Updikes a chance for a less stressful life, now centered on non-literary friends. In Ipswich Updike found the ambience he needed to write and could separate himself physically from New York. It was not the "silver town" of fun and allure evoked in *The New Yorker's* pages.

At Ipswich Updike reviewed the autobiographical novels he had begun earlier—"Willow," "Home," and "The Plot against Myself" and even finished a draft of "Home." But apparently he realized that they were all too conventional for a first novel. So instead of returning to any of these, he devised an ambitious plan to turn his first four novels away from himself and toward his parents and grandparents. The protagonist of the first novel *The Poorhouse Fair* (1959), John F. Hook, was modeled on his maternal grandfather. Hook, a 94-year-old retired history teacher, was a singular protagonist for his debut novel. It won the Rosenthal award and a grant which Updike used to support the writing of *Rabbit, Run* (1960), a departure from his "family novels" project. Next, *The Centaur* (1962) focused on his father Wesley Updike. The concentration on family ended with a portrait of his mother (*Of the Farm* 1965). Perhaps stymied by his project requiring a novel about his grandmother, Updike followed *Of the Farm* with a closet drama about Pennsylvania's only president, *Buchanan Dying*.

Now, an established writer for Alfred Knopf, Updike proposed offering for publication a novel every other year, with a book of poems, stories, or nonfiction in the "off-years." Knopf agreed, and until his death they adhered to this decision. During the "Ipswich Period," some issues of his novels were entitled "Ipswich editions." *The Centaur*, like *The Poorhouse Fair*, won a prize. While he researched *Buchanan Dying*, he wrote *Marry Me* about marital difficulties (he suppressed its publication until 1976). The sensational novel, *Couples* (1968), based on philandering Ipswich friends made him financially independent and placed him on *Time*'s cover. To avoid controversy Updike took his family to England, then used a government travel assignment to the USSR and related countries to write several stories about Henry Bech. About this time, Updike wrote two significant journalistic pieces—his first memoir, "The Dogwood Tree: A Boyhood" and his highly acclaimed sports reportage, "Hub Fans Bid Kid Adieu." In addition, Updike published three books of poems and adapted several works for children, including a libretto for an opera.

But of most significance, he continued the account of Harry "Rabbit" Angstrom in *Rabbit Redux* (1971), a novel treating the Viet Nam war, civil rights, sexual liberation, and the moon landing. Updike also began a trilogy based on Hawthorne's *The Scarlet Letter*, by basing Tom Marshfield, an adulterous minister, on Arthur Dimmesdale (*A Month of Sundays*, 1975). In this work Updike turned from writing only realism to constructing works using post-modern devices.

So the Ipswich period saw Updike continuing the "Rabbit" narrative, chronicling the adventures of a Jewish writer, and initiating a "*Scarlet Letter* Trilogy." Thus, he not only produced an immense amount of fiction, but he set in place the foundations for much more. He also became a literary celebrity at this time, receiving honorary degrees, acquiring awards, appearing on television, and giving lectures and readings here and abroad. Updike fathered two more children in Ipswich and suffered his father's passing. Also passing was his marriage to Mary Pennington (divorce, 1976), bringing this "Ipswich Period" to a close. After his remarriage to Martha Bernhard, Updike moved to nearby Beverly Farms.

24. Nicholas Delbanco
"R.I.P."

I have been the full-fledged student of a writer only once. John Updike was, I think, one of the most literate and able critics of our time. His breadth of reading, acuity of insight, and grace of expression must give most scholars pause; he would no doubt have been welcomed at any institution in the fifty states. But he remained at a stiff arm's remove from Academe, earning his living by the pen alone. In 1962, however, his resolution wavered and he agreed to teach—at Harvard Summer School. I wanted to remain in Cambridge and therefore applied for the course. It was an offhand decision. I barely had heard (more excusable then) of his name. When he accepted me into his fiction workshop, it would have been ungrateful to drop out.

By the time our first session was over, I knew how lucky I was. He arrived five minutes late—a little bit breathless, a little bit flustered, a tall and lanky personage with an intermittent stammer that seemed a mark of breeding, as if more words were clustered at the portals of his tongue and teeth than could come trippingly out. At twenty-nine he had already published. *The Carpentered Hen*, *The Poorhouse Fair*, *The Same Door*, *Pigeon Feathers*, and *Rabbit, Run* were making him famous; *The Centaur* was soon to appear. Now he was trying on the role of pedagogue for size, and the suit did not fit snugly; my best guess is he chafed at having to spend time with what he understood to be apprentice prose. In class he smoked, he doodled. That high-pitched, braying laugh of his came often into play; so did his critical eye. One afternoon a beautiful deeply tanned woman entered the room and sat in a corner, listening. I later learned that this was his wife Mary and developed a schoolboy-crush on her; if a writer could have so compelling a muse then a writer I'd try to become.

The first word I wrote for Updike was the first of my first novel. As a teacher he proved himself kind and attentive, trying hard to draw analogies with stories he admired—by Franz Kafka, Henry Green,[1] James Joyce—and writing detailed comments on our work. Had he not then encouraged me, I cannot say for certain that I would have persevered; there were many windscraps in the wind, and I followed the favoring breeze. Harvard does prepare you for the world in this one crucial way; if you succeed within those walls you assume that you will when outside. When I handed in the opening pages of *The Martlet's Tale,* and my professor's reaction was praise, I concluded that the rest must follow as the night does day. I suppose I stood out in his class; I certainly tried to; his wary approval meant much. I wrote a second chapter and was hooked.

That hook went deep. Through the years and decades to come—let me be grandiose yet literal—through the centuries and millennia to come, he remained my model. His was the opinion I most valued, the endorsement I most sought. We saw each other frequently to start with, less frequently as time went on and I moved from Vermont to Michigan. The last encounter was by happy accident, at an exhibition in Manhattan we both were walking through. I'd lunched with John not long before, at a pre-arranged meeting in

Boston and for a pre-arranged conversation, but this felt somehow more fortunate: the chance to look at art with him and see, from a shared vantage, what he saw. As always he instructed me: the context he established, the minutiae he observed, the things he was alert to that I would have failed to register or, registering, passed by. Each time we paused to focus (on photographs of post-Katrina New Orleans, in the Metropolitan Museum of Art) he pointed out something I might not have noticed, and surely not so rapidly, and surely not so well. *Just Looking* and *Still Looking,* his collections of art criticism, attest to his acuity and to his wide-ranging eye.

Once I drove him on a road near Bennington I'd driven over often—past a house I passed on an almost daily basis and that to my certain knowledge he had never seen before. John made a remark about the "shuddering roof line" of the ancient structure, and then the way the shutters hung, and I realized to my respectful shame that he in one assessing glance had captured what I'd failed to see. That Jamesian injunction—"Try to be someone on whom nothing is lost"[2]—fit Updike perfectly; nothing escaped his attention.

So my relation to him, always, was that of admiring acolyte—and though over the years and decades I did muster reservations and oppositional opinions, he was my master, first and last. He was, I think, not sorry to claim me as his student, and I was always proud to claim that as my role. There are letters exchanged, books signed and sent, postcards and photographs shared. His archive at Harvard's Houghton Library is vast, and I play only a modest part in it, but one of his last letters to me is a text I cherish and reprinted in my own most recent book: *Lastingness: the Art of Old Age.* In it Updike resoundingly writes: "Aesthetic flourishes fade and wrinkle, though they may get attention when new. A blunt sincerity outlasts finely honed irony, I would think."

His work was full of "aesthetic flourishes" and "finely honed irony"; in the end there was "a blunt sincerity" as well. R.I.P.

Nicholas Delbanco (born 1942) is the Robert Frost Distinguished University Professor Emeritus of English at the University of Michigan. His most recent work of nonfiction is The Art of Youth: Crane, Carrington, Gershwin, and the Nature of First Acts. *His most recent novel is* The Years. *Author of twenty-nine books and editor of a dozen more, Delbanco has judged such awards as The Pulitzer Prize and the National Book Award for Fiction. He was a student in John Updike's summer writing course.*

25. Catherine Hiller
"Groping for the Truth"

It was 1972, and I was finishing my doctoral dissertation about a young author when I realized that soon he'd be having a major birthday. I persuaded the *New York Times Magazine* to let me do a piece on spec for them, and a few days after John Updike turned forty, I drove up to Ipswich, Massachusetts to interview him. I had never conducted an interview before, and I had prepared three pages of questions to ask of a luminary novelist I'd admired for years.

The car took me through low hills and small ponds to Updike's front door at exactly the appointed hour, and there he was, my literary idol, hauling his garbage bins up the driveway from the road. It could have been a coincidence, but it could also have been a demonstration of a studied "just plain folks" approach.

Abandoning the trash barrels, Updike welcomed me into his large, comfortable house on Labor-in-Vain Road. He introduced me to his wife, Mary Pennington Updike, who radiated serenity and grace. He gave me a tour of his home, guiding me upstairs to his study and the children's rooms. He said he spent a lot of time with his four children, perhaps because he was home a lot. "It's hard to find men as idle as myself," he told me.

I was too shy to protest appropriately, for Updike's output was prodigious. As I followed him around the house, I scribbled notes on a clipboard so I wouldn't miss a word. (My tape recorder needed to be plugged into a wall.) When we returned to the living room, he spoke about the pleasure he took from playing golf with the village tradesmen. "Oh, but John, those aren't your real friends," chided Mary.

"They are—they are," he protested gaily. "I love them."

Our interview proper was to take place at his office, and as we drove into downtown Ipswich, he stopped at a PhotoHut to deliver some film. Although easily the most famous man in the area, he carefully spelled out his name: "U-P-D-I-K-E." We drove on and parked the car, and I followed him into a dingy frame building and up a flight of stairs to the cluttered room where he did most of his writing, 9:30 to 12:30 weekdays. Updike liked to do it all himself. He had no literary agent and no secretary. He proudly showed me his copier, an outdated machine that produced wet and messy pages.

He settled into his chair and gave me a close look. "Tell me," he asked, "How old are you?"

"I'm twenty-five."

"My goodness, that's young, and how did you persuade the *Times* to let you come interview me?"

I recognized the competitiveness of one smart young person for another—although his achievements by age twenty-five (poems and stories in *The New Yorker*, a prize-winning first novel) far surpassed mine. I explained about the dissertation I was writing at Brown and thanked him for agreeing to the interview.

I plugged in the tape recorder, pressed the record button, and the light glowed red. I was ready.

"I don't often give interviews," he began, "because they take a lot out of me. My voice gets hoarse and I get dizzy. Yet there is this desire to justify and explain myself—I become anxious to say it honestly. One is always groping for the truth." Indeed, as the day unfolded, Updike spoke gracefully hour after hour, at the smallest prompt. I scarcely glanced at my pages of questions.

He gestured toward the tape-recorder on his desk. "The best interview I ever gave was to a man with a machine like that. For some reason I was feeling good that day, and I talked, I thought, brilliantly, and things I'd never even known I knew I said, and he came back two days later saying the machine hadn't been working."

He laughed. His voice deepened, swelled, thinned, dried, and finally exploded in a juicy "Hawf." During our interview, he often laughed. When he spoke about his books and his life, he would suddenly chuckle, or giggle, or even guffaw. It was part of his homely charm, that awkward laugh. His mouth stretched to become as large as his nose, all his teeth shone, and he suddenly looked like the David Levine[3] caricature framed behind his desk.

"Now is that thing really on?" he asked, gesturing. "Yes? Very well. The morning mail."

Gamely following his weekday routine, he put on his glasses and went through his letters. A Mrs. Tarbox from Canada wanted to know why he was always using her name.[4] A German magazine wanted the translation rights to a poem. A kid in Pennsylvania wanted help in writing a paper about *Rabbit, Run*. A new Boston magazine wanted an Updike piece. And there were several birthday greetings.

These did not bring him cheer. He remarked about his mind "not being as quick as it once was," and the "slackening of ambition you feel at forty," and how he was "sloping gradually into the grave."

Yet to me he seemed shockingly young. It wasn't just that he looked youthful for his years, with an adolescent's lanky body and a schoolboy's thatch of hair, but that he had been famous for so long. Even knowing his birth date, I'd somehow expected Updike to be wrinkled and gray. But his cheeks were pink and his eyes held a flirtatious twinkle.

By forty, Updike had written eleven books for adults, including *Rabbit, Run* and *Rabbit Redux*. A shelf in his office held all of his books, including some for children. He had won the National Book Award for *The Centaur*, produced a best-seller in *Couples*, and landed on the cover of *Time*.

He seemed oddly rueful about his success. "In a dismaying way, things have come true," he reflected. "Dismaying. I had these finite hopes. When *The New Yorker* took my first story and poem, I had achieved my ambition. Everything since has been gravy."

Considering his many books, more than one a year, I was surprised to hear Updike claim it felt like "each thing is produced on the verge of silence and like each thing is the last I can think of to say."

As a child, Updike wanted to become a painter: often he drew separate objects—a toaster, an apple, a teddy bear—which he would then connect with a kind of tree. "This feeling of wanting to connect is fairly basic to the artistic impulse," he observed. Although he wrote poems, essays and reviews, fiction claimed Updike's deepest allegiance. "In some funny way, the texture of our lives, moments, hesitations, ambiguities are capturable only in fiction," he maintained. "Fiction can tell the truth better than statistics or sociology. Writing has become the core of my *raison d'être* and I feel curiously dirty and cross if I don't write my three pages or whatever: I feel I must do that to make the rest of my life O.K."

Three pages a day sounds modest, but multiply it by, say, 200, and you get a 600-page novel in less than a year. Updike's work ethic was formidable. "I see myself keeping hours like the dentist—although not as long. The American dream is somehow tied into work," he mused, "and the dream is crumbling because the work ethic is crumbling. Of course, most people do not have work as interesting and as personally glorifying as mine."

Updike approached his own work with a thorough professionalism. When he read proof for his *New Yorker* stories, he made change after change until the last minute. After all, "Prose can always be better."

Updike said that while looking at proofs, he scrutinized not only how the words read, but how they looked on the page. Occasionally, the arrangement of the sentences would create barely perceptible ribbons of space which wound through a paragraph, and when this happened, Updike fastidiously insisted on rewriting the entire paragraph to make it more pleasing visually.

When we met, Updike was working on a historical novel about James Buchanan. Noticing a certain similarity in his leading men, I asked if Buchanan would end up being like Rabbit, Bech and his other heroes: nice enough, but selfish and passive.

"We're all to a degree selfish and passive," he said, "and my men tend to be paralyzed by the enormity of action. The arena I've chosen to write about is of course the arena of at best small actions and gradual decisions." If this is frequently "a domestic arena where the biggest thing is divorce," surely that is where many of us lead our most passional lives. Updike continued. "We should seek to rejoice in our own lives and our own possibilities."

Updike rubbed his eyes, kneaded his forehead, and was silent for a moment. Then he went on. "Yet there is something irremediably perverse and self-destructive and other-destructive about us. The basic human condition of being a social animal is hard on the animal and hard on society." He stared out of the office window, at the Ipswich River. Turning back to face me, he continued, "Any story of merit has some pain in it. In some strange way, it only matters when we write with blood. Writing with ink isn't enough."

I asked about other contemporary authors and whether he'd ever met Norman Mailer. "Actually, I must be one of the few Americans with a B.A. degree who's [never met] him," he replied. "Yet I do seem to keep beating myself over the head with him." He called Mailer "a genius of perception—he can evoke like just crazy." He claimed he coveted Mailer's knowledge of "how things work, how political deals are made." Still, he went on, "Mailer doesn't do what's important to do—e.g., make a thing, make a pattern, forget himself long enough to make a character."

Unlike Mailer, Updike usually refused requests for speaking engagements. "In a curious way, speaking is a whorish thing to do. As a writer, your business is not to be a lecturer or a preacher: it's to make things, to try to crystallize something out of the random stuff of your memory and imagination, to provide vicarious experience for people and in that way to widen their sympathies. I like to feel I've done myself some sort of justice. I don't feel I've been distracted by trying to teach, or trying to make a great movie, or trying to be a Beautiful Person, but that I have set myself well as to the task ahead of me.

"But who needs it?" he suddenly asked. "You see the books on the shelf—who's read them all?"

"I have," I piped.

He smiled. "Okay: maybe you. But now that I'm forty, I have a sense that the jig's up and I must either put up or shut up artistically. I have to marshal my forces. I happily drifted through my thirties, and now I must get down to serious business somehow."

Catherine Hiller's doctoral dissertation on John Updike was written at Brown University. She is the author of five novels and Skin: Sensual Tales, *about which Updike wrote, "Good, brave and joyful writing." Shorter pieces appeared in* Redbook, Penthouse, The Westchester Review *and* The Antioch Review. *She co-produced two documentary films:* Do Not Enter: The Visa War Against Ideas, *and* Paul Bowles. *Catherine Hiller is married and the mother of three sons.*

PART IV: BEVERLY FARMS, 1976–2009

Writers, Fans, Friends and Family Reflect and Reminisce

The momentum Updike created with his remarkable production during his 'Ipswich Period" accelerated when he moved a few miles from Ipswich to an estate in Beverly Farms overlooking the ocean. Now he could devote separate rooms to correspondence, poetry, fiction, and revision. Protected by his new wife from distractions, Updike could direct his energies more forcefully than ever. He now undertook to expand the possibilities of both modern realism and post-modernism.

Updike had established himself as the master of domestic tragedy while writing in traditional realistic modes. His customary work included the completion of the "Rabbit" saga with the Pulitzer Prizes going to *Rabbit Is Rich* (1981) and *Rabbit at Rest* (1990). Updike had already explored post modernism in his satirical fantasy, *The Coup* (1978), set in an imaginary African country and told by a dictator-in-exile, and he continued his post-modern explorations in his "*Scarlet Letter* Trilogy." These three novels employ the post-modern devices of intertextuality, problematic texts, and the "absent presence." Updike's use of Hawthorne's tale of adultery featured three characters derived from *The Scarlet Letter*—the Rev. Tom Marshfield, the Rev. Arthur Dimmesdale counterpart (*A Month of Sundays*, 1975), Roger Lambert, the Roger Chillingworth analogue (*Roger's Version*, 1986), and Sarah Worth, the Hester Prynne equivalent (*S.*, 1988). He would explore textual ambiguity in *Memories of the Ford Administration* (1992), in which the chronicle of President James Buchanan's early life inter-penetrates the narrative of history professor Alfred Clayton's two marriages. His interest in stretching the limits of the novel's form extended to the inter-textual prequel to *Hamlet* (*Gertrude and Claudius*, 2000), written in three styles that tell three tales of the Danish Prince. Updike also explored gothic romance and magic realism in *The*

Witches of Eastwick (1984) and its sequel and last novel, *The Widows of Eastwick* (2008).

To show how Updike worked almost simultaneously in the two modes, traditional realism and post-modernism, one need only note that he produced a story rooted in folk magic (*Brazil*, 1994) and then followed with a novel investigating movies and religion (*In The Beauty of the Lilies*, 1995). He then returned to post-modernism with a narrative set in the future and relying, some argue, on quantum physics (*Toward the End of Time*, 1997). He returned to naturalism with *Seek My Face* (2003), *Villages* (2004), and his only thriller, *Terrorist* (2006).

Meanwhile, Updike also added two volumes of story cycles about Henry Bech. During this "Beverly Farms Period," Updike also produced four other books of stories; he collected his early short stories in 2003. His only novella, "Rabbit Remembered," concluded the life of "Rabbit" (*Licks of Love*, 2000). Updike added four books of poetry, including *Collected Poems* (1993). He gathered his essays and reviews in several volumes, two of these art reviews. He also had time to produce a book of memoirs in *Self-Consciousness* (1989) expressly intended to circumvent a biography. At his death, he was researching a novel about St. Paul. The last decade of Updike's life indicates that his surprising energy was rooted in the use of innovative and familiar frameworks.

After his mother died in 1989, Updike found fewer reasons to return to Berks County. Nevertheless, he continued to preside over his Shillington High School reunions as class president and oversaw his inherited farm in Plowville. Updike and his first wife maintained a friendship, particularly since his children had now given him many grandchildren. His terrain was now Boston and New York, with vacations in Arizona. He traveled extensively giving lectures and readings across the country, and visiting Australia, Brazil, Cambodia, Canada, England, Finland, Israel, Italy, Jordan, Scotland, and Thailand. Updike supported and actively aided many scholarly projects. In addition, he barnstormed for Knopf to promote his books; in fact, he traveled to the West Coast to stimulate sales of *The Widows of Eastwick* just weeks before he died. In the elegiac "Endpoint"[1] poems written while Updike lay dying, he expresses a moving farewell to the friends of his youth, records the progress of his illness, and affirms his certainty of an afterlife.

Appearing posthumously are books which show Updike's continuing use of Shillington as a canvas on which to limn his personal world, all published in 2009—poems (*Endpoint*), stories (*My Father's Tears*), set mostly in Berks County, and an augmented collection of republished stories (*The Maples Stories*). Other posthumous collections were: essays and reviews (*Higher Gossip*, 2011), appreciations of artists (*Always Looking*, 2012), and *Selected Poems* (2015). These books were edited by Christopher Carduff.

26. John Barth
"Remembering John Updike"

Although it was not my privilege to be among John Updike's many close friends, he and I were amiable and mutually respectful literary acquaintances for decades. I enjoyed his so abundant and eloquent publications, from the earliest fiction, verse, and critical essays right through the touching items written in his life's last weeks. We regularly sent each other copies of our books as they appeared, and our several path-crossings were invariably pleasant, often memorable occasions.

I persuaded him to have a go at something else to which he'd been habitually disinclined: John resisted public readings, but when he mentioned in a letter that he was seriously hooked up with a new woman, at my invitation he brought Martha down to Baltimore for what he happily declared to be their first public outing together. He gave a delightful reading at Hopkins that included, at Shelly's and my request, his story "Lifeguard" (one of our favorites), and we guided the new couple through such standard Baltimore sight sees as the Inner harbor area and the haunts of Edgar Allan Poe.

Over the ensuing decades, our connection was limited mainly to holiday greetings (we always enjoyed his Christmas card verses), first edition swaps (more from that so prolific John than from this less prolific one), and occasional Academy nomination business.[2] Like many another of his admirers, Shelly and I were annually chagrined at his being passed over for the Nobel Prize in Literature: an award to which he would have done as much honor as it to him. In December 2008 we were dismayed to learn of his illness in what—incredibly!—turned out to be his final Christmas note, and were much moved some months thereafter to receive from his publisher John's final three volumes—the new edition of his Maples stories, the all new story collection *My Father's Tears*, and his fine last verse collection *Endpoint*, with its so touching final poem "To Martha, On Her Birthday, After Her Cataract Operation"—together with a note from his editor, Kenneth Schneider, addressed to both of us and saying "John would have wanted you to have these."

We thank you for that, Mr. Schneider. And even more we thank you, John Updike, for being the miracle that you were—and will remain.

*John Barth (born 1930) taught at Pennsylvania State University from 1952–56, and later Johns Hopkins (1973 to 1995). Though a realistic writer (*The End of the Road*),*

Barth is known for post-modern novels (Giles Goat-Boy). *His* "The Literature of Exhaustion" *(1967) argued that* literary realism *is finished.*³ *His* metafictional *collection of stories,* Chimera, *won the* National Book Award. *Recently retired, Barth lives in Baltimore with his wife Shelly.*

27. Stephen Bergman [Samuel Shem]
"My Dear Friend John Updike"

This is a short story of a long friendship.

It was 1979, my first novel had come out, and he was 46, I, 34. We met at a party of PEN⁴ New England at the house of the writers Robie Macauley and Pam Painter.⁵ My first impression was clouded by nervous awe, but luckily it was summer and our conversation turned to golf, John's passion, and my sport at our shared alma mater, Harvard. A week later, I was out on a forlorn public golf course packed with carts-full of beer-swilling guys in T-shirts whose swings were converted from hockey. There had been a mistake and we were a five-some. A six-some, actually. Another young writer in the group, supposedly happily married, had brought along his petite blond girlfriend and spent a lot of time in the woods with her while we played on. Reappearing, flustered, they would walk along with her arm around his waist, her hand tucked neatly into the hip pocket of his jeans—a true Updikean touch.

You can tell everything about a person by the way they play a sport. Last night I calculated that in thirty years John and I spent at least 5,000 hours playing golf. We had a regular foursome, and often played with his son David, now a dear friend. But often it was just John and I, walking along together, bags on our shoulders, talking. In golf John was meticulous—our scorekeeper, cherishing those little yellow golf pencils; frugal, picking up pencils and tees all during the round; steady as a fair Christian but for an uncontrolled deviance into the raw sensuality of woods and briars and swamps and lakes and sand traps; reliable to a fault on the greens; capable of astonishing flights of golf poetry and sudden crashes into golf trash—and really funny. Once when he and I were teamed up against the other two and I complained of a bad back, on the 2nd tee he said, "Steve, I want you to know that if it's a choice between helping the team and hurting your back, I want you to hurt your back." Always on the 4th hole he and I would talk about his medical questions, and always walking up the long par five 8th fairway we had our "literature and career" chat, what we were reading and writing, the folly of both popular and literary taste, what the gossip was. Often he would repeat something I said, and I knew I would soon see it in a book. He had an astonishing eye, and in golf gathered details—one fall day he walked off the course to make sure he knew the name of the last tree to turn color—I believe ash, or hickory. Harry [Angstrom's] condo in Florida in *Rabbit at Rest* was, in fact, my parents'; John stayed with them to make sure he got it right.

Janet and I had a house in Gloucester, twenty minutes from Updike and Martha, and we became another foursome—seeing each other often for dinner, celebrating each birthday together, and Christmas at their home with their mixed families. Soon there started arriving book after book, and private editions as birthday presents, as well as cartoons and drawings—such as a set of four golf balls, on each a cartoon of the face of a member of our foursome. One night Janet, a psychologist, insisted that John and I take the Meyers-Briggs Personality Inventory; she then announced the results. I came out as a writer; he came out as an office worker or clerk. So much for psych testing. Every book he sent had an inscription, often blaming me: "For Steve, who ruined this novel by a) suggesting it, b) inquiring after it constantly and making me talk its lovely essence away." For a *New Yorker* review of *The Bible*: "For Steve, without whom this piece would have been composed with much less distraction"—but to each of these he added, "with affection and esteem." John was the most loyal friend I ever had: he would always show up at events for my books or plays, he would listen attentively to my publishing woes, and if I was going through a rough time and we hadn't talked on the phone for a while, he would always call—imagine, a *man* who always calls! When my publisher asked him if he'd write the introduction to a 25th anniversary edition of my novel *The House of God*, to my surprise he said yes, and included it in one of his anthologies, *More Matter*. Though never directly, in postcards and letters and half-joking inscriptions, he pointed out my strengths and weaknesses as a writer, always in an encouraging way.

I never saw him yawn, and he rarely lost his temper: mostly on the golf course, once at dinner at home when he was so angry that he pointedly let his napkin drop a full five inches from his hand to the table. He was the most generous of critics; only in the last few years did I ever hear him voice irritation at a writer—one in particular, who shall remain nameless. He talked freely with me about the craft. I learned an enormous amount from him.

We had a secret joke: in *The Witches of Eastwick*, he wrote, "The new young editor of the *Word*, Toby Bergman, slipped on a frozen stick outside the barber shop and broke his leg." In my next novel, *The Spirit of The Place*, I wrote, "The new young editor of the *Crier*, Toby Updike, slipped on a frozen stick." ... And when last year I received his last novel, *The Widows of Eastwick*, sure enough there "Toby Bergman" was again. In my new novel there is a final, leg-rebroken, "Toby Updike."

The last few years of our friendship, because of various orthopedic surgeries on my part, were not on the golf course. Rather we would meet for lunch at the Harvard Faculty Club. He timed our lunches to his delivery of boxes of his personal papers to Houghton Library. He always seemed shy when he announced himself to the librarian—John was always wonderfully humble. He was modest, but with a rock-solid confidence. Once, after a novel of his had gotten panned, I asked how he handled it. "They're talking about my *novel*," he said, "not about me."

Last summer (2008) we had a belated joint-birthday lunch at Myopia Hunt Club, John's exclusive old-Yankee golf course at which he never seemed quite comfortable. I noted his old man's wrinkled and scarred face but then— when I looked into his eyes—(those eyes!)—I recognized the signature boyish joy at being alive and at play for another great day. He and I, two small-town boys sitting there in a grown-up's exclusive club eating our BLT's off bone China on a starched white tablecloth. The sun shone hot on the 18th green, lighting it up as if it were made of crushed emeralds. Over lunch we laughed, hard, happy to see each other again and delighted with our good fortune in life, talking about everything as best friends do, and then parting, he with his gentle handshake and slight stammer. As I drove off I turned and saw him walking away slightly stooped, snowy hair shining in the sunlight, but with a bounce in his step as he swung his putter along, heading toward the green to practice.

That was the last time I ever saw him.

There was a last postcard, in November. He told me about his diagnosis, and a few other things, and about the care his family was showing him. After that, he drew back, into himself. I knew that the suddenness and aggressiveness of his cancer had been a shock to his self-image, an end that simply does not happen to those who, despite their bodies, feel young, feel in touch with, in his transcendent line in one of his last poems: "our heaven at the start and not the end of life." I kept in touch through David, and the notes I wrote John. There are all different kinds of love in the world. And John wrote brilliantly about most of them. He taught me a lot about the love in a friendship. And I find myself thinking about him most days as if he's still around, and then, realizing he's not, missing him pretty badly. When you don't get to say goodbye, there's a hole in your heart, sometimes for a long time. So I just want to say, "Goodbye, John. I loved you. You will live with me, and all of us here today, for the rest of our lives."

This essay was originally read in slightly different form as "Tribute to John Updike" at The John F. Kennedy Presidential Library and Museum, Boston, June 7, 2009.

Samuel Shem, pen-name of Stephen Bergman, is a doctor, novelist, playwright, activist. His first novel The House of God *is now a "medical classic"*; The Spirit of the Place *won two national "Best Literary Novel of the Year" Awards; the play* Bill W. and Dr. Bob *ran Off Broadway for a year. A Rhodes Scholar, Visiting Scholar at the American Academy in Rome, he is Professor of Medical Humanities/Literature at NYU. His 2016 novel,* At the Heart of the Universe, *is set in China.*

28. William H. Pritchard
"John Updike"

John Updike's recent, quite unexpected death last January prompted me to review our correspondence over the past thirty-six years. It was a correspondence initiated by my bothering him with a couple of things I had written, partly about him. I was emboldened to continue bothering him when he responded—and continued to respond, unfailingly—with a brief letter or a packed post card. So I pretended that he found it salutary to begin his morning by some clearing of the correspondence desk before settling in with the novel, story, poem, or review he was currently at work on. Of the two items I sent him in that first missive, one consisted of paragraphs from a fiction chronicle about his 1972 story collection, *Museums and Women*, paragraphs ending with a rather pompous sounding prediction that he was "putting together a body of work which in substantial, intelligent creation will eventually be seen as second to none in our time." (For some reason he liked the ring of praise enough to use it on the back of one or another of his books.) I also sent him a talk I'd given on nostalgia that quoted a question he raised in one of his writings: "What is nostalgia but love for that part of ourselves which is in Heaven forever removed from change and corruption?" In his letter back he surprised me by claiming, in himself, a "waning of even the ability to feel nostalgia," which, he said, "maybe is freshest when we are in our twenties and for the first time faced with a great block of subjective time forever set aside."

When I reviewed *Rabbit Is Rich* in 1981, *The New Republic* sent a galley to him, and he made my day with a postcard announcing that I had given "a passable impersonation of that favorite ghost of mine, the Ideal Reader." Meanwhile I had asked him whether, if it were offered, he would accept an honorary degree from Amherst College. He said he would be willing, "providing no speaking (speechifying, I mean to say) is involved," and suggested further that "Just as a nation should conserve its fossil fuel, a writer should try to conserve his face and voice." In 1983 the invitation came through, and although there was no speechifying required, he had to deal with two speech-challenges, both of which were met fully and gracefully. The first occurred as we ascended steps to the president's garden where drinks would be served. At the top stood a friend, the wife of a faculty colleague, whom I introduced to Updike and his wife, Martha. Without a pause, the friend informed the novelist that her mother had very much disliked his latest, *Rabbit Is Rich* (doubtless for its sex). A smile, a twinkle, and "I trust she won't be here tonight?" asked Updike. A few minutes later as the party began, I introduced him to a rather thick-headed trustee whose business success had left small time for literary matters. He gave his name and number, then asked Updike, "And what do *you* do?" "Oh, I'm a freelance writer," was the mock-modest reply. The trustee appeared satisfied and the evening continued without event. Later that evening we had arranged a small party at our house, among those in attendance two novelists—Alan Lelchuk,[6] then teaching at the college, and Maureen Howard,[7] whose daughter was among the graduates. When Updike wrote to thank me for looking after him, he noted

> Your post-dinner party was a lot of fun. Maureen Howard had panned *Marry Me*, I had called Lelchuk's *American Mischief* "more trash than truth," and God knows what other slights had been perpetrated, but we sat down cozy as kindergarteners on their first day, determined to be good. A study in craft loyalty.

In anticipation, he had pictured the commencement ceremony itself, held outdoors, as "sun-drenched and laced with chamber music"; alas, the only music consisted of two hymns to Amherst, and soon after things commenced a steady rain began to fall.

It would be wrong to reduce him to the polite, charming, obliging man with only good will in his heart. I had a glimpse of a different Updike than the genial host of my solicitations when, over-eagerly, I sent him a letter I'd written to *The New York Review of Books*, attempting to rebut some negative aspersions cast on his work by Frederick Crews. In the midst of an otherwise friendly reply, Updike suddenly (I had to look twice before it registered) wrote apropos of the letter "It's really your friends that hurt you. You credit me with 'a couple of dozen engaging, sometimes moving short stories,' when I've published well more than a hundred that I hoped were rather more than engaging." Never had the word "engaging" looked shabbier to me, but it was too late to substitute a better one. While never again being so reprimanded (as I felt it), he more than once reminded me of the difference between being a writer of fiction and a teacher of, among other things, fiction. When I published a book about my life as a student and teacher, mostly conducted at the same institution, he reminded me that he was not a teacher:

> I found your gracious memoir about all those Amherst years slightly harrowing, in the way that I find colleges anywhere harrowing. Why, I wonder? Everything is so dear— the neo-Gothic buildings, and the intelligent and witty faculty, and the shiny-eyed students looking up and being fed.

It was a point to be taken and considered by all celebrants of the golden haze of college days to which our hearts presumably keep turning back. He was careful not to sentimentalize his own not-unhappy years as a Harvard undergraduate.

But he was willing to read, with good grace, so it seemed, the occasional exemplary student paper about his work. One of them, directed at the Maples stories collected in *Too Far to Go*, received as his comment, "Yes indeed, I could hardly have said it better myself," and he went on to say that he "certainly could not have written a paper so sensitive and free (bringing in her own parents, divorce, etc.) when I was her age." When I taught a seminar divided equally between his works and those of Philip Roth, he professed to be made nervous by the syllabus:

> Just looking at it aroused flutters in my stomach, suspecting that I wouldn't do very well in it—better, perhaps, on the Roth half than the Updike—and thinking of all that reading. I picture you and your 21 students a bit like those people in Gericault's *Raft of the Medusa*,[8] gesturing and staring in different anguished directions while the damn thing sinks under you.

He also delivered a question that caused a slight flutter in me: "I keep wondering, if I were an Amherst student would I sign up for your course in Roth and Updike? ... I would learn a lot, no doubt." No doubt, but just a smidgen of doubt surfaced. What *was* I doing, harrowing him with a course syllabus from one of those "dear" American colleges with shiny-eyed students looking up and being fed? Maybe I should have been giving them Spenser's *Faerie Queene*.[9]

When in the middle 1990s I determined to write a book about him, I asked if he had any objections to the enterprise: no, he said, blessings on me as long as it wasn't a biography. As the book went along (I did *not* provide him with progress reports or questions), he professed concern for my situation: "The thought of you conscientiously trudging through my oeuvre, making sharp, fair adjudications, haunts me to the point that paralysis has at last afflicted my pen." Had I really done that to this unstoppable producer? Hardly, since the next sentence was "Well, not total, I have cooked up one more book on the misadventures of Henry Bech." So I spared myself any guilt about gumming up the wheels of creativity. His response to the finished book was full and generous. Apropos of his picture on the jacket he began, "Well, there I am, thanks to you—my name 2½ inches high and my youthful self posed in hip-high marsh grass." He guessed that perhaps he was more heroic back then, "burdened with sharp angsts but sufficiently far from death to give the question an abstract gloss, and making, Norman Podhoretz[10] be damned, some music that hadn't quite been heard before in American letters." Later on, he suspected he might have stayed "too long, and too garrulously, at the party." Five years after my book was published, it was reprinted with a brief introduction in which I commented on the books he had written since my first account. Rather pointedly, though as always humorously, he noted that as I "whisked" through the last five years, he "got the reluctant impression that I had become a burden to you, a task that never ends, a kind of hectoring taskmaster like the schoolmaster who awaits Shakespeare's 'school-boy with his satchel / And shining morning face, creeping like snail / Unwillingly to school.'"

We saw each other in Cincinnati, 2001, at a symposium in his honor. He gave a public interview, two public readings, signed books endlessly, talked to graduate students, and endured 20-minute talks on his work by me and Donald Greiner—all while giving at least 108 percent effort. I heard from him last in June 2008 when he was pleased to have delivered a book of stories for publication a year later. Like others who cared, I was stunned at the beginning of this year to learn he was seriously ill. I had recently sent him something I'd written on V.S. Naipaul,[11] and he never acknowledged it—which should have told me something. When a few years ago I had mentioned to him my sadness at the death of the poet, Anthony Hecht,[12] he replied that he was sorry to hear of Hecht's death: "At the age of 81, how bad are we supposed to feel. Somewhat bad, I think." About his own death, coming a couple of months before his 77th birthday, we may be justified in feeling more than somewhat bad. But the books are there.

William H. Pritchard is Henry Clay Folger Professor Emeritus of English at Amherst College. He has published a number of books including literary biographies of Robert Frost and Randall Jarrell,[13] a teaching memoir, English Papers, *and various collections of essays and reviews. His book,* Updike, America's Man of Letters *(University of Massachusetts Press, 2005) is a survey and criticism of Updike's novels, stories, poems, prose essays, and criticism considered in chronological order. He began a correspondence with Updike in 1973 that continued until Updike's death.*

29. Jack De Bellis
"Updike in Sync"

I was in a Florida bookstore, searching an anthology of poems for one by Updike for my bibliography, when my wife Patty whispered the searing words,

"John Updike has died." A friend had phoned her from Pennsylvania; she had heard the news while driving only a few miles from where Updike had been born. I didn't weep, but I pressed my hands against my eyes, fell to the floor, and tried to stop time.

His voice appeared: "That's a Bradford," as he glanced at a pear tree in the park across from our home. He was thinking of Rabbit, beguiled, among the Edenic pear trees in *Rabbit at Rest*. I must have blended Updike to Rabbit, both now in "paradise." When I felt better I remembered our first meeting.

At Moravian College in Bethlehem, Pennsylvania, in 1982, Updike read from *Bech Is Back*, the section in which a fan named Fedderbush revealed that he had not only pestered Bech to sign his books, but wanted them only so he could sell them. Afterwards, Updike answered questions from the audience and was interrogated on stage by two professors. Following this outpouring of energy, Updike signed books. I joined the long queue with nine hardbacks I had acquired from thrift stores and yard sales. Since this brazen armload made me self-conscious, I asked my wife Patty and her friend Peggy to convey three apiece. They inched forward, and as Updike asked engagingly, "Who should I sign these books to?" they gave my name. Updike grew more interested as he inscribed their six books. When I stepped forward I was cowed by his stern voice, "I suppose you're Jack De Bellis?" Worried, I croaked I was, and before I could apologize and withdraw the books, he said quietly, "I have a question for you." I guessed he would ask how I had the gall to unload nine books on him, and I quaked as his eyes caught mine and he asked, "How did you get two such cute girls to carry your books? I've been trying to do that for years." While I laughed with relief, he picked up my used copy of *A Month of Sundays* and popped it open to the title page. The seller had marked "50" on the first fly. Updike paused, looked up with mock-hurt and asked, "You mean you only spent fifty cents for my book?" I was numb at being discovered, but Patty rescued me, "That means he read it fifty times!" "Oh, sure," was Updike's pseudo-indignant reply, as he circled the "50" and wrote alongside it, "What a bargain," and below it he penned, "for that old/Skinflint/Jack De Bellis." I had not only gained an inscription, but had provoked Updike's wit. I vowed that day to build a collection of his books worthy of the man, while dedicating my scholarship to exploring his work.

During the next twenty-five years, I carried on a professional correspondence with Updike, and he astounded me more than once. For example, I was gathering reviews of the "Rabbit" books for an anthology and he suggested sending me his files of commentary. Another time he made what must have been an arduous trek to his attic to retrieve old peeling galleys to clear up a point or two for a bibliography. And he regularly sent me signed foreign editions, which I paid for; after all, he was a Depression child.

He could be almost alarming with his praise. Writing to me about an essay on his use of movies, he remarked, with typically ambiguous modesty, "I marvel at the fanatic, Book of Kells–like care with which you scrutinize my poor work." In 1994 he was kind enough to contribute a preface to a bibliography I had compiled, saying it showed an "eagle eye," while simultaneously scolding me for missing several essays on golf. So he could be chiding as well as charming, and I would see this pattern countless times. I felt his wrath as he accused me of betraying a trust when I asked if I could publicize a particularly quotable reaction to another of my books. He was my hero but a hero made of flesh and blood with little time for mistakes.

In 1997 he honored our home by having breakfast with us, and we discussed some enigmatic passages in *The Witches of Eastwick*. He complimented our breakfast, we saved his napkin, and then I drove him to the airport. Four days after his departure, I received Xerox pages from books he had used in his research which settled the weird witchy issue.

When Updike came to my school in 1998, I ushered him into the rare books room where I had organized an exhibition of books and broadsides from my collection. When I indicated a typo in the broadside "Styles of Bloom," he deftly unhooked it from the wall, freed it from its glass and frame, and inked in the correction, placing his initials in the margin.

For a luminary he usually wore no mask to meet the inquisitive, adoring, or obnoxious, but when he gave the Pennsylvania Speaker's Millennium Lecture in 2007[14] in Harrisburg he shrugged off the cloak of celebrity, indicating that on this date (April 23) not only were Shakespeare and James Buchanan[15] born, but also Shirley Temple.

In October 2008, before we knew of his terminal illness, Patty awoke me with the news that she had had a lovely Updike dream. Incredibly, I too had dreamed of him, so I wrote to tell him about this amazing synchronicity. Updike replied on Thanksgiving, 2008, and in the last sentence of the last letter I received from him he said, "May you and Patty continue to dream in synch." Unforgettable words. Unforgettable man.

Jack A. De Bellis (born 1935) is professor emeritus of English, Lehigh University and the first John Updike Scholar in Residence at Alvernia University. He helped found The John Updike Society and served on the board of directors (2009-14). De Bellis taught at UCLA and the University of Toulouse, France. He has authored or co-edited John Updike's Early Years; John Updike: A Bibliography of Primary and Secondary Materials, 1948-2007; *and* The John Updike Encyclopedia. *In 1998 John Updike visited his seminar, "Should John Updike Receive the Nobel Prize?"*

30. Burl N. Corbett
"The Centaur's Son"

I was born in 1947 and raised on a farm only three crow miles from the Plowville home of John Updike. From the time I learned to read I wanted to be a writer, and after years of delay began to write my first short stories in the late 70's. Then in 1983, I read in the Sunday *Reading Eagle* that John had returned home to attend his high school reunion. I decided to call him at his mother's and ask if he would read my work, offer an opinion. Hungover with a bit of the Irish courage still coursing through my veins, I dialed the listed number, and when Mrs. Updike answered, asked if I might speak with her son, hoping she would think me one of his classmates. She asked my name and I told her, hoping that my unfamiliar name would ring a bell she had forgotten she owned. "I live near Geigertown," I hastened to add, "and was wondering if he'd be kind enough to look at a few of my short stories."

"Just a second," she said pleasantly.

When John said hello, I quickly explained I was a writer, and that I'd appreciate it if he'd read some of my stories and tell me if I had talent or was just wasting time and paper. Much to my surprise, he asked if I knew how to find my way there. I assured him that I did, thanked him profusely, and promised I'd be there, within a half-hour. He said he'd watch for my truck.

Wow! Here was my chance! I selected three or four of my favorite stories, put them in a self-addressed 9x12 envelope, and put on some decent clothes. I was so nervous I was almost trembling. At the last minute, I decided to take along my three-year-old daughter, Amber, hoping that her innate charm would deflect attention from my anxiety. We got in my truck, and off we went.

I drove past Geigertown and up a long hill to Weaver's Orchards, whose owner leased his strawberry field from Mrs. Updike. Just past the strawberry field, I turned left on Moyer Road. A few hundred yards on the right, sitting among some trees, was the Updike homestead. The famous barn of "Pigeon Feathers" sat a few yards off the narrow road. I parked behind Mrs. Updike's Dodge Dart, a decrepit vehicle only a failed state inspection away from a junkyard or destruction derby, and got out, clutching Amber's hand and my stories. When I knocked on the front door, John answered, wearing a tweed jacket and a white turtleneck sweater. He was much taller than I expected.

He smiled and shook my hand, but little Amber quickly stole his attention. He bent over and picked her up. With her in his arms, he led me inside. His mother was sitting in the living room, and with a smile welcomed us into her house. John motioned for me to sit, put down Amber, and we began our talk. Mrs. Updike listened attentively but said nothing. It must have been a familiar role for her, watching her renowned son hold court, while she—a published short story writer herself and the author of *Enchantment*, a lovely book of childhood reminiscences—sat quietly in the wings, ignored. Throughout my short visit, she remained in the background, or as much as she could in a tiny room that, although taking up half the downstairs area, wasn't much bigger than twelve by sixteen feet.

The furniture was well broken-in, the rug threadbare. The chairs were the same style my parents had owned, old but comfortable. Along the wall behind John was a room-length bookcase, about three feet high, filled with first editions of all his books, a treasure of incalculable value that Mrs. Updike would later bequeath to the Morgantown Library, one of the few places she habitually visited. (They are now at the Reading Public Library.) Amber sat quietly in my lap, but I was afraid she'd soon tire of all our yakking and begin acting up.

I mentioned how John's father had once been my substitute teacher at Daniel Boone High, adding that my wife had also once had him for a sub at Exeter High, another nearby school district. This elicited John's interest, but I steered the subject back to my stories. I shudder now at my rudeness, but as I handed him my stories, I thoughtlessly advised him to "take his time," as if I were a lenient teacher handing out an assignment. Perhaps my tone didn't strike him as presumptuous then, but the memory still makes me cringe.

John took the envelope without looking inside. He asked which writers I liked, and I mentioned Henry Miller, Erskine Caldwell,[16] and Ernest Hemingway. I had recently read a lengthy excerpt from *The Grandmothers* by Glenway Wescott[17] and said that I had liked it very much, adding that I hadn't been able to find a copy at the Reading Public Library. John seemed surprised I had read him and said, "I just saw him last week in New York. The next time I'm in Boston, I can buy you a copy at the used book store I always stop at." His generosity was impressive, but I assured him that he was already doing me a huge favor by agreeing to look at my short stories. He asked if I were sure; it would be no problem at all, and I politely (foolishly?) refused his offer again. I was hesitant to impose upon a stranger.

He asked if I wrote poetry, and I said no. He beamed with delight as I then quoted Faulkner's famous remark that he had taken up short story writing after having discovered poetry was too demanding, only to learn that it, too, was beyond his capabilities. Finally, he turned to writing novels, which he claimed were much easier. As for me, I said I didn't particularly care for much of the current poetry I read; I felt that it was devoid of music, John agreed, commenting, "It just seems to spill down the page, doesn't it?"

I wanted to keep our conversation on literature. I was there strictly for business, so I asked nothing about his personal life, and I already knew all I needed to know about his public life. I held the country notion that a man's private life was exactly that. John didn't pry into my life, either, although he did ask how old I was. I told him, and he observed that thirty-six wasn't too old, that plenty of other writers had gotten published rather late in life. During my visit, he was solicitous, respectful; I had the feeling that he genuinely wanted me to succeed. His warmth was deeply moving.

John spoke slowly and deliberately, carefully choosing his words before speaking, while I, in my nervousness, had been verbally stepping on his toes from the start, mistaking his oral commas for periods. I adjusted quickly, however, and learned to give him ample time to finish his sentences. His great intelligence was evident; I had sensed it right away. It was tangible, almost a physical presence, and his calm self-assurance lent him a dignified aura of authority. We had once lived only three miles apart, sleeping in second-floor bedrooms in old stone farmhouses that creaked in the night, and our parents may even have picked peaches side by side at Weaver's Orchards. Now we were separated not only by age but experience. I instinctively liked him, although I couldn't picture us spending a weekend together on the Chesapeake Bay, for instance, boating and fishing and carousing in the harbor bars.

I stood up and thanked him, apologizing to him and his mother for intruding, although I had a hunch that he was more amused than annoyed. He escorted Amber and me to the door, where we said goodbye. Then I went home to await his judgment of my stories.

A month or so later, my envelope arrived. I tore it open and devoured John's page-long, typed report. He had crossed out a word or two and added others; his hand-printed corrections perched atop each caret like pigeons on a barn roof.

His opening sentence got right to the point, observing that I'd picked a hard row to hoe, and what other advice could he give but to keep hoeing it? I assumed he was referring to the ill-bred, unrefined, and downright uncouth rural grotesques who populated my tales, and the difficulty he foresaw in finding editors willing to invite them into their magazines and quarterlies. But this I already knew.

John's second comment, however, gave me the jolt of adrenaline I needed. If he had ended his letter then, I would've been amply provisioned for my future campaign against the literary bastions that I proposed to storm. With a stifled cry of joy, I read that, in his opinion, I didn't write badly, my stories moved, and I didn't get bogged down in just words. Wow! I was ecstatic!

He went on to mildly rebuke me for my excessive use of vernacular, commenting that I seem to get bogged down in the rough talk of my male characters and my awkward attempts at Southern dialect. He felt that perhaps I had concentrated too much on their colorful-but-disgusting aspects, and neglected to bring the reader any "news," as he tactfully put it. And he wisely pointed out that even the most disgusting character has other attributes too.

I was guilty as charged! But in my defense, I had only begun to write; I was still discovering my voice, testing out the instruments which would allow it to sing. After that advice and his gentle admonitions, he made the remark that gave me the encouragement to continue writing. Apparently, one of my stories had affected him strongly. He confessed that it had made him feel sad and wounded; he sensed that humanity was crying out! Well! Upon reading that, *I* cried out! My gamble had paid off: I'd consulted the oracle and been sent on my way, brimming with confidence. The fate of the journey was dependent upon me.

John went on to give a few practical hints, mainly about usage and punctuation and manuscript preparation, things that a proud autodidact such as I should've already known. After warning me not to take anything he said too seriously because we are all groping in the dark, he not-too-subtly reminded me of the nature of our tenuous relationship. It wasn't his business to conduct a writing course by mail, even if he thought he could. He signed off, "Best Wishes, John Updike."

So, there it was: my visa to the exotic land of literature, hand-stamped by one of its preeminent suzerains. As he suggested, I kept hoeing my row, and a year later I sold my first short story to *Crosscurrents*, a California literary magazine. At the editor's suggestion, I bought extra copies for my children, plus one I intended to give to John.

I called his mother and asked if she would give it to John if I brought it over. She replied that he'd be home in a week or two, and asked if I'd like to give it to him myself. I agreed, and a couple Saturdays later I once again sat in Mrs. Updike's living room. This time I talked to John without Amber squirming in my lap. When I gave him his dedicated and autographed copy, he thanked me politely. He hefted it and leafed through it to my story, which, at twenty pages, was too long for him to read just then. He commented favorably on the quality of the printing, then laid it aside without reading my dedication. He asked how Amber and the rest of my family were, and I asked about his. Again his mother was content to sit quietly in her rocker, listening alertly. John appeared preoccupied, so after a short, inconsequential chat, I excused myself and left. Much later, through Mrs. Updike, he conveyed his enjoyment of my story, a tragedy about an old woman who loses both her freedom and her farm, and with them her life.

In 1986 I began working for a local weekly as a reporter, outdoor columnist, and occasional photographer. I asked Mrs. Updike if I could interview her, and she said yes. I met her at her home and photographed her seated in her chair, petting her dog, Tessie, using only the natural light streaming through her living room window. At some point during the interview, I put down my notebook and we simply talked, like the neighbors that in fact we were. We hit it off so well that we became casual friends. When the interview was published, she loved the photograph so much that I had the newspaper make several 8 × 10 prints. I then made four or five handcrafted wooden frames to mount them. I gave them to Mrs. Updike to pass on to John and his children. In return, he sent me an autographed copy of *Of the Farm*, a book I'd always liked. And I suspect that it was his mother's favorite, too.

I saw John twice more in my life but only spoke with him once. On an early June evening in 1985 or perhaps 1986, I had been picking strawberries with my wife and two of my oldest children. When we were done, I asked my wife to drive past Mrs. Updike's house. There in the driveway loading his suitcases in the trunk of his car was John, preparing to leave for his home in Beverly Farms. My wife stopped, and I shouted greetings from the road, offering him some berries.

He remembered me, his rustic "competitor," and grinned. "No, thanks," he said. The Weaver family always kept his mother well-supplied.

"Are you sure? I have a hundred and fifty pounds."

Laughing, he asked, "What are you going to do with that many?"

"Make a barrel of wine," I said. "I'll drop off a gallon next winter, when it's ready to drink," I promised.

"Thanks, anyway," he replied, "but I haven't drank in years."

"OK, have a safe trip home," I told him. He wished me well, and my wife drove away.

The last time I saw him was at his mother's funeral in October 1989. I entered Plowville's Robeson Lutheran Church shortly before the services began at 11 a.m. I squeezed into a pew near the back of the packed church and looked around. There were no famous faces, no members of the press, only those who remembered her as simply Linda, a kind and loving woman who had been their friend. The fact that she had given birth to a celebrated author was secondary. She had been theirs in life, part of their community, and they had come to bid her farewell. Her coffin, of cherry and bronze, sat before the altar. It was closed. Through the stained glass windows, the brilliant autumn sun fell in slanting bars across the burnished oaken pews.

Suddenly, John and his two sons and two daughters appeared at the rear of the church. They swept down the center aisle, their husbands and wives in tow. Their expressions were serene, devoid of anguish. After they were seated in the front pew, the minister began his eulogy. From behind, I saw John's face in profile as he listened, smiling gently or nodding in agreement as the preacher recounted his mother's life. When her favorite hymn, "This Is My Father's World,[18]" was sung, I was silent, but John carried my weight, singing loudly enough for us both.

Afterwards, I followed the cortege down a narrow asphalt lane through the heart of the old graveyard. Visible on the right, maybe seventy-five yards away, was the Little League baseball field named after John's father—Wesley

Updike Field. The pallbearers stopped under a tall pine, less than a hundred yards from the stone church that Mrs. Updike's father had helped build. They put the coffin on its bier and stepped back. There were fifty, maybe sixty people around the grave. The minister urged everyone to gather closer to the coffin, and some did. I stood twenty feet from John; his mother lay between us. As the preacher delivered a brief final homily, I studied the somber expressions of the mourners, then looked up to the sky for an omen: perhaps a circling hawk or a passing crow or just a songbird that had overstayed summer just to chirp a goodbye to a wonderful lady. I saw none, only the rolling blue hills stretching north, toward Reading, the city her son had made famous as Brewer.

If John noticed me at the grave, he gave no sign. His attention, understandably, was on other matters. His children, whom I had never met, stood by him talking softly. When the ceremony ended, I walked slowly to my truck. There was a reception in the church's social hall, but I didn't go. What could I have said that wouldn't be said by everyone else? No, it wasn't for me. I left John standing in the lovely hilltop cemetery, surrounded by his family. I never saw him again, yet when I finished my first novel in 1990, he graciously wrote, sight unseen, a short letter of recommendation.

Many years ago I read in one of his essays that he didn't believe in helping neophyte writers, that it was an impossible task, or words to that effect. At the time I was working as a newspaper reporter, and I knew that you can't believe everything you read, even if you wrote it yourself. Refuse a polite request for help? Naw, that wasn't the John Updike that I knew. His momma raised him better than that!

Burl N. Corbett (born 1947) grew up near Reading and attended Governor Mifflin Middle School in the 1960s. He has four children, six grandchildren. He has lived in Greenwich Village and Haight-Ashbury, tended bar on the Bowery, picked fruit with migrants, chased the sun as a pipeliner, and drove the big rigs, and worked as a reporter. His novel, A Haven from Violence, *appeared in 2002.* Coon Tales, *a children's book, has been accepted. Corbett has won 4 PEN awards and the 2013 Eaton Literary Agency Short Fiction contest.*

31. Jay Parini
"Updike and the Numinous"

When I was in my late teens, I read *The Poorhouse Fair, Pigeon Feathers,* and *Of the Farm,* and they made a huge impression on me. As his reviews and essays, stories, and poems, emerged in *The New Yorker*, which I read each week in my school library, I sought them out eagerly. The tang of his voice, with its barely controlled opulence, appealed to my innocent ear. Now *here* was literature, I told myself. I found myself rereading sentences, saying them aloud, amazed by their shapeliness, their perceptiveness. Updike attended to the surface of life in ways nobody else did; it was the life of ordinary Americans, the middle and lower-middle classes, evinced with loving detail.

As a young man I wrote several letters to Updike, just to make contact with a writer whose work I admired. We shared many things beside[s] Pennsylvania: a middle class family, a Christian orientation, a love of reading and writing. I liked the fact that he read and wrote on Karl Barth and Paul Tillich[19]—German theologians who had caught my attention. I wrote to him with a feeling of kinship, and he wrote back with shocking swiftness. His natural fluency was such that he could almost not fail to write sentences that reflected substantial, and original, thoughts. He wrote to me, about his theological adventuring, which he described as having gone from Chesterton[20] to Kierkegaard[21] to Barth. He told me that Tillich, whom I had been reading closely at the time and mentioned with enthusiasm, offended him as an attempt to avoid the scandal of faith. He made that point to me that God cannot be pressed into making a revelation of Himself, and that one should cultivate in one's life work an openness to joy that, almost by reverse effect, brings God into play.

I did, once, have a long lunch with Updike in a restaurant outside of Boston. I was much taken by the warm flame of self, unabashedly on display. He was a man who never had to reach terribly far to find an apt phrase, to characterize the work of another writer, to formulate his ideas in sentences that held together in natural paragraphs. I don't think anybody who ever talked to Updike for any length of time didn't feel his intimacy with language: he spoke as he wrote with an almost eerie ability to summon an image.

In our single long personal conversation, he mentioned Emerson, and we talked happily about that section in *Nature* (1836) that dwells on language, and Updike called my attention to the declaration that every word was once a bright and original picture, and that all language is fossil poetry. In a way, this explains Updike as well as anything I've ever seen. For him, language is fossil poetry, and he works as an excavator, digging up the roots of words, marshaling them in ways that re-grounds the prose in the physical world– yet without losing the numinous sense, as in the last magnificent paragraph of "His Finest Hour," an early story, where he writes of his hero, George: "His mind, swept clean of assertion, knew nothing but the flowers; they pour through his eyes" [*The Early Stories* 287]. That is, the physical world ultimately sweeps us beyond language; but we must step through that looking-glass medium, into eternity. Updike the poet reemerged with astonishing poignancy at the very end, with the aptly named *Endpoint* (2009), surely one of his fine accomplishments, a deep cry of mortality tinged with wisdom. Here fossil poetry is made numinous.

Theology—or, at least, a sense of the numinous—is never far from Updike's mind, and that also sets him apart from his contemporaries. His distinctly theological bent was out of fashion in his time, and yet it's what makes the work (for me) shimmer in its best moments. That he had a Lutheran tinge should surprise no one who reads him carefully: he regards the human comedy as a grand display of unoriginal sins. People mate and separate. They worry and resolve to do better. They flourish or fail according to laws that seem strangely out of their control.

As a critic, Updike wrote at length on Hawthorne, and he had a particular fascination with *The Scarlet Letter*, a novel about adultery and guilt—subjects that Updike took on with his own ferocity, in story after story, novel after novel. He saw himself as part of the American procession, as a writer who understood his Puritan roots. Updike was in perpetual conversation with the writers who went before him, adding his own fresh voice to debates already underway, running in his head.

He was part of the mental furniture of my time, and I can hardly imagine he is not there, on the North Shore of Boston, adding pages to his daily pile of fresh compositions. That productivity was, for me, inspiring. And he reached for sublimity, for what the theologian Rudolf Otto[22] called the numinous, exhibiting a sacred and mysterious sense of the world. That Updike actually tried to reach for this is worthy of celebration.

Jay Parini, a poet and novelist, is Axinn Professor of English at Middlebury College. His novels include The Passages of H.M., Benjamin's Crossing, *and* The Last Station. *The latter was made into an Academy Award-nominated film in 2010, starring Helen Mirren and Christopher Plummer. He has written biographies of John Steinbeck, Robert Frost, William Faulkner, Jesus, and Gore Vidal. His five books of poetry include* New and Collected Poems: 1975–2015.

32. Claude Clayton Smith
"Touching Genius: John Updike's Odd Obsession"

My sharpest memory of John Updike is the time we spent together as "inspectors" witnessing the process of putting together footballs. I was able to observe not only Updike's startling personal responses, but discover later how he imported this experience (along with me) into his writing.

In Updike's "Foreword" to his 1988 three stories, "The Football Factory," "Part of the Process," and "The Lens Factory," he remarks, "in August of 1988, oddly obsessed by the vistas that my visit to an Ohio football factory opened up, I wrote a ten-page non-fictional memoir, called 'The Real Story,' which has never been published." He admits he was "entranced and repelled ... overwhelmed" by the "savage precision" of machines and workers. As the person directly responsible for Updike's visit—a member of that "party of inspection" who appears in both "The Real Story" and "The Football Factory"—I would like to describe what Updike made of the unusual but prosaic outing I had arranged, what he called, "subject matter out of [his] usual path."

Before providing my recollection of that unusual path, I would like to ask your indulgence while I describe the history of my acquaintance with Updike and his work. I became aware of Updike during my sophomore year at Wesleyan when I assigned *Rabbit, Run* for a course in contemporary literature. The book electrified me. It was 1964, I was twenty years old, and Updike, twelve years my senior, seemed as ageless as God. A former high school basketball player like Rabbit, I knew the very songs Rabbit heard on his car radio as he fled south from Pennsylvania on his impulsive "road trip." I knew the roads, too. I envied Rabbit's sexual escapades and shared his inarticulate longings. *Rabbit, Run* was quite simply the first piece of literature that ever seemed personally relevant to me.

So, when I bought a paperback edition of *Pigeon Feathers* at a bookstore in Oxford, England, during the summer of 1965, I was delighted to learn that Updike himself had spent a year at Oxford after Harvard and that some of the stories in the book were about his experiences there. The collection included "A&P," and I encountered it again in a short story course as a Wesleyan senior. The following year, pursuing an M.A.T. at Yale, I read that story aloud—and many others from *Pigeon Feathers*—to the students I was teaching as part of my program at New Haven's Hillhouse High School. At the end of that unit, when I offered a suitcase of my own books to the students for their book reports, *Rabbit, Run, The Centaur, The Poorhouse Fair, Of The Farm* were the first to be claimed.

A year later I was teaching Updike at Churchill High School in Potomac, Maryland, where I insisted that the English Department purchase a class set of *Pigeon Feathers*. The book room would hold multiple class sets by the time I left. Each new Updike book in those days was for me an annual gift from heaven. I would buy the hardbound first edition at the Saville Book Shoppe in Georgetown and repair to the Tombs beneath the 1789 restaurant on the Georgetown University campus to read the afternoon away over a pitcher of beer.

In 1970, pursuing an M.F.A. in the Writers' Workshop at the University of Iowa (among other things I had published a poem about a high school teacher teaching a John Updike short story from *Pigeon Feathers* ("Hinc Illae Lacrimae," *English Journal*, Oct. 1969), I encountered negative criticism of John Updike for the very first time. William Price Fox, a Southern novelist complained, "Updike can't get a character down the stairs without having him count every whorl in the banister," and a fellow graduate assistant declared, "Updike never got over being the most sensitive guy in Shillington, Pennsylvania." All this, of course, was blasphemy to me, and I asked John Leggett, who had just succeeded George Starbuck as the Writers' Workshop director, "Why should anyone else bother to write when we have John Updike?" Leggett only smiled.

Then Leggett did something that changed my life. Apparently, Leggett showed my poem to Updike, because he wrote to me expressing his pleasure at the unequal reactions to the story shown by teacher and students. I had touched my hero, who, unlike Ted Williams, was a god who answered letters.

In 1975 I pursued a D.A. at Carnegie-Mellon, and, as fate would have it, Updike appeared in September. I was first in line for tickets with my fiancée, who disliked Updike's unflattering treatment of women. A few years later, when dining with Updike at Virginia Tech, where I was then an assistant professor, my wife said, "I'm going to shake his hand, then kick him in the shins." But Updike charmed that impulse right out of her. That Pittsburgh reading (the first time I ever saw Updike in person) was highly successful. Moved by the experience, I wrote him a letter, inviting him to play golf at the Yale course that summer. He replied, as he always did, by postcard, his message rendered on a manual typewriter, declining the invitation by offering a vivid contrast between winter in Massachusetts and summer at Yale.

I saw Updike again in the spring of 1982, when he was the keynote speaker at the annual meeting of the Associated Writing Programs in Boston. With several Virginia Tech colleagues, I had driven the sixteen hours from Blacksburg to Boston, only to leave on the final afternoon to get back to our classes just as Updike was entering the hotel. I passed within a few feet of him in the corridor outside the auditorium, and the near miss emboldened me. I wrote him from Blacksburg, inviting him to read at Virginia Tech, enclosing copies of my poem and his postcard to remind him that we had touched base before. I proposed a "John Updike Week" for May of 1983, and he accepted. He read before more than two thousand people,

In person John Updike was warm, gracious, self-effacing, and accommodating to a fault. His eyes sparkled, as did his wit, and he noticed everything. At the time, I was teaching workshops in poetry, fiction, and creative writing for young audiences. My first "Little Golden Book" had been published, the second was forthcoming, and Updike, who had published several children's books, said that he had once submitted a "Little Golden Book" but it had been rejected. Oddly, he seemed more anguished than entertained by the vast number of Bikini-clad coeds studying on the May grass.

In October 1987 I hosted Updike again for a reprise of "John Updike Week" at Ohio Northern University. Now an associate professor, I described, over dinner, how the "times" seemed to account for the student response to "A & P," which he intended to read later on. From 1967 to 1977, my students, like me, had considered Sammy a hero for quitting his job in defense of three girls that the manager had embarrassed for entering the grocery store in bathing suits. From 1977 to 1987, however—the Vietnam War having ended and the economy having soured—the students thought Sammy a fool. My students had forced me to see, after ten years, that Sammy was not a romantic anti-hero. I saw Updike's eyes twinkle, perhaps in appreciation that the story had defied both teacher and time.

The morning after Updike's Ohio reading we visited the Wilson Sporting Goods factory, exclusive makers of the NFL football. My neighbor, a manager there, arranged a VIP tour. The facility seemed to me a Victorian sweatshop, and it had a dramatic effect on Updike, who later indicated that he intended to write about it. Two years later I toured the factory twice in order to write "Made in Ada: The NFL Ball" (*The Gamut* [1990] *Ohio Outback* [2010]). His story, when I came to read it, overwhelmed me.

In 1999 I read *More Matter*, savoring several pages each night, and at that pace it was more than a year before I encountered Updike's "Foreword" to *Love Factories*, stunned to recognize myself on p. 770, where Updike quotes from his unpublished essay, "The Real Story": "I was taken by my host ... to the local factory where footballs were made... I was entranced and repelled." But *Love Factories* was difficult to find; copies available only from special bookstores cost more than three hundred dollars, so it was 2003 before I had it all in hand. The wait was worth it, because in "The Football Factory" the "visiting dignitary" (Updike) provides a meticulous rendering of the Wilson operation, for example:

> The ... workers ... seemed no more conscious of the visitors than the machines were ... the hides ... went to a young woman at a machine that stamped big pumpkin-seed shapes from them. It was wonderful to see how quickly she placed the oval die, snatched back her hand, let the machine descend and lift with a hollow plucking sound.... When the pieces were stamped out, the waste remnant, minimal and tangled like a wet bikini, was tossed into a barrel [21–22].

The detailed descriptions amazed me. They are interspersed with exchanges between "the dignitary" and "the company president" who is giving the tour, while "the liaison" (yours truly) looks on. I was even more surprised when, in the spring of 2003, Updike acknowledged he had written "The Football Factory" from memory. This had to be so because he took no notes and was quite busy after the factory visit. I had been with him climbing Mad River Mountain then visiting the Columbus Museum of Art, where I trailed him from room to room for an hour, thrilled by his astute commentary.

The football factory was miles behind us, yet it had been indelibly stamped on Updike's mind, just as the Wilson logo had been stamped in gold and black foil on the tanned-and-pebbled top-grain leather panels of the NFL footballs. It had taken me three trips through the Wilson Sporting Goods factory—taking notes on two occasions while interviewing both workers and management, checking and rechecking my facts—just to get the steps in the process straight. But Updike had done it months later from memory.

The only letter I ever received from John Updike (besides intermittent postcards) was in response to my question about researching the football factory. It arrived in a padded envelope that contained a surprise, a copy of *Love Factories* #43 in a signed limited edition, with a note saying that no one deserved it better than his football factory tour guide. Needless to say, that left a memory that touches me still.

Claude Clayton "Bud" Smith, professor emeritus of English at Ohio Northern University, is the author of eight books and co-editor/translator of two others, most recently, Meditations After the Bear Feast: The Poetic Dialogues of N. Scott Momaday and Yuri Vaella *(Shanti Arts Publishing, 2016). His own work has been translated into five languages, including Russian and Chinese. He has been cited as a "Friend of Native Peoples by the UN Committee for the Decade of Indigenous Peoples (1994–2004).*

33. Nicholson Baker
From *U & I*

… [I]f he hadn't felt enough fondness for his old school magazine [the Harvard *Lampoon*] to show up that day, I wouldn't have had my chance to wait for him near the ham tidbits, steeling myself to be pushy. I knew it was pointless, but I wanted to talk to him more than anyone else I didn't know. I spied on him as he stood in a rearward room, giving serious advice to an exceedingly tall person who was editor or president of the *Lampoon* that year. Then he took his leave of everyone and briskly walked along the long neomedieval table of hewn food toward the door.

"Hi, I'm Nick Baker."

"I'm John Updike."

"I know." (This "I know" is a faint source of shame to me now, but it is nonetheless what I said.).

He nodded, still thinking he could escape by giving the general appearance of hurry. But I wasn't going to let him go. "I, um, had a story in *The New Yorker* a long time ago." Resigned to this standard interchange ... he asked me what the story was about. I told him, and he said, "Mmm," but he didn't look as if he remembered. He asked me my name again. I told him and mentioned the long story I had had in *The Atlantic*, too. Closing his eyes, pressing on his forehead with his index and thumb, he forced himself to recall who I was. "Didn't you also write a story about some musicians on the West Coast?" he suddenly asked.

Surprising as this may sound, I had to think for a second. It was a work I didn't want to exist. Both *The Atlantic* and *The New Yorker* had rejected it.... So when Updike finally remembered who I was on the strength of that *Little Magazine* story I was taken aback—I didn't know for an instant what he was talking about. "Musicians on the West Coast?" I said, puzzled, and then, realizing that I probably appeared to him to be pretending to have to make an effort to remember something that I really knew right off the bat, I said, "Yes! Right! I did!"

"A lovely thing," said Updike. He also praised something else of mine that appeared in *The Atlantic*. And *he said that I should keep writing because I had a gift*. Should I not be including this pronouncement here? Is it self-serving? No, because mainly it shows Updike to be civil and generous in person, which is a thing worth knowing.... Anyway, how can I not retain Updike's moment of encouragement, when it is one of the very few *events* I have to offer in this whole plasmodium? It isn't as if Updike said, "Nick *Baker*! Holy Moly! Congratulations on being you. You're going to *fly*!" Still, "a lovely thing" was a lovely thing for him to say—it helped me; it altered my opinion about that story, which I now will certainly include if I ever put out a book of stories. But did it also, I now discover myself wondering—and even my suggestion of such a possibility should serve as a warning to all eminent and tolerant writers not to be nice to people who pounce on them at parties—did it also to lower him ever so slightly, in the old Groucho Marxian manner, in my estimation, since I can see, rereading the story now, that it is replete with false touches? Why didn't he see through it? I wonder; in seeing through it myself I suspect for a minute that I have found a blind spot in him to the kind of cheapness it exhibits—when really he was simply doing what he knew I wanted him to do, which was to recognize my existence as a writer, to bless me by remembering who I was.

He asked me how I made a living, and I told him. "When I first got out of college..." I started to say.

"College *here*?" he interrupted, raising his eyebrows as if to settle an important question, and pointing at the floor.

"Myeah," I said. A lie! A pathetic lie! ... I went on talking about my employment history. He said his son was thinking of taking a teaching job, but he, Updike, wasn't sure it was such a good idea. "It's hard," he said, meaning hard to make a living at writing.

"It is hard," I said. "But when I get deflated I go back to one of your early stories and I'm all fired up again!"

He had been backing away by then, knowing the obligatory praise-heaping and groveling scene was coming; at this he shook his head and waved and walked out. Had I insulted him by saying "early stories"? I had meant it as an allusion to his own statement on the PBS show that his early stories had the best chance of surviving; and I meant that I went back to them in particular because they were stories written when he was my age. (In 1984 I was twenty-seven.) But what I didn't understand then was that he might not want his assessment of his work taken at face value.

When *Roger's Version* came out a year or two later [1986], with its nice pale blue cover faintly inset with crosses, I stood in Lauriat's in downtown Boston and read the first few pages. My single powerful reaction was: *I was Dale*. Updike was describing me. I actually believe (and still do believe, though with less conviction) that Updike got Dale's extreme gawky tallness, his thinning hair, his bad skin, his overeager technotalkative, slack-but-smart way of speaking, and Roger's own immediate sense of being threatened by and mildly disliking Dale, all from that one time encounter with me. Updike had broken free from my chatlock, I figured, gone home muttering to himself about pushy younger writers, gotten up the next morning, and written me into the first scene of his novel as a computer nerd.

Nicholson Baker (born 1957), B.A. in philosophy, Haverford College, is noted for his post-modern novels: Vox *(1992) and* The Fermata *(1994),* Double Fold: Libraries and the Assault on Paper, *and* Substitute: Going to School with a Thousand Kids *(2016).* Double Fold *received the National Book Critics Circle Award in 1997 and the James Madison Freedom of Information Award.* U and I: A True Story *(1991) is a non-fiction study of John Updike.*

34. Nicholson Baker
"The Nod"

What I think of now, though, is a time more than 20 years ago, when I saw him in the Boston Public Garden. It was a cold, overcast late afternoon, in the eighties, and there was a man walking toward me on the path. We were over past the statue of George Washington, in a part of the garden that has fewer trees, that's always colder and windier than other parts—and I had to figure out what to do. He was wearing a tweedish jacket buttoned up and a scarf and a hat and he obviously had somewhere to go, as I didn't, really. If I stopped and I said, "Mr. Updike?" he would of course politely stop and we would have had a brief conversation. I would maybe say that I liked his writing and that he'd signed one of his books for me once and that I'd sent him a fan letter once that I hadn't put a return address on because I didn't want to compel him to answer it and that in the letter I'd told him that my girlfriend, who had since become my fiancée, had dug out of a wicker basket of *New Yorker*s a story of his and given it to me to read and I'd read two-thirds of it and had decided, walking under the awning of a tuxedo shop in a moment of passing shade that I wanted very much to write him and tell him about how happy it made me to *know* that he was out there working. But I couldn't stop him on his path and tell him all that. He was on his way somewhere. So I decided instead that I would just nod. I would pack in everything I knew about him in my nod, all the memories I had of reading about packed dirt and thimbles and psoriasis and stuttering and Shillington, Pennsylvania, and the Harvard *Lampoon* and the drawing class at Oxford, and his little office upstairs in Ipswich—and the letters that he and Katherine White had exchanged when he was writing his early stories for the *New Yorker* that I'd seen behind glass in a display case at Bryn Mawr College—all that knowledge of him I would cram into one smiling knowing nod. And that's what I did. And he nodded back, a little uncertainly, I think. He wasn't sure: maybe he knew me?

And then later, in a letter, he said, didn't we meet once on Arlington Street? He remembered my nod.

What a memory on that man.

35. Lini S. Kadaba
"Who Was John Updike?—Ask His Driver"

As the first conference of The John Updike Society began last October on Alvernia's campus, an unassuming man of 60-something, dressed neatly in coat and tie, fidgeted in the rear of a filled lecture hall. Unbeknownst to most who had gathered, David Silcox, Updike conference organizer, good friend of the university, and retired engineer, was far more than a casual observer. Depending on one's point of view, he was a confidant, handler, helper, heckler, friend, or just plain driver for the revered writer. Maybe he was all these, or perhaps none. To Silcox he was just Updike's gofer or grunt. But across two decades, Updike the man unfolded before him—vulnerable and quirky, thrifty and testy, sometimes funny, occasionally witty, but always a gentleman, and always brilliant.

David Silcox is a born collector. The Shillington resident enjoys the hunt as much as the acquisition, especially when it involves books or memorabilia from the youth of famed author John H. Updike. For a stretch in the late '80s, Silcox made a 12-mile drive on a regular basis between the Reading Airport and the Updike family farm in Plowville, Pa. His trips, however, didn't focus on building his broad collection, which he has begun to donate to the [Alvernia] university archive, to be housed in [the] Frank A. Franco Library. Instead, he was intent on building a relationship and store of unforgettable memories with Berks County's favorite son.

Then in his 40s and an industrial engineer, Silcox jumped at the chance to "chauffeur" Updike during visits to his mother. Every couple of months between 1988 and 1989, he shared the front seat, and casual conversation, with one of the greatest American fiction writers of his generation. As they traveled through the rolling hills that dot the highways and byways of Greater Reading, the two chatted in the sprawling '84 Crown Victoria Silcox inherited from his uncle. Sometimes, Bradley, Silcox's then 8-year-old son, would tag along in the backseat and shoot the breeze with the distinguished writer. Talk amongst the trio was often of the mundane; Updike's travels, Silcox's job, town news, property taxes, Bradley's autograph collection. But now and then the Updike fan, who often planned potential topics ahead, turned the conversation to the writer's childhood or literature.

"I was never his buddy," says Silcox, 63, an affable man, sturdy with white, wavy hair and wire-rimmed glasses. The retired Carpenter Technology executive speaks with a gravelly voice as he drives us around in his red Honda CRV (the Crown Victoria long since traded in) and points out the old locations of Stevens' [Stephen's] Luncheonette, Becker's Garage, and other favorite Updike haunts in the Shillington of old. "My wife used to say, 'You're his grunt.' But I enjoyed being his grunt."

Scholars may dissect Updike's works to analyze the author, as they did at October's John Updike Society Conference; Silcox, though, came to his conclusions from his regular rounds of small talk and a gradual conversation that unfolded over 20 years, first as a driver, then as a "contact" in town until the writer's death in 2009.

Who was John Updike? Celebrity? Cultural icon? Demure recluse? According to this accidental chauffeur, the guy was amiable, modest, and always frugal. In fact, the multimillionaire who pulled in about $30,000 per speaking appearance sought rides to and fro in large part because he fretted over what it was costing him to travel to visit his mother, even after his tax advisor told him that he could deduct those expenses as research. After all, he would be incorporating memories from those trips into his future writings.

Updike also refused to subscribe to the *Reading Eagle* (the very same newspaper he worked for in his younger years) when he moved away, prevailing on locals to send clippings. And he was known to prefer postcards over letters to save postage, even to reuse a stamp on occasion. "That was John Updike," Silcox says as he shares the details. "He had a Depression-Era mindset."

Silcox delights in talking Updike. He has not yet, however, read all his masterworks. "He's a hard read," he says, adding his favorite is *The Centaur*. And it should come as no surprise that he was at the meeting—it was held in his dining room, no less—when the notion to establish The John Updike Society was kindled, an organization that the author wouldn't allow while he was alive. Silcox also helped organize the inaugural Updike conference at Alvernia, where he had a ready audience for his tales. He served as a tour guide for participants and retraced part of the route taken with Updike those many years ago. True to form, the detail man that inspired the meticulous author's trust was charged with conference site particulars, handling goodie bags, organizing itineraries, and ensuring buses ran on time. (They did, naturally.)

In October 1989, the Silcox shuttle service screeched to a stop when John's mother Linda Hoyer Updike died, but by then a comfortable bond connected the two men. Soon Silcox was called upon to handle various affairs. He would suggest a lawyer, pass on information about former classmates, attend his lectures and readings in the region, or keep tabs on local politics, he says. "I was Updike's go-to man," he adds with obvious pride. For a decade starting in 1999, he clipped articles on local news and gossip from the *Reading Eagle* and mailed the thick packets to New England, where the writer had settled. Updike used details from the articles to inform his rich portraits of Middle America.

Silcox came by his "in" with Updike through neighbor Thelma Lewis, who taught with Updike's father Wesley, at the local high school and was a friend of Linda, who Silcox also got to know. Lewis also served as an adviser for *Chatterbox*, Updike's high school newspaper to which he contributed editorials and cartoons as a teen. She recommended Silcox for the chauffeur role, and as her health deteriorated, she passed on the clipping job. Before Lewis died in 2006, Silcox, who helped with her affairs, was given many of her prized Updike items, including yearbooks, correspondence, and a few first-edition books, several of Updike's inscriptions indicated that Thelma Lewis was his finest editor.

Silcox was a natural for the job. "He seems to know everybody," says

Alvernia's sitting Updike Scholar in Residence Jack De Bellis, professor emeritus of English at Lehigh University and author of *The John Updike Encyclopedia*. "He's a man in motion. He's constantly involved in multiple projects." One of his latest is a book with De Bellis called *John Updike's Early Life*. Silcox tracked down teachers and classmates. "He's the kind of person who gets things done. He's really a dynamo."

Silcox, though, doesn't care for the attention, perhaps a quality of Updike's that rubbed off on him over the years. On a drive around town, he prefers not to focus conversation solely on him but include Updike's former classmates, particularly Barry R. Nelson, laid up from a series of strokes. Nelson, 78, met Updike in ninth grade and became his closest friend. The two worked together on the *Chatterbox*, where Nelson, a basketball player, contributed sports stories. "I taught him how to shoot over his back, without looking at the hoop," he says from his recliner. Once, he also researched Updike's questions about sandstone quarries, information used for the short story "A Sandstone Farmhouse."

As we take our leave, we drive past Grace Evangelical Lutheran Church, where Updike was baptized, and Silcox recounts the time 9-year-old John was walking to Sunday school, a nickel clasped in his hand. As he crossed the street, a car hit him. "Fortunately, in those days, the cars didn't move very fast." Even as the boy was sprawled in the street stunned, he kept a tight grasp on his nickel. "Who, but John Updike, would still be clutching their nickel after they got hit by a car?" he wondered.

We pass the local library, and Silcox remembers his efforts to get Updike to make a large donation to the renovation project. In return, a room would be named in honor of his parents. Updike declined; instead, he purchased a brass nameplate for $500. His tight purse strings left some Shillingtonians to gripe that the two-time Pulitzer Prize winner never did much for the communities that inspired his oeuvre. Silcox bristles at the suggestion. "Shillington is internationally known but for whom? John Updike," he says. Updike was a stickler for accuracy. For the 100th anniversary of Shillington, Silcox wrote a headnote about Updike, with his permission, to be included in a town history book. "I told him, 'I'll work something up, and you can rip it apart.' I have the rough draft," which Silcox says had a few extra errors "for John to find." He did his editing in red. Updike complimented his work and asked for another draft.

The book also reprinted a well-known Updike poem, "In the Cemetery High above Shillington." He instructed Silcox to ensure that the verse was typeset accurately. Updike distrusted printers. When the book came out, he offered compliments. "When someone like John Updike says, 'Good job,' that means a lot."

Those who knew the writer always describe him as friendly but seldom called him friend. "John's relationship with most people was a professional relationship," says De Bellis, who knew the author for three decades but never became close to him. "John was an extremely private person. He was always cordial, honest, and delighted that people took an interest in his work."

As Silcox says with no hint of malice: "I was on the periphery. I consider myself very fortunate." The two would never discuss Updike's many health problems, including a stutter (which made a reappearance whenever he spoke to the locals), psoriasis, and asthma. Or the woes of his first marriage. Or anything else truly intimate. Yet, the two Pennsylvanians shared common ground that could have led to a deeper relationship. Silcox, like Updike, is an only child. He grew up in Pottsville, in coal country. "I grew up a poor boy," he says. "My dad had a little print shop.[23] My mom worked in a factory." Silcox also suffered a speech impediment not unlike Updike's stutter. "I would always withdraw. He was more of an extrovert. He would make fun of himself."

Updike, of course, left the area for Harvard University and his career. Silcox graduated from Penn State University in 1967 with his engineer's degree and married a Shillington woman, Mary, in 1977. The next year, the couple moved to town. Unlike the Harry Angstrom character in *Rabbit, Run*, however, Silcox has always remained content with his small-town life, satisfying any wanderlust with vacations to China, Russia and other exotic locales. "I love Shillington," he says simply, echoing Updike.

By now, we're near the Plowville farm, where Emerson and Marlene Gundy live. (Emerson is a second cousin to Updike and bought the place 20 years ago.) The red sandstone farmhouse was built in 1812—and Marlene allows a peek inside. "This was where he sat and read," she says, showing the living room with its broad plank floor and built-in book cases full of Updike. The room is cozy with knickknacks and country charm, but when Silcox used to visit Linda Updike, he says the room was bare and sparsely furnished.

One of the Gundys' favorite memories was the time Updike, who hated the farm as a child but grew fonder as an adult, visited them on a wet day. His shoes were muddy, and he took them off to pad around barefoot, settling in the enclosed sunroom. As he shared tea with the Gundys, he remarked, "Isn't this blissful—sitting here listening to the rain on a tin roof?"

"We always liked the tin roof, but I never used that adjective," Marlene says, laughing. "Anyone else would have said, 'Isn't that a neat sound.'" It was one more tale for Silcox to collect.

The collector in him has amassed books by local authors John O'Hara[24] and Conrad Richter,[25] autographs of baseball greats, presidents, Medal of Honor winners and cosmonauts and astronauts. But his true passion is Updike. In Shillington, some might argue that's a rampant condition. Silcox, though, has more determination than most. He is proud of the breadth of items that showcase Updike's early days.

"I was always planning ahead," says Silcox, who realized the value of keeping certain mementoes. To that end, he has begun an inventory, after which he plans to turn his collection over to Alvernia where it will be housed in the Updike archive room with the other remnants of the John Updike Society Archive. "The rest of it can be sold off, split up," he says of his other collectibles, "if I pass away and my son doesn't want it. But the Updike pieces are near and dear to my heart, where they came from and how I collected them, and the personal association. I want it to stay together."

Besides the first editions, all autographed, Silcox has personal correspondence dating to the 1950s as well as his own written exchanges with the author. He rattles off his finds: honorary awards, Updike's high school yearbook, Wesley's and Linda's college yearbook, *Chatterbox* issues thought lost, sermons given at his parents' funerals. "A lot of little stuff like that," he says. Silcox always kept a stash of items handy for Updike to sign—adding value to them. The busy writer always obliged. Silcox is still on the hunt for Updike's .22 caliber rifle used to shoot pigeons in the barn as described in the short story "Pigeon Feathers."

"His collection is really very impressive," said Alvernia archivist Gene Mitchell of Silcox's Updike collection. "From a scholarly perspective, the pieces add to what we know already exists and shed further light on Updike the author and Updike the man. We are grateful to Dave for his donation and thankful for the foresight he had to collect items that have such significance."

In fact, Updike, himself, was apparently impressed with Silcox's tenacity when it came to the collection. One time, the go-to guy got his hands on the last football program that Updike wrote in high school. Even he didn't have a copy in his personal files he told Silcox.

"He said, 'Dave, you're always finding things.'" In the process, Silcox discovered far more than a prize-winning author and a trove of valued memorabilia. His experiences revealed Updike the Everyman, and for his trouble, he was rewarded with a collection of memories that will endure for a lifetime.

Yes, that's David Silcox. Always a collector.

David R. Silcox was born in 1947 and raised in Pottsville, Pennsylvania. A Penn State University graduate, Silcox spent his career at Carpenter Technology Corporation in Reading, Pa. He has published numerous books and articles and was Updike's contact in Shillington for many years. He donated his Updike collection to Alvernia University in 2011. Silcox served as Site Director for the first John Updike Conference in 2010. He has been active in the purchase and restoration of the Updike home in Shillington.

Lini S. Kadaba is a freelance journalist and former Philadelphia Inquirer *staff writer based in Newtown Square, Pennsylvania.*

36. Harry Charles "Buck" Niehoff
"John Updike: Gentleman"

Having read the "Rabbit" quartet, I wasn't looking forward to meeting John Updike, our speaker on October 25, 1991. Exposing the turmoil of a white suburban American male, Harry "Rabbit" Angstrom, the four volumes are disconcerting. As Updike acknowledged in an *Enquirer* article about the final volume, *Rabbit at Rest*, "You might say it's a depressed book about a depressed man, written by a depressed man."

But Updike turned out to be much brighter than his books ... he was humble, considerate, and "immensely polite ... a pathologically polite man," to borrow words he used to describe someone else.

When I met him at the airport, he mentioned with shy satisfaction that he managed to find a "super-saver ticket," even though we had offered first class travel arrangements. He is, by the way, the only author in our series to travel coach.

His humility seemed genuine and refreshing. Before lunch he commented that his hotel suite "was far grander than I deserved."

When the sound system seemed to fail, he asked, "Is this microphone dead? I wouldn't blame it if it died." Perhaps the best example, though, of his humility occurred when my son, Peter, then six years old, and I arrived at the hotel the morning after the lecture to drive him to the airport. When I asked Peter to move to the rear seat, Updike said he wouldn't think of taking Peter's regular place. As he squeezed into the back, Updike added that he had treated himself to room service for breakfast and he hoped that was ok for the budget. When he saw the stuffed rabbit that Peter was holding, he recognized it as one of the table decorations from the lecture and autographed its ear which a felt-tipped pen.

Updike's thoughtfulness seemed unlimited. With open fascination he moved modestly and attentively through a daunting series of activities the afternoon before the lecture. During lunch at the hotel, he talked with Dr. James Schiff, Library Board member, about his recent golf trip to Ireland. At 2:15 he was interviewed by Maureen Conlan of the *Post*, and at 2:45 he recorded a piece for WVXU radio. At 3:00 Patti and I took him to Union Terminal, where DeVere Burt, Director of the Museum of Natural History, showed us the newly renovated facility that was to open to the public the following week. About 4:30 we went to the Zoo's Center for the Reproduction of Endangered Wildlife where Patti volunteered. We also checked out the Zoo's Komodo dragons. In all these things, Updike was a curious and thoughtful observer. More important, he seemed appreciative, like an art history student being shown a private collection of masterpieces.

During dinner at the Hall of Mirrors, he talked golf with Dr. Joe Steger, President of the University of Cincinnati. Unlike many speakers, who merely nibble nervously before lecturing, Updike ate everything, including a piece of rich chocolate cake. At lunch he had also enjoyed dessert, crème brûlée, and when I talked about my Graeter's ice cream, he eagerly accepted a heaping spoonful. Perhaps playing golf keeps him slender.

The theme of his talk was leaving home, and he read two of his stories and four poems dealing with that topic. His first story was "The Parade," written in 1976, about a celebrity returning to his hometown, the fictional Haysville, similar to Updike's birthplace of Shillington, Pennsylvania, for a parade commemorating the 75th anniversary of the incorporation of the municipality. The main character's comment about his fame seemed typical of Updike's humility. Celebrity was "welcomed at first but ... has become as far as my actual work goes a burden upon both my time and imagination."

He also read "The Rumor," published in the June 1991, issue of *Esquire*, about a couple who has moved to New York from their hometown, which was Cincinnati. Although Updike had never been to Cincinnati before, he had gathered details from friends who knew the city. He concluded with the poems "Movie House," "Small City People," and two about Shillington.

During the question period he recognized one of the two special guests at the dinner, Pulitzer Prize winner Edward Albee, as "one of America's preeminent playwrights." He was in town for the production of one of his plays. Also with us was Jim Borgman, *Enquirer* cartoonist, who like Updike, had just won a Pulitzer Prize.

Updike's politeness continued even after he returned to his home in Beverly Farms, Massachusetts. About 4:30 on the afternoon following the lecture, I was slightly dozing, listening to a recording of his 1963 novel *The Centaur* when the phone rang. "Hello, Mr. Niehoff, this is John Updike. I am home." It was magical to hear the actual voice of the author interrupt the reading of his written words. Like a well-mannered houseguest, he had called to thank me for an enjoyable visit. He was a gentleman start to finish.

Harry Charles "Buck" Niehoff (born, 1947) practiced law at Peck, Shaffer & Williams from 1973 until his retirement in 2012. Since 1997 he and his wife Patti have sponsored an annual "Evening with a Great Teacher," which highlights outstanding faculty members of the University of Cincinnati. He has written three books, and with Patti has sponsored for 25 years the annual Niehoff Lecture at The Mercantile Library, featuring distinguished authors such as Joyce Carol Oates.

37. Roxana Robinson
"John Updike"

I don't know when I started reading John Updike, but it was probably when I was in my teens. I sank into his beautiful prose as though it were a summer-high meadow. I hadn't known you could write like that. I hadn't known you could use language so precisely and elegantly, or speak from a heart so compassionate and generous, or reveal life that was so daily and so unpretentious, so authentic.

For years I read every story he wrote. They seemed essential. They seemed what writing should be. They showed that this was the way to look at the world, with a gaze that was thoughtful, attentive, and generous. The generosity was what moved me most, and it seemed that Updike was the true heir to Chekhov,[26] a writer who accepted every kind of behavior—selfish, stupid, arrogant, tender, wounded, idealistic, wise, brave, brutal, loving—as part of the human story.

Years ago, while teaching a writing class, I told my students that the best way to learn to write well was by reading good writing. If I can write, I told them, it's because John Updike taught me.

After class, a student came up to me. Have you ever told John Updike that he taught you to write? She asked.

I told her I had not.

You should, she said.

When my next book came out, a collection of stories,[27] I sent a copy to Updike. In a letter I explained what my student had said, and told him of my debt. He wrote back at once, a type-written post card, in which he was friendly and direct. He said he'd never thought he'd actually influenced another writer, and ever since Leslie Fiedler had called him "curiously irrelevant" he had managed to carry that burden. What he'd heard from me had changed this, and it delighted him. It made my day to get that post card, and I framed it.

I kept on reading his stories and novels, which seemed to illuminate our lives. Who else was looking so closely at the way we really lived? Who else was so tolerant of our frailties, so aware of our vulnerabilities, so interested by our failures, so respectful of our passions? Who else wrote such breathtakingly beautiful prose?

I sent him a copy of the next book I wrote, but didn't receive another post card.

A few years later I met my hero face to face. It was at a literary party, and I saw him standing alone. It was my moment. I drew a deep breath and walked up and introduced myself.

My conversation with him had been going on throughout the whole of my writing life. I read his stories, I taught them, I remembered characters and scenes and phrases, and I carried his sentences around in my mind. My understanding of marriage and divorce and parenthood was influenced by the way Updike had rendered them. I felt a certain kind of tenderness towards husbands and wives and children, because of the way he had written about them. I felt his constant presence in my world.

That evening I told him who I was. I reminded him of my letter, his postcard, my book of stories. He smiled, that courtly V-shaped smile we know so well from the photographs. I could see that he had no recollection of our conversation, of my book, or the post card with his kindly response. I had been thinking about him for twenty years. He had never thought of me.

What have you done since then? He asked politely. Have you published anything else?

I had published several books since then, but I was unable to answer.

I had been thinking of him for twenty years, and he had never thought once of me, he had never read any of my books or even heard of them, and suddenly the extreme one-sidedness of our conversation was too much for me.

I'm sorry, I said, I can't talk to you anymore. I turned away.

I wanted, of course, to continue our conversation, but it was better to continue it in the way we'd always done it before—me thinking of him when I was alone, and reading his work. This was better than trying to carry it on at a party, when only one of us even knew about it.

I walked away that night, never imagining that it would be our only meeting. I thought of course we'd have another chance, and this time I'd be better prepared, or that he would. Maybe he'd have read something I'd written, or maybe I'd be able, this time, to start another conversation.

But maybe the real conversation between writers was the longstanding one we'd always had, the one in which I read each of his words, alone, encountering them deep in privacy and silence, which is the best way to meet another writer. It was a conversation for which I was profoundly grateful.

In a century famous for irony, for disaffection, for cynicism, for bitterness, for existentialism, for surrealism, for post-modernism, and metafiction, for literary currents that favored experimental approaches to form over emotional connections between people, Updike remained steadfast to the literary institution of humanism. He wrote in the tradition of Homer, Shakespeare, Tolstoy,[28] Woolf[29]; he was the greatest American writer of the twentieth century.

Great fiction is about the power and complexity of human engagement. Updike understood the glowing bond that links people so irrevocably, he understood the costs and the rewards of this deep linking, and he revealed all this in nuanced, powerful, and exquisite prose. It's rare for a writer to combine, in such sumptuous abundance, the gifts of wisdom, grace, and *caritas*.

We were lucky to have him. We were lucky to have all those stories, those novels, dropped so quietly into our collective unconscious. We were lucky to be part of a conversation, however one-sided, which, for six decades, offered us new ways to understand the lives we were living.

Roxana Robinson is the author of nine books. Her latest novel, Sparta, *won the Maine Fiction Award, the James Webb Fiction Award from the USMC, and was a finalist for the Dublin Impac Award. Four of her books were* New York Times Notables. *She has written for* The New Yorker, The Atlantic, Harper's *and* The New York Times, *and is an NEA and Guggenheim Fellow. She teaches in the MFA Program at Hunter College, and is President of the Authors Guild.*

---

38. James Schiff
"Updike as Correspondent, Literary Performer, and Composer of Sentences"

My primary contact with John Updike, as for many, was through letters and postcards. Much has been said of John's generosity and responsiveness as a correspondent. His immediate and extended reply to a list of questions I posed in January 1989 about his retelling of Hawthorne's *The Scarlet Letter* was very important to me. I'll never forget the surprise, as a graduate student living in Greenwich Village, of finding his letter in my mailbox, his name and return address stamped in blue on the envelope's northwest corner. John's response provided me with a new way of viewing Hawthorne's novel; as he explained. "*The Scarlet Letter* is not merely a piece of fiction, it is a myth by now, and it was an updating of the myth, the triangle as redefined by D. H. Lawrence, that interested me" (*Updike's Version* 132). In his answers and throughout the letter there was considerable playfulness, perhaps tinged with a touch of annoyance. To my question about first-person unreliability in his

Scarlet Letter novels, he wrote: "What's unreliable about them? They're as reliable as I can make them. Even Roger's visions of his wife and her lover, which might be taken as a pornographic fantasy, are borne out in the end, essentially, by her pregnancy. I know the phrase 'unreliable narrator' is popular critically these days, but I have nothing to do with it. A narrator who's unreliable, why listen to him/her?" (*Updike's Version* 131). Both comic and illuminating, John's response was energizing; whether or not he knew it, he had given a fledgling graduate student a leg up.

Most writers, I later learned, are not as likely to write back, at least not that quickly. John's generosity—to me and to hundreds of writers, critics, and readers—was unusual, and though not something he had to do, it was clearly something he wanted, or needed, to do. Perhaps the gesture was inspired by the writers and cartoonists who had generously responded to his requests when he was an ambitious, artistically-driven teenager—Saul Steinberg, for instance, sent him an inscribed drawing. Or maybe it was due simply to good manners and disciplined work habits. Whatever the case, twelve years later, when we knew one another better, I was again grateful when John responded to what felt like a sizable request. John had just spent several days in Cincinnati, where I live, giving readings and interviews, participating in a panel discussion, dining with professors, graduate students, and donors, and being a generally good sport. Enormously grateful, I nevertheless wanted more of him and sent him—I cower in confessing—nearly a hundred pages of written transcripts of these events which, prior to publication, required editing. Within a couple of weeks John graciously returned the package, what he called "this mountain of manuscript," with careful emendations in red ink. In an accompanying letter that couldn't fully conceal an edge of aggravation, he opened comically with a question: "Don't you think it's cruelty to dumb authors to get one to a conference, have him spout thousands of impromptu and haphazard words, and then submit for his pained scrutiny these words in their disgraceful incoherence, repetitiveness, and virtual idiocy?" (*Updike in Cincinnati*, xxviii). I did. Yet I also believed that publishing the material was important because it provided a clear picture of him as a public literary performer. It's hard to imagine the degree of good will and professionalism that led him, in spite of other work and commitments, to complete such a task.

In our correspondence, John was almost always funny and light in tone. In December[,] 1992 he sent me a rare black-cloth edition of his recently published novel *Memories of the Ford Administration* (incidentally, his inscription on the front endpapers also noted corrected typos on seven separate pages, so that I could turn to, say, page 24, and see that "front-wheel drive" had been crossed out in pencil, replaced with "a rear-end engine"). In his enclosed letter he indicated that the new novel, like the trilogy of novels about which I had written, was not only interested in Hawthorne but actually included the author as a character, to which he added, "Well, enough Hawthorne, and enough adultery. I'm going to devote the rest of my life to writing boys' adventure books." On another occasion I sent him, as requested, a packet of photographs taken of him by two Cincinnati photographers, to which he responded, "I seem to have an expression I maintain through most of these authorial appearances—mouth half open, as if mulling a salient point or recovering from a sharp blow to the back of the head" (*Updike in Cincinnati* xxvii–iii).

If I was having a problem with a writing project, John often expressed concern or advice. On some occasions a slight edge of annoyance would slip through, usually directed at the weather or a publisher, though perhaps it was aimed at me for interrupting his day. I'm not sure whether John's letters to me reveal all that much beyond his professionalism, conscientiousness, and playful sense of humor. In many ways, I believe his correspondence with those of us who were readers, writers, and critics may have been simply a warm-up exercise for the real writing of the day, just as a golfer spends a few minutes on the driving range hitting practice balls before heading to the course where the shots actually count. The longer and more personal letters John composed to family and friends, however, are different and reveal a more fully engaged and unrestrained writer. When his personal correspondence is ultimately published, the public will discover another side of him and his writing, as if gaining Updike in yet another genre.

As for our personal, face-to-face interactions, I spoke with John on a few occasions, and we spent a fair amount of time together during his two visits to Cincinnati in 1991 and 2001. What struck me most was how good-tempered and willing John always seemed. Over the years, I've had the opportunity to spend a day with many visiting writers, and I cannot think of one who was as relaxed, accommodating, and good-natured as John. During pre-visit planning, many writers balk at certain requests—lunch with graduate students, participation on a panel—and most express concern about preserving a few hours of personal time, whether to write, go for a run, or check email. In contrast, John, during one of his days in Cincinnati, spent more than twelve hours with us, participating in a morning museum visit and panel discussion, lunch with students and professors, a public interview, an evening reception and reading, and finally, dinner with academics. Most writers would have recoiled at the prospect of doing half as much, yet throughout the day John was agreeable and voiced few if any complaints. He mostly seemed to enjoy himself and was willing; perhaps because he had been well-compensated, to do whatever was required.

What also struck me was what a natural and versatile social performer he was, adept in front of a crowd of hundreds, or at a small dinner with critics and patrons. As to the former, when an audience member in a packed auditorium asked about his answer to a question on *The Charlie Rose Show*, he explained that on that show "one is apt to say almost any crazy thing that pops into one's head. Charlie Rose has a way of looking more orange in reality than he does on television, and when he leans toward you his face, already long, gets even longer, so that you undergo a kind of panic" (*Updike in Cincinnati* xxii). As to the latter, while dining at the Maisonette, a fashionable and expensive French restaurant, he smiled as the waiter lifted a silver serving dome to present him with a lovely piece of fish; he then picked up its accompanying half-lemon, elegantly wrapped in a gauze dressing held in place by thin white strings, and remarked, "it looks like a see-through nightie," then added, "Or perhaps an Amish woman's cap" (*Updike in Cincinnati* xxvii). So good was he in social situations—funny, clever, eloquent, and intelligent—that upon his return to Massachusetts, I somehow imagined him, on a daily basis, attending parties, dining out with friends, and chatting with neighbors. Perhaps for a brief period of time during his Ipswich years John partially resembled such a social creature, but the reality, particularly over the final three decades of his life, is that he was mostly at home working. John spent the bulk of his lifetime at a writing desk or in front of a book, so perhaps these visits, which included interacting with audiences, provided him with more than simply a generous pay check.

Though I first met John after a brief talk he delivered at the Plaza Hotel in New York City in 1987, it wasn't until four years later, during his first luncheon in Cincinnati, that we had an extended conversation. What struck me almost immediately were two things. First, his manner of speaking. Anyone familiar with John's writing is aware of his eloquence, ranging intelligence, and deft use of metaphor, yet one is slightly taken aback to see those same gifts on display in casual conversation. What was also unusual is that John spoke at a pitch that remained fairly constant in both rhythm and emotion. Most people I know display greater variation in their speech patterns, whether in raising or lowering their voice, expressing a range of emotions (sometimes through exaggeration), or perhaps pausing before landing on a certain word. In contrast, John's manner of speech was remarkably even keeled and understated. His language and perceptions were dazzling, but the consistency of pitch and tone made it all seem less astonishing, while keeping his listener at a slight distance. I should add that while his speaking resembled his writing, it was more the writing of, say, "Packed Dirt, Churchgoing, a Dying Cat, a Traded Car" than of *Rabbit Is Rich*, by which I mean his speech was elegant and refined but without any trace of the graphic, more vulgar interiority of the Rabbit novels. Though John could be candid, there was always a professionalism and genial distance in his delivery.

My second observation, which I've already addressed obliquely, was really more an enigma. The relaxed, smiling author sitting beside me, I learned, had just returned from a golf trip to Scotland and Ireland. He would be spending the rest of the day touring Cincinnati with literary patrons, followed by a reading, reception, and dinner. In a few days he would be doing something similar in another city. It didn't make sense. Here was one of America's most prolific authors and what was he doing: spending his days golfing and giving literary performances. When did he write? As I have acknowledged, there was something illusory about John as a public performer, in that he was so adept and charming that it was easy to forget he devoted most of his waking hours to reading and writing. What was odd, though, in light of all the recent obligations that had pulled him away from his writing desk, is that John, while admitting he may have overscheduled travel, gave no indication at our luncheon of anxiety or irritability. In fact, when I mentioned that a local radio sportscaster, Dennis "Wildman" Walker of WEBN, had been camped out for weeks on the scaffolding of a downtown rooftop billboard (he was refusing to come down until the Cincinnati Bengals, who would ultimately begin the season 0–8, won a football game), John expressed a keen desire to visit "this Wildman Walker" (unfortunately, our literary patron had made other plans). Most writers I know, particularly when away from the writing desk for a considerable period of time, are prone to irritability. Yet John seemed so relaxed and unperturbed. One could almost imagine him returning to his hotel room and, upon finding he had a spare hour before the next performance, dashing off a new short story. It all seemed so effortless.

What also became apparent to me during his second visit to Cincinnati was his generosity, though I don't necessarily mean financial. There are ample stories about John's frugality, which also manifested itself on several occasions. For instance, during negotiations for his visit, he didn't hesitate to ask for an extra $1,000, and during that same post-reading dinner at the Maisonette, he balked at ordering the exorbitantly priced sole meunière, though he encouraged my wife to do so and later asked if he could try a bite of hers. He also expressed concern in Brooks Brothers at having to pay fifty[-]some dollars for a necktie, an item he had forgotten to pack. However, by his generosity, I mean, perhaps, his magnanimity. To elaborate, on our drive to the airport at the conclusion of his 2001 visit, he presented me with an inscribed copy of his new volume of poetry, *Americana*, then handed me a British edition of Nicholson Baker's *U & I*, which had been given to him the day before by a fan—he asked if I would send it to Don Greiner, who for years had been amassing one of the largest collections of Updike's published writings. The generosity continued as he offered to tell me about his dream from the night before which, sadly, I've forgotten. Further, two nights earlier, when I was driving John and a few guests back to their hotel, John indicated he was coming down with a cold and asked to stop at a drugstore for medicine. A few minutes later he emerged from the all-night Walgreen's, smiling and holding a plastic bag. Inside was a bottle of Nyquil for him—"I think I'm becoming addicted," he confessed in mock fashion—as well as a roll of lifesavers for everyone in the car, and for me, his host: a green plaster turtle (*Updike in Cincinnati* xii).

While the world has been without John for several years now, I think it's fair to say that I do not miss him in the way, I imagine, his family and closest friends miss him. I don't because I never really knew him all that well as a person. John has often been in my daily thoughts, particularly when I was writing books about his work, but the John Updike I think about and knew was primarily a composer of sentences, literally black marks on a white page. So it is the writer, more than the person, I miss. I miss seeing John's stories and reviews in *The New Yorker*, and I miss the occasional surprise of discovering an essay or poem in an unlikely place, such as *National Geographic*, *Architectural Digest*, or *Van Gogh's Ear*. Although his literary estate has done an admirable job with posthumous publications and reissues, there is still a hollow feeling upon acknowledging that we will never crack open the spine of a new Updike novel. That said, the reality is that John left us with so much. In my study, a half[-] dozen shelves are filled with his books: a lifetime of reading and rereading. John poured much of his life into those books, and though the writing must at times have seemed a selfish act to those closest to him, to a distant reader like myself John's fiction was life-changing. Middle and middling America, the world in which I was raised, had always seemed so familiar and mundane—hardly the stuff of great fiction. Yet in John's writing, the quotidian was lifted and lovingly described so as to become beautiful and mysterious. I had never before seen my own world limned in such a way—John's transformation of the ordinary seemed an act of genius. While the person who answered my letter twenty-five years ago and gave me a leg up as a young scholar is gone, my real relationship has been and continues to be with the composer of sentences. I remain grateful to him for the many pleasures and moments of recognition, and for the continuous lessons in seeing, knowing, and celebrating the world. His writing has made a deep and lasting impression. To not remember John Updike, and I speak here for myself and also, I hope, for posterity, seems literally impossible.

James Schiff (born 1958) is the author or editor of five books on contemporary American fiction, including John Updike Revisited, Understanding Reynolds Price, *and* Updike in Cincinnati. *He holds degrees from Duke University and New York University, teaches at the University of Cincinnati, and serves as editor of* The John Updike Review. *His correspondence with John Updike began in 1989, and they spent time together during Updike's two visits to Cincinnati, in 1991 and 2001.*

39. Stephanie Vanderslice
"My John Updike"

Updike was one of my heroes when I was a young writer. I read haphazardly, as I did then (and perhaps, still do), through his oeuvre: *Marry Me*, *Trust Me*, the *"Rabbit"* books, awed by his capacious, lyrical portrayal of the middle class, his middle class, my middle class. But like any hero, he remained rather abstract, the snowy-haired icon (as a Generation X'er, my John Updike was never anything but gray) smiling genially from the back of a book jacket. Until 1992, when he came to read at *George Mason University*, Fairfax, Virginia, where I was studying fiction writing, and [he] became real.

The *George Mason MFA* program routinely brought in visiting writers to read from their work; the midlist writers usually workshopped our stories as well. It was in this way that I was fortunate to receive the fleeting advice of writers like Lee Smith, Madison Smartt Bell and Faye Moskowitz, and it was in this way that my lifelong literary crush on Charles Baxter began. But among all of these writers, John Updike stood out.

He was our headliner that year, the big gun brought in with extra funds from the campus bookstore. As such, he commanded a considerable fee simply to read in the auditorium, smile that genial smile, shake a few hands, and then catch the train back to Massachusetts.

But John Updike wanted to do more. He had asked if he could meet with "some students, some budding writers, perhaps." He liked, our director told us, to meet with young people.

So about a dozen or so of us gathered in a nondescript classroom to sit in uncomfortable molded chair-desks and bask in the glow of this famous American man of letters. To ask him tentative questions and listen to his kind, patrician wisdom, because he had *requested it*.

Updike himself never sat but rather leaned at the edge of an enormous metal and wood veneer desk at the front of the room. I remember when he spoke wistfully about how difficult it is for writers to make a living solely from their writing anymore, which struck me as unusually empathetic because for the most part, he still did. He went on to reminisce about his early days as a writer when he could "support a wife and family by publishing a handful of stories in *The New Yorker* every year."

Even then, we knew his request was special. Now, two decades and countless writers' visits later, I have never known it to happen again. For a writer, of Updike's stature especially, to ask, "Could I meet with some students as well?" when such a meeting was most definitely "not in the contract."

After this gathering, a few of my friends took Updike to the metro station so he could catch the train home. At his request, they stopped at a Dunkin' Donuts for coffee along the way. The next day they returned to the graduate student bullpen brandishing John Updike's coffee cup, a modest paper cup which they promptly labeled with a black Sharpie and tacked to the wall.

I like to think that it's still there.

Stephanie Vanderslice writes creative nonfiction and fiction and contributes The Geek's Guide to the Writing Life *column to the Huffington Post. Her most recent book is* Rethinking Creative Writing. *She is currently working on* Beautiful, Fragile Things, *a novel about, among other topics, survivors of the sinking of the steamship General Slocum in New York Harbor in 1904, as well as a memoir,* Dear Madeleine: Letters to the Daughter I Never Had. *She is also Professor of Writing and Director of the Arkansas Writer's MFA Workshop.*

40. Terry Gross
"The Problem I Had in Common with John Updike"

At some point in the 1990's, a writer doing a magazine article on me contacted several notables who'd been guests on *Fresh Air*—including John Updike—for their comments on my interviewing style. I don't remember now all of what Updike had to say about me or the show, except that it was very gracious and that he pointed out we had something in common—we both occasionally stuttered. I think of mine more as a stammer; still, my first reaction was ... *what?* Why call public attention to something I've worked hard to conceal? Then I realized this was part of what I loved about his writing: the unsparing precision with which he confronted exactly those traits that usually go unremarked because they might be awkward or embarrassing, but that play a large role in making us who we are to ourselves. Nor did Updike spare Updike. In his 1989 memoir *Self-Consciousness*, he examined his stutter, his "deplorable skin," and other "physical handicaps, neurotic symptoms, aberrant thought patterns, and characterological limitation" with the same "scientific dispassion and curiosity" he brought to his descriptions of the physical world. It's perhaps my favorite of his books—one I read with wincing pleasure, just glad he never wrote about me at greater length.

Terry Gross is the host and an executive producer of Fresh Air, *a daily radio program of interviews and reviews, which is produced at WHYY in Philadelphia, distributed by NPR and broadcast on nearly 600 stations. The program received a Peabody Award. Gross has received the National Book Foundation's Literarian Award, Columbia University Graduate School of Journalism's Columbia Journalism Award, the MLA's Phyllis Franklin Award for Public Advocacy of the Humanities, and the Author's Guild award for Distinguished Service to the Literary Community.*

41. James Plath
"Fringe Benefit"

In 1985 I wrote to ask John Updike if he would grant an interview for *Clockwatch Review*, a non-profit journal of the arts I edited and published using my own money. His response was gracious—many writers, after all, ignore such requests—but Updike nonetheless made it clear on a postcard he sent that he couldn't oblige because interviews were an intrusion on his writing time. Plus, he added, they make you feel as if you have dirt under your fingernails.

I was undeterred. Besides being a literary magazine editor, I was also a graduate student at the University of Wisconsin–Milwaukee with a dissertation to complete. Updike, I had decided, mattered enough for me not just to try to feature him in the magazine, but to devote five years of my life to writing *The Painterly Aspects of John Updike's Fiction*. Here was a man of my father's generation, yet he was writing about things that I thought, things that I feared, things that I obsessed over, and things that I believed. This guy Updike knew me inside and out, without ever having met me. His characters were restless and often a mass of walking contradictions, as was I. When he wrote about religion, sex, and art as being "the Three Great Secret Things," I knew instantly that if I were to compress all of the thoughts and feelings that were swirling around inside me into a tidy top-three list, it would be those same three things—with death (as it seemed in Updike's world) coming uncomfortably close to being a fourth.

With some hesitation I decided to contact Updike again in May 1986—and I use the word "hesitation" because Updike's Jewish alter-ego, Henry Bech, responded to such inquiries with a rubber stamp that read, "It's your Ph.D. thesis; Please write it yourself."[30] Still, I mustered the courage to tell Updike about my topic and ask how much of a connection he felt between painting and his writing. What came back was the first of many "no ... but" responses. In a letter he explained that he hadn't had any particular visual artist or painting in mind for any of his fiction, but conceded that a person might be subconsciously inspired by artwork to which he has been exposed. Though he was skeptical of the approach I was taking, in the very same letter he steered me toward art movements that affected him and also pointed me in the direction of fictional passages that I should consider.

As I got more deeply into it, I wondered if he'd be even more forthcoming, and in summer 1990 I asked if he'd consent to an interview that I might refer to in my dissertation. But John Updike, as I came to learn, was a very private person. He wrote back with another "no," yet he still offered to meet me in Boston—not at his house—to talk about my project. Knowing how he felt, how could I take him up on that generous offer, especially when he questioned in the same letter whether it was advisable for writers to talk about their works, which he felt should really do all the talking? Still, I had piqued his interest and he asked me what questions I might pose. We ended up talking by phone quite a few times—always in the afternoon, because his mornings were reserved for writing—and what struck me about Mr. Updike, as I called him then, was that despite his concerns about his own time, I never felt that our conversations were rushed. I won't pretend that it was more than it was, because Updike believed in the value of literary criticism and was just as gracious and intimate with others who contacted him about the dissertations and books they were writing. Yet, it always impressed me that he took the time not only to respond to my questions, but to ask about my two sons and two daughters, then ages 13, 14, 15 and 17. We may have been a generation apart, but we had this much in common: four children, two of each gender, with a woman who was now an ex-wife. I was a custodial single parent, and I think this fascinated him enough to where he actually seemed eager to hear details of my life apart from the academic. If I expressed regret that I didn't have the money to give the kids things other parents managed, he told me, "The time you spend with them is most important. I envy that." Often he would ask me about them and what it was like to raise them by myself, or he would share stories about his own four children. That a friendship of sorts grew out of our professional relationship was really a pleasant surprise—a fringe benefit of the most wonderful kind.

Our contacts became even more frequent after I proposed *Conversations with John Updike* to the University Press of Mississippi. The press editor phoned me and said they had wanted to do an Updike volume for years, but had a policy of not moving forward with a book unless they received the author's blessing and cooperation. Updike had apparently turned them down several times, but I was told if I could get him to agree to it, I could edit the volume. I sent Updike copies of *Conversations with John Cheever* and another volume in the series, then proposed a timetable for the project that would put the book four or five years into the future. He wrote back that yes, it's a worthy project and said he'd share a file of his interviews he'd collected, but wondered who besides academics would care to read it. He also expressed relief that the project was not projected to begin for a handful of years.

Over the course of those years we talked by phone and exchanged letters. No longer the passive author whose only task was to grant permission, Updike continued to send me interviews he wanted me to consider. He reread some of the translations of his foreign interviews that I'd passed along and made substantial changes to them, adding that perhaps he should proofread the whole manuscript. It was my baby, he conceded, but it still "aroused a paternal interest in him." Updike eventually collaborated on biographical and bibliographical details that he wanted included, and playfully chastised me for confusing two of his children's books and leaving out *Cunts*, which he said was prized by collectors. So *that's* what he meant when he said he wasn't sure he was emotionally up to it when I first proposed the project, I thought. He knew all along that it was his nature to become totally involved if the project bore his name.

I finally met John Updike face-to-face in July of 1993. At the time I was director of the Hemingway Days Writers' Workshop & Conference in Key West and, as a member of the Conch Republic Prize selection committee, I floated Updike's name as a possible honoree. The committee voted to invite him. His response? He loved the idea, though he sensed (correctly so) that it was a way to get him to appear for much less than his normal speaker's fee. He agreed to accept the prize on Sunday and give informal remarks the following afternoon. Later, when the Hemingway Days Festival director asked me to get a few comments from him to put in the festival booklet, as we'd done with previous winner James Dickey, Updike balked when I phoned to ask him. "Now I'm having to do an interview? I thought I only had to go down there and say a few words and sign books," he said. "This is already expanding." We don't have to do the interview, I told him. It was just something the festival director preferred. We can forget about it. "No no," he said. You have me now, so let's just get on with it."

When he arrived in Key West, Updike remarked that it was his first time there. "It's all very tropical, isn't it?" At the reception he was extremely gracious, and everyone was struck by the elegance with which he carried himself—though he was the only person in Key West wearing a plaid sport jacket. Updike partly agreed to come to Key West because it gave him a chance to reunite with friends from Ipswich, and he in fact declined our offer of a hotel suite to stay with them. Nonetheless, I got to spend a lot of time with him during the days. Part of the Conch Republic Prize for Literature was a portrait painted by Edward Hemingway, Ernest's grandson, and I took Updike to what would have been his suite at the Ocean Key House, where Edward had his easel set up. "All this would have been mine?" he asked, looking around. I slid open the glass doors so we could step out onto the balcony, which overlooked the spot where the Atlantic meets the Gulf of Mexico. Then we leaned over the railing and looked down at the hotel swimming pool. "Oh my," Updike said. "You can see cleavage from here. Maybe I made the wrong decision. Maybe I should have stayed *here*," he joked.

As he posed for Edward we continued to converse. Some writers like to talk about themselves, but that wasn't the case with Updike. He liked to hear what others had to say. He wanted to hear, for example, how Edward's classes were going at the Rhode Island School of Design, and what media he preferred. Acrylics in Key West, Edward told him, because oils take far too long to dry with the humidity. "Of course," Updike said. "I hadn't thought of that." From me, he wanted to know how the festival operated and how I got involved, and I told him. He wanted to know if the residents were knowledgeable readers, and I told him the story of a Hemingway scholar who shared entries from the log of the Pilar that had just been made available to researchers and how rattled she became after she matter-of-factly told the audience she didn't know what a group of whales was called, and the entire room shouted, in perfect unison, "POD!" He laughed, and when Edward left to use the restroom Updike abandoned his pose on the couch and walked to the easel. "Let's see what the young genius has been up to," he said, then, "Well, that's actually quite good. I think it needs a little something though." He picked up one of Edward's paintbrushes. "Maybe a mustache?" His eyes twinkled and he started to laugh, then caught himself. "I think maybe I should just stand here and see what he says when he comes out and sees me."

When Edward finished the sitting I offered Updike a ride to his friends' condo, and we walked to the hotel garage, where I noticed my Chevy was gone. "One of the kids must have taken it," I said. "What do we do now?" Updike asked, with almost clinical calm. I wondered if he was okay walking the length of Duval Street with me to the Lucky Street Gallery, where there was a car I could borrow, and where Edward was having his first one-man show. Maybe we could take in the show, I suggested. "That sounds like it could be fun," he said, and along the way we talked more about my kids and his kids when they were teens as we walked in the Key West heat, with Updike eventually removing his jacket and carrying it over his shoulder. Along the way, I asked him about his Ipswich friends, whom I'd met, and wondered aloud if they were the inspiration for any of the characters in *Couples*. "Which character does Frank remind you of?" Updike grinned, taking obvious pleasure in tantalizing a literary critic. But when I guessed Freddy Thorne he said, "Oh, no, not even close," adding how his friends have been utterly faithful to each other and there was no resemblance. "Frank would be quite hurt to hear you say that."

At the gallery, we looked at Edward's paintings and Updike was kind enough to offer a gentle critique to the artist, pointing out the strengths of his work and what he called the best painting of the show (which I later purchased and donated to Illinois Wesleyan University). At the show we ran into my children, who had taken the Chevy, and Updike talked with them as well, joking about the missing car and our long walk while I was speaking to the gallery director to borrow her car so I could take him to his friends' condo on the Atlantic side. "Ready?" I asked. "No," he said. "I've been speaking with your children, and it's clear that you've been neglecting them. I want you to spend time with them instead of me. I can walk there," he insisted. "Besides, I could use an adventure."

The next morning at the opening conference session, a woman came up to me and said, "I just wanted you to know that I rescued John Updike yesterday." "*WHAT?*" I said. It turns out that she saw him staggering as he made his way along Atlantic Boulevard, and she pulled over to offer him a ride. Before she could even identify herself as a conference participant, he was already opening her car door, lifting a leg inside, and saying, "Oh, thank you, madam." I teased him about it the next day, and he laughed and said that he had no idea how far of a walk it was, or that Key West could be so oppressively hot.

After we returned to our homes I received a long letter from him in which he asked me to call him "John" from then on, because of our shared time in Key West, adding that he enjoyed himself. In a follow-up letter, he sent another batch of interviews and told me that if there were too many I should ask the university press to give me more pages.

Conversations with John Updike finally came out in 1994, but John and I kept in touch afterwards. When friends of mine from college started mysteriously dying before their fortieth birthdays and I was having one whale of a mid-life crisis as I approached that mile/millstone, John calmed me down by telling me, "I'm sure they've passed along all their unlived years to you." Another time, though I never asked for his opinion, when I sent him a signed chapbook of my poetry as a thank-you for all the books he signed for me, he followed up with a note telling me which of the poems were his favorites, and why. He didn't have to, but it always impressed me that he actually took the time to read them and comment. But the thing that really endeared him to me was that he helped me propose to my wife.

Since both Zarina and I were writers and readers, I wanted to do something special involving books, and handing her a copy of John's novel, *Marry Me*, seemed like a fine way to propose—especially, I thought, if I could get him to write an inscription for the occasion. I phoned John to tell him my plan and asked if he'd help. Before he would commit, curiously, like the chaplain who would marry us, he asked how our relationship was going. "You *do* know that the couple in *Marry Me* doesn't exactly live happily ever after, right?" That's okay, I assured him. It was the title I was after. "Okay," he said, adding, "This could be fun." So at the top of the Empire State Building I took out a small tape recorder and played "Arthur's Theme" and began slow dancing with my now-wife. When I told her I had something to ask her and reached behind my back, she was expecting a small ring box. Instead, it was a plastic bag in which there was a copy of *Marry Me*. "Read the inscription," I told her. Inside, John had written something to the effect that if she agreed to marry me I'd put a ring on her finger at the Rainbow Room, where we had dinner reservations. He post-dated the inscription to the day I was to propose: April 28, 1995.

Later, he sent us a wedding present, and when I saw him again in person and he finally got to meet Zarina, he told us how glad he was that our marriage has lasted longer than the characters in *Marry Me*. "I was afraid the book might jinx you," he said. John had come to Bloomington at my invitation to speak at the dedication of the Ames Library at Illinois Wesleyan University, and although we hosted a dinner for him at our house with some of our faculty colleagues and spouses, what stands out in my memory once more isn't the wonderful reading and remarks he delivered, that fun dinner, the way he charmed our university president and the people he met, or even how apologetic he was about the $15,000 fee, which he modestly said was "too much." It was a single moment at the president's house when he was leaving a reception in his honor, and the president's wife, a rather forward and outspoken woman, shall we say, started telling him in her East Coast motherly voice how cold it was outside and that he'd better wear his hat. Before John could respond, she dug into his coat pocket, took out his knit cap, and, as he looked helplessly to me, she pulled it onto his head, right down to those bushy eyebrows. "There," she said. "And you liked the Beer Nuts, didn't you? They're made right here in Bloomington. Here, take some with you for the plane ride," she said, and proceeded to dump the contents of the nut bowl from a hall table into his coat pocket. Now, Rabbit may have run, but John was as gracious as ever. Flashing me a disturbed-but-sly look, he grabbed her by both hands—probably to keep them from causing him more mischief, I thought—and thanked her for hosting such a wonderful evening.

When I proposed the idea of a John Updike Society sometime in 2000, John wrote back, "no, no, no," because he said the whole idea brought to mind a Max Beerbohm[31] cartoon of a literary gathering with admirers forming a worshipful circle around an author. He made it clear that such a thing would embarrass him, but added something very telling. "Not in my lifetime." It was yet another "no ... but," and clearly the part of him that looked toward the infinite future was secretly delighted that we would choose to honor him like that.

As it turns out, the honor was all mine.

James Plath is R. Forrest Colwell Chair and Professor of English at Illinois Wesleyan University, where he received the university's highest teacher-scholar-service award in 2004. He is the author or editor of Conversations with John Updike, Native Son: John Updike's Pennsylvania Interviews, *and numerous essays in critical anthologies. As president of The John Updike Society he is responsible for overseeing the restoration of The John Updike Childhood Home in Shillington, Pa., and its conversion to a literary center and museum.*

42. Adam Begley
"Updike's Dangerous Charm"

In the late fall of 1993, I trailed behind John Updike, playing Boswell for a day and a half. We were in Appleton, Wisconsin, at Lawrence University, where Updike's younger son had studied in the eighties. Updike had been invited to give the convocation address, dine at the home of the university president, and talk with students in a writing seminar. It was the sort of well-paid trip Updike made over and over again. He was on display as America's preeminent man of letters, showing off what he called his "public, marketable self"—a wonderfully controlled and pleasing performance that revealed, it seemed to me, a good deal about his private, hidden self.

We were at a buffet supper at the president's house, plates balanced on knees, guests in armchairs or perched on footstools, and Updike had barely sat down when a well-dressed woman sitting near him asked in a sweet Midwestern voice, "Mr. Updike—did you write the wonderful story about the man who swims from pool to pool?"

"I wish I had," he answered at once, his voice honeyed like his interlocutor's; "that was John Cheever, 'The Swimmer.'" He grinned, and contained in that wolfish grin—his small mouth a sharp V in his long, narrow face—was a mixture of pure amusement, malice, and forbearance. "Perhaps now that John [Cheever] is dead I could lay claim to some of his stories." The assembled company exhaled with a long, relieved laugh. They were relaxing, surrendering to his charm.

Encouraged, the same lady spoke up again, asking if Mr. Updike, so famously prolific, was slowing down, thinking of retirement. Again, the response was instant: "Do you think I should? At sixty-one?" His tousled hair was nearly white, his eyebrows scruffy like an old man's. A network of fine wrinkles surrounded his eyes—but the eyes themselves were bright and lively ("he had a bona fide twinkle in his eye," said Jane Smiley,[32] "maybe the only person I've ever known to really have such a thing"). He was tall and lanky but not remotely feeble or doddery. On the contrary, he exuded a vigorous self-confidence, an almost palpable centeredness. His voice, still sweet, had taken on a flirty, comically submissive edge, as if the advice of this Midwestern Cheever fan could hasten his retirement and shape the end of an illustrious literary career. "I *have* been tidying up," he offered, along with another friendly, wickedly acute grin.

That moment of teasing social agility sparked my suspicion that the playfully mischievous, dazzlingly clever John Updike was a potentially dangerous individual, and that a gamut of conflicting emotions, not all of them kindly, were hidden behind the screen of his public persona. I think it was the hint of danger, subliminally communicated to the clutch of listeners in the president's blandly elegant living room that made his performance in the role of celebrated author so appealing. Yes, he was a professional writer being professionally engaging, but he was also signaling—how? with that clichéd twinkle?—that his good behavior, his forbearance, had its limits.

At the time, I'd read only a few dozen Updike stories and a couple of the novels; when I finally read his memoirs, I found this apposite passage about an earlier trip to a Midwestern university:

> I read and talked into the microphone and was gracious to the local rich, the English faculty and the college president, and the students with their clear skin and shining eyes and inviting innocence, like a blank surface one wishes to scribble obscenities on.

Suspicion confirmed. Of course there was an undercurrent of aggression in all that expertly deployed charm, a razor edge to his ostensibly gentle wit. In one of the dazzling self-interviews with his alter ego Henry Bech, he lamented his own eagerness to please and ridiculed the whole notion that a writer should be "nice": "[A]s Norman Mailer pointed out decades ago, and Philip Roth not long afterwards, niceness is the enemy. Every soft stroke from society is like the *pfft* of an aerosol can as it eats up a few more atoms of our brain's delicate ozone, and furthers our personal cretinization." A nice, happy author? No, thanks. I found I liked him all the more.

It's possible, I suppose, that I was programmed to like him. My father and he were classmates in college, both of them majoring in English, and for a while after graduation, when my parents were living in Cambridge, Massachusetts, and Updike and his first wife had moved to Ipswich, less than an hour away, the two couples were friendly. Fifty years later, when Updike died unexpectedly (very few people knew that he was ill, let alone dying), my father sent me an e-mail version of an anecdote I'd heard before:

> One day for some reason John came to see us alone, in the early afternoon. We were in our living room, which was flooded by the afternoon sun. You were in your Easy

Chair, a contraption in universal use then among advanced couples, which allowed the pre-toddler to recline rather as though he were in a barber's chair having his hair shampooed. One of John's less known talents was his skill as a juggler. He took three oranges from a bowl on the coffee table and began to juggle for you, and you began to laugh. Astonishing belly laughter.

According to this family legend, Updike was the first person to make me laugh. Part of me believed it, and believed it was a natural consequence of this early imprint that I found him congenial when I met him as an adult, the baby in the Easy Chair having grown up to be a literary journalist.

I interviewed him again, ten years after our Appleton encounter, in the bar of the Ritz Hotel in Boston, at a table pressed up against a vast picture window looking out over the Public Gardens. We talked for two and a half hours, a tour of the Updike cosmos that took in golf, girl-watching, body-piercing, George W. Bush, J.M. Coetzee, Manhattan in the 1950s, and a joke he picked up on a recent tour in Germany. (What comes between fear and sex? Fünf.)

I was amazed and delighted all over again by his gracious, professional manner, and by the sly undercutting of his public, marketable self. He wanted to let you know that he was perfectly aware of the falsity of the situation, and perfectly prepared to be amused by it, for the moment. He wanted to let you know that his real self was elsewhere. This wasn't just a targeted trick, like juggling for a baby, deployed for the benefit of an admiring journalist. Even with old friends and colleagues, he was there but not here—just as he was kind but subversive, and charming but dangerous.

Adam Begley is the author of Updike, *published by Harper in 2014. He was books editor of* The New York Observer *from 1996 to 2009; a Guggenheim Fellow in 2010; and a Fellow at the Leon Levy Center for Biography in 2011. He lives with his wife in a village in Cambridgeshire, England.*

43. Lynne Davis
"My Night with John Updike"

It's not what you're thinking. It's not at all what you're thinking.

It started with a flyer in the mail room. On cream-colored paper, a man with a teacup. John Updike. He was coming to our rural Midwestern University.

You could hear the whispers in the hall. "John Updike? *The* John Updike?" "Why is he coming *here*?"

I fell in love with him in college, when I read one of his stories in *The New Yorker*, "The Music School." His phrasing was precise, so delicately balanced—like a Mozart piano concerto.

Later I worked as a copy editor at Houghton Mifflin Publishing Company in Boston. I was the proofreader on *Enchantment* by Linda Grace Hoyer. When they told me she was John Updike's mother, I was star-struck and probably spent too long checking to make sure I'd caught all the typos.

In a creative writing class I took (a few months after the birth of my child, Nora) our assignment was to imitate the style of an author we loved. I chose Updike's "Wife Wooing."[33] Sensuous and lyrical, it spoke poetically about the juxtaposition of male and female bodies in a marriage bed, and ended with the sentence, "*Oh.*" In my story, I changed the theme from married love to mother love. Updike's prose gave me a way to express my feelings about the intense physical connection of my body and my baby's, and our emotional bonding.

When I saw the Updike poster in the mailroom, I knew I would be there.

He spoke to a large crowd in the Student Center. Handsome and refined, he read poems, a story, and an excerpt from his most recent novel.

Then he took questions. I had never raised my hand in a room full of academics. This time, though, I had to.

"Would you mind talking about your writing routine?" I asked. Shivers went through me when he heard my words, and he replied precisely to them.

"Would I mind? No. It's a little boring, though." He proceeded to recite, as I'm sure he had done thousands of times, how he wrote from 9 am to 1 pm, in the maid's quarters of his big old house. He wrote by hand, he said, and then revised on the computer.

After his lecture, there was a book-signing. When I reached the table, I told him that I had been the proofreader for his mother's book.

"*Enchantment*," he said, looking up. To find a Boston publishing person in the middle of *Moo* country must have been perplexing to him, and perhaps—dared I hope?—even a little enchanting.

I didn't sleep at all that night.

I met John Updike. *Oh.*

Lynne Davis (born, 1944 in Evanston, Illinois) received her Master's Degree in Teaching English as a Second Language at Southern Illinois University-Carbondale in 1975. She took writing classes with Richard Russo at SIU in the nineteen-eighties. Her writing has appeared in Modern Haiku, Turnstile, The Sun Magazine, *and* Global Study, *as well as the anthology* Women on Poetry. *Davis encountered John Updike in 1997 when she met him at Southern Illinois University.*

44. Avis Grey Hewitt
"Knowing John Updike"

John Updike was the plenary figure at the 1998 Festival of Faith and Writing at Calvin College in Grand Rapids, Michigan. Having a temporary teaching connection with that school that year, I was part of the local crowd invited to attend a reception for him the night he gave his reading. I watched him from across the room, admiring the grace with which he made good-natured talk with equanimity, regardless of the comer's stance—adulation, self-importance, or studied "serious engagement." His dramatic comeliness with that shock of thick hair now white, the hawk-like nose, and the lithe physique remind an onlooker of how he must have, since coming of age and coming into his own with vast literary success and steady fame, found himself relentlessly attractive to others. Remembering descriptors of himself that he provides in *Self-Consciousness*, I considered the extent to which he had surely always been and always felt himself to be loved. He speaks of his "docile, good-child nature" (32), of his sense of his own "nagging specialness" (37), but also claims having done a creditable job with his "impersonation of a normal person" (54), and finally frets over his anticipated revelation that "in my dying I will become hideous. I will become what I am" (78).

The next morning he did a book signing at our local Grand Rapids hub. He was again rugged *GQ* dapper and handsome, smiling and genial. A long line formed, armed with books already treasured or books just purchased. He sat at a small table in his elegant suit, flashing each patron his enthusiastic greeting. Like Gatsby's,[34] his was "one of those rare smiles with a quality of eternal reassurance in it," one that "concentrated on you with an irresistible prejudice in your favor" (52). Thrilled when my turn to stand in front of him finally came, I handed this much-larger-than-life figure from our American literary pantheon my much underlined, annotated, and Post-It noted—that is to say, my beloved copy of *Self-Consciousness*. Seeing its hardback edges deckled with paper markers, he deftly rifled its pages and surmised how frequently and hungrily they had been read and pondered. Then raising his face to meet my gaze, he offered what has struck me at each remembrance as the most gracious and generous of hyperbolic responses: "Why, it looks as if you know me better than I know myself."

Of course, I hardly know him at all. But I have longed to know him and been enriched by knowing him the little that I do. He once commemorated

Ben Franklin's legacy with an essay titled "Many Bens."[35] That first-rank private citizen of the eighteenth-century had, of course, a Boston Ben and a Philadelphia Ben and an English Ben and a French Ben, in addition to Ben the scientist, the statesman, the rhetorician, the *bon vivant*. It strikes me that even without the kite and the key, an essay on "Many Updikes" is in order. One of the most literary and learned men of our time, the breadth of his intellect and the depths of his soul will provide critics material to explicate for as long as Western Civilization, for which he was a mighty repository and representative, abounds. In the shorter run, we can be grateful for any brief encounters. Though the gracious site of his personhood, his bodily self, is gone from our midst, he lives wildly and madly among us, just as he had planned in his obsession with immortality, in his books. Masterful at his specialty, "On Being a Self Forever," we have only to turn on our e-books or open the materially real pages of one of that dauntingly long row of novels, short story collections, essay collections, poetry collections, art books, and children's books that he created to be yet again in his lyrical presence, as he paints creation with words that make us resoundingly alive to our own lives. "Being human," he wrote, "cannot be borne alone" (*SC*, 233). We bear it better with the prop and pillar of his work.

Updike's contributions to American letters have made being human an experience more replete with intensity and discernment than it otherwise would have been. Like Henry James, Updike's is the art of all that is happening when we think nothing much is happening. Dickinson wrote, "To live is so startling it leaves little time for anything else." Updike wrote, "Existence itself does not feel horrible; it feels like an ecstasy, rather, which we only have to be still to experience. Habit and accustomedness have painted over pure gold, with a dull paint that can, however, be scratched away, to reveal the shining underbase. The world is good, our intuition is, confirming its Creator's appraisal as reported in the first chapter of Genesis" (250). Thank you, Updike, for empowering us to re-envision the deep goodness of God's creation in your splendid half-century powerful prose.

Avis Hewitt is a professor at Grand Valley State University in Allendale, Michigan, where she serves as president of the Flannery O'Connor Society. She has co-edited Flannery O'Connor in the Age of Terrorism *and published a comparison of Updike and O'Connor as well as articles about "Pigeon Feathers" and* Self-Consciousness. *Her essay on* The Maples Stories *appeared in the* John Updike Review. *Avis Hewitt includes an Updike story collection in her "Studies in Fiction," course and* Self-Consciousness *in her "Studies in Nonfiction."*

45. Donald J. Greiner
"Creating John Updike"

"Nobody belongs to us, except in memory"
—John Updike, "Grandparenting"

The above epigraph is the closing sentence of the final story in *The Afterlife*,[36] John Updike's collection of tales that parse the complex relationship between loss and memory. The sentence speaks to an enduring truth: memory is creative. Given the impossibility of fully knowing another person, we create that individual via imagination and remembrance. We become, in effect, the artists of our own lives. Such is the case when I recall my journey through the world of John Updike.

The journey began during an evening of bad beer and worse pizza. At the time I was a student at the University of Virginia, where I studied textual bibliography and Shakespeare with the fearsome but helpful Fredson Bowers, Poe and Whitman with the esteemed and patient Floyd Stovall, and Faulkner with the thorough and generous Joseph Blotner. In those days most living writers were not considered appropriate for serious research, particularly by a student. These were the years *after* the deaths of such masters as Hemingway and Steinbeck, Frost and Eliot, and most of all the incomparable Faulkner. Following library work late at night, my peers and I would gather at a nearby tavern to engage in spirited discussions about how to read the great American Modernists. A question certain to spark voice-raising argument was, who would take the place of Hemingway and Faulkner as the supreme American fiction writers during the next decades? We thought the answer could be Saul Bellow, surely not Norman Mailer, and most likely J. D. Salinger, author of *The Catcher in the Rye*, which taught us that we were indeed a group of Holden Caulfield's phonies, and of the Glass Family stories, which challenged us. We did not know, of course, that Salinger had already retreated into a long-kept silence. Only later did I learn that Updike had similarly experienced the magic of Salinger's fiction, conjured when a professor read "Just before the War with the Eskimos"[37] to an English class during Updike's student days at Harvard.

My tavern-haunting classmates and I were wrong about Salinger. Bursting with indignation while spilling his mug of beer, a friend first insisted that Updike "would be the guy" before he thrust his copy of *Pigeon Feathers* across the messy table. I read it the next weekend, and my understanding of the genre of short fiction changed. It is not that I became an Updikean overnight but that I was in the presence of something new. Professor Bowers still hammered me with the textual conundrums of Renaissance plays, Professor Stovall still demanded that I master Poe and Whitman, and Professor Blotner still guided me through the massive Faulkner archive at Virginia; but I found myself remembering "Wife-wooing" and "The Lifeguard" and particularly "Packed Dirt, Churchgoing, a Dying Cat, a Traded Car." These stories were as radical as "Just before the War with the Eskimos," as much signposts to the possibilities of fiction as Hemingway's tales in the 1920s and Faulkner's novels in the 1930s.

But who *was* John Updike? Knowing nothing about him except what we could occasionally glean from a short biographical profile printed on a dust jacket, we "created" him during our discussions. We had not heard of *The Poorhouse Fair* or *The Same Door*, much less *The Carpentered Hen*, and I had not read *Rabbit, Run*; but *Pigeon Feathers* persuaded me to stop placing my bets on Salinger. The professors, however, did not encourage research on living writers. My fellow students and I burned to create Updike as the emerging giant of American fiction, but our instructors pointed to the lack of primary and secondary sources. How, they asked, could we research a contemporary author when there was little on the library shelves and nothing in the archives? So I followed the paths of my mentors and later, following graduation, published first a book that was a textual study of Stephen Crane and then a book on Robert Frost, thereby assuring my new faculty colleagues that I was sane and practical. All along I kept buying trade editions of Updike's books as they were published, but in a desultory fashion. I missed, for example, *Buchanan Dying*, but I eventually realized that I owned a modest shelf of Updike books, that I knew little about him beyond what I had imagined, and that a way to counter my ignorance was to begin work on what I called "the other John Updike."

My professors were correct. Little did I foresee the extent of the challenge I faced, the sheer and all but unending frustration of committing to research on current writers. When one of my doctoral students gave me an inscribed copy of Robert Wilson's *Modern Book Collecting*, and I read the following comment, "Among living novelists ... John Updike is far and away the most collected fiction writer," I knew I was in for a struggle that would probably send me back to the relative safety of Stephen Crane and Robert Frost. The lion in the path was the following question: what had Updike written? I thought that familiarity with his trade editions, the kinds of books available at Barnes & Noble, would answer the question. It took me months to understand that the Updike canon contained an astonishing number of rare broadsides, limited signed editions, bound proof copies, uncollected essays, children's books, introductions to the work of other writers, and a library full of uncollected appearances in magazines. The first question led to a second: where could I get help to answer the initial query? Jack De Bellis and Michael Broomfield had not yet compiled their comprehensive bibliography. Jim Plath had not yet collected the Updike interviews and conversations. In effect, I was back in the tavern with my buddies and beer, creating Updike from the ephemeral words of our late-night debates.

The scholar researching a living writer is likely to be stymied the way I was because there is no reliable biography; no collection of letters; no journal(s); no notebook(s); no typescript material, much less access to manuscripts of the kind I had ready access to when working on Crane and Frost; no bibliography of primary material; and no bibliography of secondary material. All I had was Michael Olivas's useful checklist. It was as if I had begun researching Updike back in Frost's or even Crane's time because there was no Google, no Internet, and no electronic connection to other libraries. Yet even on-site access to university libraries would not have helped because libraries did not then assemble extensive research collections of living writers. Major libraries rarely keep dust jackets, but dust jackets are critical when committing to this kind of scholarship because the jacket often supplies at least a modicum of biographical information and a blurb or two to hint how the author is being received, not to mention a photograph of the writer. Thus, I had to buy the books I planned to study. I contacted a rare book dealer in order to purchase the scarce first edition of *The Carpentered Hen* in the first state of the dust jacket. From the jacket I learned that Updike lived in Massachusetts and had two children. But then a bookseller called to tell me that there was also a first edition, *second* printing of *The Carpentered Hen* with a *second* state dust jacket. He did not have a copy, and he did not know where I could find one, but he thought I should know. The second printing of Updike's first volume is even scarcer than the first printing: approximately only 500 copies were published over a half century ago. When I finally located a copy, I learned from the jacket that Updike still resided in Massachusetts but now with four—not two—children, an apparently insignificant bit of information that meant, however, I would have to collate the two volumes to determine whether the author had changed the text as well as the jacket material between the publication dates of the two printings. Fredson Bowers, the primary American theorist of textual bibliography, would have been pleased.

Similar challenges loomed. Most readers of Updike know and admire "Hub Fans Bid Kid Adieu," but many may not realize that four distinct states of that great tale exist. Further, a few years ago when Updike learned that I was preparing to teach *Of the Farm*, he sent a letter advising me not to use the standard Fawcett paperback edition because he had made substantive changes for the forthcoming Ballantine edition. Another collation awaited me, a collation which revealed, for example, that Joey calls Peggy "stupid" in the Fawcett but "simple-minded" in the Ballantine—a significant emendation. My years of writing about Updike confirm that, when publishing scholarly articles and books about living authors, textual puzzles complicate the research because the author's canon has not yet been accurately established. It is still, as it were, being created: *which* edition? *which* state? *which* variant should we use? The problem is even more acute with Updike's many but rare and expensive broadsides, particularly if one has access to the several proofs and thus can determine the changes he made as each proof was printed. A similar challenge complicates *The Witches of Eastwick* because Updike radically revised the novel in proof. Thus, an Updike scholar needs copies of both the first and second states of the proof, even though the first state is difficult to find.

As I committed more and more time to Updike, my closest colleagues began to lay on good-natured teasing. After all, I was supposed to be publishing on safely dead writers, but now I had sunk into the murky waters of the living. One of my firmest friends was Matthew J. Bruccoli, the biographer of (dead) John O'Hara (dead), James Gould Cozzens, and most of all (dead) F. Scott Fitzgerald, not to mention author or editor of thirty or forty other books on Fitzgerald and Hemingway. Professor Bruccoli's reaction was typically funny and blunt. During a break in an interminable meeting, he nudged me and asked, "Why are you wasting your time on Updike? All his characters do is screw and pray." He soon proposed—with a grin—that we should team-teach a doctoral seminar titled "Bruccoli's Drunks and Greiner's Crazies," so named to include my interest in Updike as well as in John Hawkes[38] and Frederick Busch[39] who, at the time, were very much alive. When I gave him a copy of my first book on Updike, he handed me his biography of Fitzgerald with the following inscription: "For my friend and colleague Don Greiner—who has strange tastes in everything except biography." Later, when, at his request, I shared reprints of several Updike articles, I asked Professor Bruccoli to inscribe his textually revised edition of Thomas Wolfe's *Look Homeward, Angel*, now titled *O Lost*. Here's what he wrote: "For Don, who has strange tastes in literature—but not in wives." He never stopped teasing me about researching Updike.

I did not send copies of my books and articles to Updike, but other people did, with the result that a friendly, long-distance relationship began. The "John Updike" whom I had begun to imagine years ago in the noisy student tavern was finally beginning to take shape beyond the limitations of my creation of him. His responses were always generous, as illustrated by his witty reaction to *The Other John Updike*: After complimenting what he called my homework, he lamented with amusement that the negative reviews of his work I had dug up were better off permanently buried. Equally generous were his comments about *John Updike's Novels*. Reading the book while recovering from a cold, he explained that he particularly appreciated the discussions of

The Coup and *A Month of Sundays*, and that my musing about the end of *Marry Me* nudged him to reread the unusual conclusion to that underrated novel. By now our relationship, while still long distance, was comfortable enough to encourage collegial debate, as illustrated by his response to *Adultery in the American Novel: Updike, James, Hawthorne*, a book in which I write favorably about Henry James's long and intricate *The Golden Bowl*. Confessing that other than *The Scarlet Letter* he did not read much Hawthorne before 1970, he comically denigrated *The Golden Bowl* as an insufferable novel that merely confirms James's inability to understand how people typically behave. I, of course, disagreed.

We finally met in 1998 when Updike came to my university to deliver a talk. My imagined creation, born years earlier of beer, pizza, and *Pigeon Feathers*, became a tall and friendly man with soft voice and ready smile. His grin was as wide as mine when we shook hands for the first time. After examining a library exhibit of his work curated from my collection, he spoke to the admiring crowd. Luckily, his informal remarks were recorded and soon published: "A loved child has the sensation that everything he or she does is precious.... The sensation of being infinitely cherished can translate into a religious sense, as in the old phrase 'God is watching you,' a sense that all you do is noted and recorded." Then he brought down the house with a big smile and the following quip: "Whether or not God is watching me, Don Greiner *is* watching me."

Three years later, Jim Schiff invited William H. Pritchard and me to the University of Cincinnati. Our assignment was daunting: to join Updike on the stage, where Pritchard and I were to read papers about Updike's fiction, to which he would respond. The weather was damp and chilly, the lovely city of Cincinnati was recovering from racially charged riots, and Updike had a cold, but he glided through multiple public sessions with the same good humor and generosity that he displayed at my university. Similar comfortable exchanges were the hallmark of the inscriptions he wrote in his books. Indirectly aware of the burdensome amount of mail he received, but familiar with his Henry Bech stories in which such burdens are a comic but troubling issue, I still refrained from mailing books to Updike for signing, but then he began to send inscribed copies. I agree with Matthew Bruccoli, who always insisted that substantive inscriptions are primary material, worthy of study in their own right as part of an author's biography. Updike occasionally added hand-drawn cartoons beneath his inscriptions, a reminder of his years as the unofficial in-house cartoonist for *Chatterbox*, his high school newspaper, and for *The Harvard Lampoon*: a Valentine's heart in *Gertrude and Claudius* because he sent the novel on Valentine's Day; an "arf" coming from the mouth of the Borzoi dog in *The Widows of Eastwick*; an eye-catching, colorful Santa Claus in *The Music School*. More important, the inscriptions confirmed a growing friendship and trust. For example, in the British edition of *Couples*, he referred to the cover and urged me to ponder William Blake's drawing of Eve and the snake. This inscription reinforces the necessity of examining American and British editions in dust jacket because Updike often selected the illustrations for the jackets of his books. By calling attention to Blake's painting of Adam and Eve, he indirectly noted his primary theme in *Couples*. For the British edition of *Bech Is Back*, he pointed to the amusing photograph of him on the back of the dust jacket, which, to my regret, is not featured in the American edition, in order to stress his pin-striped suit complete with vest and his glass of champagne. For the paperback edition of *Villages*, he ironically called himself a sociologist. I laughed when I read his word portrait of himself as the social scientist of small town America. Yet my favorite inscription is in the first trade edition of *Rabbit at Rest*, when he claimed with delightful irony that I knew more about him than he did. But no, I did not know more about him than he did.

Updike was correct: nobody belongs to us. Still, the second half of his observation—"except in memory"—is a resonating affirmation of imagination and remembrance. To say that memory is creative is both to concede loss and to celebrate art. The "John Updike" I recall with such pleasure could never be *the* John Updike, but "he" was substantial enough to stride through my memory for decades. I know now that I began creating him when a spilled mug of cold beer led to a dog-eared copy of *Pigeon Feathers* and a never-ending fascination with the artist who wrote "Wife-wooing." *My* John Updike was not *the* John Updike, but he was always enough.

Donald J. Greiner is the South Carolina University Distinguished Professor of English and the author of John Updike's Novels, The Other John Updike, *and* Adultery in the Novel: Updike, James, Hawthorne, *as well as many essays about Updike. When Updike was invited to USC, Greiner met him for the first time, and in 2001 at the University of Cincinnati Updike responded to a paper Greiner read. Here Greiner describes a "bad beer and worse pizza" session from 1963.*

46. Robert M. Luscher
"John Updike: Short Fiction, Long Impression"

I knew John Updike primarily through his short stories, consuming a steady diet of them when I wrote *John Updike: A Study of the Short Fiction*. The more

I read by and on Updike, the more daunting a figure he became in my mind, with his wide-ranging knowledge of theology, art, and literature and a polished, exacting style that set the gold standard for prose. I had hoped that a short interview about his short stories might be included in the book, but Updike deflected my inquiry with a postcard response, wishing me the best in my endeavor but claiming that he felt it best for there to be some distance between a critic and his subject. Until the book was finished, I respected that distance, developing my understanding of his aesthetic directly from the fiction itself, from others' interpretations of his work, and from comments Updike had made in other interviews, reviews, and previous commentary on his own work.

After my book on his short fiction was published, I was surprised to receive a letter from him. Although I had put his name on the list of those who should receive a complimentary copy of the book, I never thought he would care enough about academic treatments of his work to respond. The note I received was most kind and clearly personal, typed on 5 × 8 piece of paper (I was pleased to have rated more than his usual postcard), with x's through errors, type overs, and various quirks of the typewriter on which it was hammered out. Updike expressed pleasure at receiving the book—which treated a substantial number of his over two hundred extant stories—noting the wariness with which he first cast his eyes about it, but praising the sensitivity and thoroughness which I had brought to his work. He had obviously inspected my book closely, as he mentioned being impressed with the care I had taken in matters of bibliography—quite a compliment from one who tracked his work so diligently to produce hefty compendiums of his own assorted prose.

Updike had clearly scrutinized my interpretations. While I had strived to illuminate his mastery of craft, to foreground his astute commentary on human experience, and to praise his reach as an artist, he unearthed one of the few negative remarks I had made. He commented about the fact that I did not seem to like "Leaf Season"—which I had characterized as having a dissipated focus and noted that "its actors seemed curiously static, and the weekend's events without lasting significance" (151)—and noted that all attempts to show a group dynamic had an unsettling plurality, citing *Couples* and Sinclair Lewis's *Main Street* as examples. He also expressed mild disappointment that I had not treated his recent unpublished stories as well as several scattered in the non-fiction collections, unaware that I had already left a fair amount of the initial manuscript on the cutting room floor to meet the space limitations of the Twayne series. Nonetheless, his report of having enjoyed my sympathetic readings of the considerable number of stories I did treat overshadowed any minor quibbles he had.

He went on to update me about his current plans for a new short story collection, once a novel on his desk made its way to New York, and went so far as to say that my guidance would be welcome on whether to include certain stories he felt to be borderline: "Tristan and Iseult" and two sketches about a burglar alarm. Seeing an opening, I responded in a short letter, and was gratified to see that when *The Afterlife* was published, he had taken my advice, including the former and omitting the latter. What I appreciated the most was the warm personal element with which Updike closed the letter, noting that—after my exercise in delving into his fiction—I was most likely eager to read someone else. Even though he had filled the page efficiently, he took the trouble to add a postscript in the lower left corner, making maximum use of the available space in a quick apology for his haste, noting that he was rushing outside, like one of his middle-class suburbanites, to work in his thawing yard. In one easy stroke, he had collapsed the distance between subject and critic, humanizing himself as he paused in getting the words out to ready his yard for the emergence of spring.

I only met John Updike once, in April 2001, at the gracious invitation of Jim Schiff, who had scheduled a Short Story Festival at the University of Cincinnati at which Updike had consented to be a headliner. Years before, after my book on Updike's short fiction was finished, I had driven two hours from Catawba College, where I was teaching at the time, to my alma mater— Duke University—to hear Updike give a reading. My memories of that event have faded with time, but I recall that he talked a bit about his research on Buchanan that had been conducted in Duke's archives before the reading. What I recall most vividly, however, was standing in line at a book signing before the event, never even getting close enough to the front of the line to get a glimpse of Updike, who did not reappear after the reading was over. Given this experience, I was definitely eager to meet the man behind the soaring sentences, precise prose, and textured depictions of the sensory details of everyday life—to collapse the distance between critic and subject even further.

A little over a week before the event in Cincinnati was scheduled, riots broke out there in the wake of the fatal shooting of a young black man, Timothy Thomas, by a white police officer, resulting in a city-wide evening curfew that was lifted only a few days before the event. Coupled with a pilot's strike that had made airline travel to Cincinnati problematic, there was some doubt about the status of the festival; despite the unrest, which cast its shadow over the proceedings, the event went on, affirming poetry's significance as a "momentary stay against confusion," as Robert Frost once characterized it. During some car travel with Updike and others through parts of the city, he concurred with these sentiments as we passed boarded up windows and bustling activity in the streets. I can only add some brief personal impressions gleaned from the events I attended and from my brief interactions.

What I recall most vividly was Updike's modesty and his patience: here we all were, assembled to celebrate his short fiction, to listen to his musings on literature, to lionize his achievements as a man of letters—one of the few in the United States who could genuinely wear that label. Yet despite all his accomplishments, Updike did not possess a super-size ego; in fact, he was genuinely self-deprecating. Unlike his literary alter ego Henry Bech, he did not seem to feed off the adulation that accompanied literary celebrity status. Rather, he exuded a sense that travelling to read his work, meeting with critics who analyzed his writing and with teachers of his works, submitting to interviews, and giving public readings are what the dutiful writer who has been deemed successful by the reading public does. Though the schedule for the conference was busy, Updike's energy never flagged; he was determined to give us what we came for, and actually enjoyed himself in the bargain. I got the sense that—despite his Harvard education, his erudition, his substantial publication, and his reputation—Updike was still solidly in touch with those humble Pennsylvania roots, about which he spoke fondly during the interview. He repeatedly mentioned the fact that in his packing he had forgotten a tie, abashed that someone who had been through such experiences hundreds of times still suffered such packing miscues. Every time he mentioned the tie—and the replacement that he had purchased (on sale at Brooks Brothers, but still pricey to him), it seemed that he was trying to assure us that he was, finally, one of us.

During the social events in which I was graciously included, Updike was attentive to everyone; I noted that during a lunch on campus, attended by a number of graduate students, he made sure to sit with them so that he would not be consigned to the margins and engaged in animated conversation with the group. My chats with Updike generally concerned his short fiction, and he amiably shared his thoughts about the form's importance and demands with me, somewhat flattered that someone placed such value on this component of his oeuvre; he welcomed my acknowledgment of the variety in his short fiction and the fact that I singled out his experimental stories for praise. He seemed glad to meet the person behind the explications of which he had once been wary, and generously answered my questions. I commented on my fondness for his early selection, *Olinger Stories*, lamenting that it was no longer in print—a sentiment with which Updike concurred. As a Vintage paperback not done by his regular publisher, Knopf, he speculated that it would most likely not be reissued.[40] However, when *The Early Stories: 1953–1975* was later published, Updike led off the collection with the Olinger Stories as a group, expressing gratification in his foreword that they were once again available together in print.

Overall, for Updike, the second day of the conference was a full one, and he kept up good humor throughout, patiently enduring as a listener and participant. In the sessions where academic critics spoke about his work, he praised their efforts and jumped right in during the discussion afterward. Given his chronicle of overcoming his difficulties with stuttering in the essay "Getting the Words Out," I was impressed with his articulateness, especially during the public interview with James Schiff. Again, during that event, he consistently displayed his modesty; there was an evident continuity between the man of letters onstage and that young Pennsylvania boy with rural roots and humble ambitions to enter the world of art and literature. I knew that he disliked interviews, but his responses were ample and gracious, and when he entertained questions afterward, I risked trying his patience with one more near the end of the session, asking him something I had not broached in our conversations: whether he had plans to put together a collection of his short fiction, and—if so—how he might approach the task and draw our attention to his short fiction beyond "A & P," by which he was most often represented in anthologies. Initially, he seemed to be a bit peeved by the question, as if I was prematurely consigning him to the role of a mere collector of previous work rather than an artist producing new pieces, though he admitted to being at that age when writers create such a gathering. After wondering aloud whether such a task might smack of vanity, he warmed to the question and gave it serious consideration, outlining a potential two-volume work[41] that might be called "Earlier Stories"; interestingly, three years later, *The Early Stories: 1953–1975* was published and met with a warm critical reception.

    I stood in line for every book signing, mindful of his Bech story in which a book-collecting fan besieges Updike's literary alter ego to autograph his copies of Bech's work, and is roundly satirized for his persistent efforts. Nonetheless, Updike displayed his characteristic patience toward this task as he chatted with each autograph seeker in turn, personalizing many of his inscriptions. Not wanting to seem opportunistic, I brought only a few select volumes to each event, relishing the chance to talk briefly with him once more and to obtain his signature, especially in those volumes of short fiction that were meaningful to me. Being particularly fond of *Olinger Stories* and having published an article about it, I owned multiple copies of the out-of-print paperback, which I spaced out over various signings. As he inscribed the second copy I had brought to him, Updike was quick to connect with our earlier conversation about the book, noting with a grin that it was perhaps no surprise the book was difficult to get, because I owned such a number of the extant copies. In his inscription to another volume of short stories, he kindly acknowledged my status as a short story expert, but the most meaningful volume he inscribed is one in which he dubs me *his* expert, validating the previous work I had done and encouraging me to continue my efforts to understand and elucidate his works, keeping in touch with him as I illustrate his oft-reiterated theme that art and memory serve as guarantees of our endurance.

Robert M. Luscher is Professor of English at the University of Nebraska at Kearney. He has authored John Updike: A Study of the Short Fiction, as well as extended biographical/critical essays on Updike's short fiction in American Short Story Writers Since World War II and in the Blackwell Companion to the American Short Story. His published essays on Updike include "Updike's Olinger Stories: New Light among the Shadows," "John Updike and the Montage Story: Farraginous Narrative," and "Teaching Updike's 'A & P': Shopping for Significance."

47. D. Quentin Miller
"All the Clever Young Men"

I imagine that most of the writers in this volume actually knew John Updike, meaning conversed with him, face-to-face. As Nicholson Baker charmingly and memorably argued, though, it was possible to know the man deeply through his books while only glimpsing the actual creator of those books fleetingly, or in my case, not at all. What follows is the story of one young scholar who wrote to Updike with the request to meet him in person, who was gently rebuffed, and yet who was given the rare opportunity to get to know him on an even deeper level through examining his archives. Updike's relationship with his readers, fans, interviewers, and scholars was, from my perspective, somewhat hot and cold. He certainly courted fame and the attention that came with it, but also felt nervous in the public eye. His memoirs, after all, were entitled *Self-Consciousness*, and reveal someone hyperaware of his own flaws, like a teenager scrutinizing himself in a well-lit mirror. Like the Great and Terrible Oz, Updike preferred to remain behind the curtain, and desired that we should pay no attention to him, but rather to focus on the grandeur of what he had created. When the curtain was pulled back, though, he was, as Dorothy said of Oz, much gentler and milder than he seemed initially.

I had just entered graduate school in 1989 when something startling, monumental, and a little anticlimactic happened: the Cold War ended. I was born at the precise midpoint of the Cold War. I grew up with the understanding that the Soviets were our national enemy, and that the world could end in the middle of the night if the massive stockpile of nuclear weapons the Superpower nations had amassed were to be deployed. Updike was of an earlier generation, and yet we had the Cold War in common. Its abrupt conclusion in the whirlwind era of *glasnost* and *perestroika* took the western world by surprise. Updike didn't expect it. I didn't expect it. He continued to chronicle the American scene. I got to work writing a dissertation about the effect of the Cold War on American fiction, eventually winnowing my list to one writer. The fact that Updike was that writer made perfect sense to me, even though he might not have been the most obvious choice. He had lived through the whole era, and it loomed in the background of his writing.

I corresponded with Updike intermittently over a period of seven years while I wrote my dissertation, and later while I revised it into a book. For a man whom I regarded as one of the finest American writers alive, I found his letters extremely generous and prompt, but also somewhat guarded and wary. I first wrote to him in 1995 when my thesis was beginning to come together, asking for an interview. He politely declined, but offered a number of pithy quotations and suggested that I look in particular at a few of his works. At the same time, he seemed surprised that I was writing on this topic, having grown accustomed to scholars writing about his work thematically in terms of what he called in his memoir "The Dogwood Tree" "the three great secret things: sex, religion, and art," which, along with literary influence, had become the backbone of Updike criticism. Cultural history was a context that he hadn't thought much about despite his insistence that his fiction "has more history in it than history books" (*Picked-Up Pieces*, 482). But, he told me, "It's your baby."

Receiving that first letter was a formative moment in my professional career. It was raining when I fetched it from the mailbox, and the raindrops blotted the ink on the envelope, ink that I quickly realized had been put there, handwritten there, by *the subject of my dissertation*. Like the end of the Cold War, I wasn't quite prepared for Updike's letter that day because I had sent my request to him just two days earlier. Yet here it was. A primary document. A gift. A direct connection to the magical world of letters I had devoted my career to understanding. It certainly gave me a bit of much-needed confidence. My peers were grinding away at their dissertations on historically remote figures like Shakespeare, Henry James, or Maria Edgeworth. "Nice," I would gloat, "but the subject of my dissertation just wrote to me, and gave me some advice."

It was only the first of a number of letters Updike sent me over the next decade, as I pored through his archives at Harvard's Houghton Library. In his first letter, though he declined my request for a face-to-face interview, he had offered to answer my questions in writing. I didn't want to annoy him with anything obvious. I saved my questions until I really needed them, framing them cautiously, like the three wishes that genies grant. I waited until I was ready to conduct archival research, and after asking his permission to dig through his papers, I cashed in my three questions, all to do with the year 1978: what did he make of the second Soviet/U.S. Writers' Conference? What were his impressions of the Soviet dissident author Andrei Sinyavsky[42] whom he had met that year? And just one more: in a manuscript version of *The Coup*, when he typed "Hippie Rift" instead of "Ippi Rift," was that a Freudian slip related to his infamous declaration of cautious support for American military involvement in Vietnam? His awareness of an ideological distance between him and his peers? His feelings of alienation from a burgeoning, politically motivated younger generation?

It was Updike's turn to be caught off guard. In his prompt and polite response, he conjured up a couple of impressions of Sinyavsky and of the conference, but felt exposed by my question about his typo. It was just a typo, he insisted.[43] Were young scholars going to scrutinize him that carefully? I had touched a nerve. He had been anxious about allowing me to dig through his papers, and all of our correspondence from that point on reflected this anxiety. In one letter he decorated his reservations with witty alliteration. Later, when I was asking for permission to quote from the papers, he expressed some reservation about allowing clever young scholars like me to access his papers. My wife was delighted: "He thinks you're clever!" I insisted that he was obliquely alluding to, and distinguishing me from, the "meek young men [who] grow up in libraries" described in [Ralph Waldo] Emerson's "The American Scholar."[44] In my mind, Updike had just dubbed me a scholar, even as he expressed his trepidation about the relationship between scholars and the writers they write about.

I know why he was anxious. The boxes and boxes of material he had deposited at the Houghton were revealing and maybe a little embarrassing, like a garage sale of the soul. To someone learning how to become a scholar, they were a treasure trove, but looking at it from his point of view, I imagine that I wouldn't want anyone to go through the drafts of everything I'd written. On the other hand, I would probably be flattered that they found me important enough to do so.

Like all great writers, Updike was a private person who was thrust into a public role. In his first letter to me, when he declined my request for an interview, he indicated that it wasn't personal: he didn't want to be interviewed *ever*, by anyone, and he said as much. During this middle batch of letters during the time when I was going through his archives, he made it clear that I was walking a thin line between scholarship and intrusion as I sorted through his drafts, letters, and random scribblings with more scrutiny than he ever had. In the final letter he wrote to me in 2002, he declined my invitation to speak at Suffolk University in Boston, because he declared a preference for avoiding local venues when he gave readings.

Fair enough. I knew that his gruff alter-ego Henry Bech had once manufactured a rubber stamp to use on letters from graduate students that read, "It's your PhD Thesis: please write it yourself" (*Bech*, 134). Given that fact alone, I was surprised, actually, that he ever wrote back. But he always wrote back, and with much more grace and delicacy than Bech would have. Moreover, while he didn't give me everything I asked for, he gave me plenty. His letters always contained quotable bits of wisdom and insight that I treasured, and used. After casting a wary eye toward a clever young man who was digging through his papers, he seemed to relax and to trust me, to a point.

But there was clearly more going on as Updike and I exchanged letters in terms of his anxiety. I was simply becoming a scholar, doing what I thought scholars did—archival research—and doing so with one of the last authors for whom such research will be possible since Updike wrote the old-fashioned way: with a typewriter. In the Information Age, ironically, authors have largely ceased to leave a paper trail of their creative process as editorial changes are made on the fly and drafts contain invisible emendations, without cross-outs or marginalia.

For his part, though, Updike was coming to terms with his own mortality. The bulk of our exchanges took place in 2000 and 2001, less than a decade before his death. It was around the time he composed the first part of his elegiac poem "Endpoint," wherein he reflects, upon turning seventy, that he is entering "that decade in which, / I'm told, most people die" (4), which looks like a chilling prophecy in retrospect. My book was published in 2001, and I sent him a copy that he graciously acknowledged in his penultimate letter to me, praising it while also pointing out an indentation error. I'm sure many scholars must have sent him books about his work. I thought that he would have never thought about me again. But my request to poke through his papers pre-posthumously and his troubled acquiescence—and I am positive about this—was one of the catalysts for his late novel *Seek My Face* (2002), which takes the form of an elderly artist being interviewed at length by a younger woman. As was often the case, Updike would render even a minor encounter into fiction. Though the novel has much to do with visual art, it also has a good deal to do with privacy and the control over one's legacy.

Hope Chavetz, the protagonist of *Seek My Face*, is at first reluctant to answer questions posed by the young interviewer, known only as Kathryn. Hope is clearly threatened by Kathryn, whom she refers to as a "burglar" and, on more than one occasion, an "intruder" with a capacity to "pounce" (105). "Who was this young woman, Hope wonders, to come pushing ... into her life, reading it back to her from her studious sheets of printout? As Hope ages, the outer facts of her life ... seem to have less and less to do with her inner life" (22-23). This tension between one's inner and outer lives—what the individual sees and what the rest of the world sees, sometimes with what must feel like a penetrating stare—is exactly what Updike felt when I got too close to his unconscious [mind] through examining his archives. Kathryn is eager to see a couple of telegrams between Hope and her husband, but Hope lies and tells her that she hasn't kept them; the narrator admits, "Both telegrams are upstairs in a steel drawer.... Why should she go rummaging for this common-minded intruder to see them, to paw them, these antique telegrams ... which had once had the force to knock the breath out of her?" (111–112). I flushed when I read this. He had called me a clever young man in a letter; I became a "common-minded intruder" in fiction.

Why would I assume the character Kathryn is based on me, and that this book was inspired by Updike's trepidations over what scholars like me were going to do with his papers posthumously? An exchange late in the novel makes the connection abundantly clear. Hope brings up the atomic bomb, and Kathryn suddenly springs to attention; she says, "Thank you for mentioning the A-bomb. In all this Cold War period, '45 to '89, did the threat of nuclear annihilation affect your thinking? Were you ever afraid?" (216). These are the very questions that informed my study, which Updike had read the year before the novel was published. Hope initially reacts as Updike initially reacted to my first letter: with surprised denial. She responds, "A bit in '62, the Cuba crisis ... but not really.... People are optimists. They must be. I could never believe the world's leaders would be so stupid as to blow it all up" (216). The phrase "people are optimists" is evasive, for if all people were optimists, the word "optimists" wouldn't exist. Hope clearly means, "I'm an optimist," by which she further means, "I don't want to confront the possibility of nuclear war." The final sentiment about how the world's leaders wouldn't be stupid enough to "blow it all up" has an eerie ring to it in a novel published in the immediate aftermath of the terror attacks of September 11, 2001, to which Updike was an eyewitness. As he imagined in his novel *Terrorist* (2006), the "world's leaders" might not blow it all up, but some rogues might.

I can only conclude that my request to plunder his papers unsettled him more than I had imagined. What is interesting, though, is that Hope's prickliness is only on the surface. She repeatedly asks Kathryn to stay so she can tell her more, fixing her tea and sandwiches in a lonely person's attempt to keep her audience. Hope is a common type in Updike's fiction: the elder, powerful figure seemingly scornful of the younger generation, like Roger Lambert in *Roger's Version* or Tom Marshfield in *A Month of Sundays*. In all these cases, the Great and Powerful Oz turns out to be an old softie once he actually starts talking to a member of that generation. This is the precise structure of his letters to me: "Why do you want to know?" followed by, "Here's what you need to know."

The fear of mortality is a theme throughout Updike's career, from David Kern's emotionally charged pigeon slaughter in "Pigeon Feathers" (1961) or Harry Angstrom's morbid ruminations about childbirth in *Rabbit, Run* (1960): "The fullness ends when we give Nature her ransom, when we make children for her. Then she is through with us, and we become, first inside, and then outside, junk" (194). The Cold War just framed one way of contextualizing the ephemerality of human existence. Kathryn tries to interject an opinion in response to Hope's "people are optimists" comment, but Hope cuts her off and rambles on: "In describing the post-war period you younger people keep telling us how haunted we were by the threat of nuclear Armageddon, but the fact is it hardly ever entered my head, and if it did what could I do about it? It was like being hit by a trolley car—that could happen, too" (217). In his first letter to me, Updike said something similar, almost verbatim: "The thing about the Cold War was you ignored it if you could." He continues by admitting, "no doubt [the Cold War] was there" in his fiction. After he read my book, he no doubt felt the depth to which it was *there*, whether he wanted it to be or not. "You ignored it if you could," Updike said; "it hardly ever entered my head," Hope echoed. But it certainly showed up on the published page. Everything he had written, he must have realized, was no longer in his control. His *oeuvre* in the age of context-based criticism was not just something that his readers would or would not "get," but rather a complex body of work that readers would make something of, whether or not that something was his intention. No doubt this left him feeling vulnerable.

Yet in *Seek My Face*, Hope's initial resistance to Kathryn gradually turns to tenderness, and even need. Symbolically, Kathryn at the end of the novel is revealed to be an angel, nearly ready to usher Hope across her final threshold, but not quite ready. She keeps insisting that Hope stay inside her house at the novel's conclusion rather than join her on her journey. I'm certainly not suggesting that Updike regarded *me* as angelic or important in any way: he didn't know me, and our brief exchanges were only a catalyst for his novel. But my requests to delve through his archives did get him thinking more broadly about his relationship to the world he was leaving behind, and about the future generations of readers who would encounter his work. Updike insisted on approving the archival quotations I wanted to use in my book, and, as I said, he pointed out an indentation error that I should have caught, but Hope seems to reflect Updike's growing willingness to let go of such control, as we see in the following exchange between Kathryn and her:

> "Shall I send you a transcript when I have one made?"
> "Oh my goodness, no. I couldn't bear to read it."
> "Would you like to approve of the quotes I use in my article?"[…]
> "Not really, dear. I'm sure you'll get them right enough" [259].

A few pages later, Hope is almost parental in her attitude toward Kathryn, who has developed from an "intruder" into a person with her own story that Hope seems to care about: "'*Have* your life,' [Hope] says, in a whisper pushed from within like a shout, 'go and have it, dear. It won't be mine, it can't be mine, we were all so naïve in a way, thinking we were so important to the world: but it will be yours, your own. Don't hang back'" (261). As I read it, this is Updike's valedictory message to all the clever young men and women of my generation. His letting go of the story of his own life and of the meaning of his life's work did not come easily, but I believe it came.

D. Quentin Miller *is Professor and chair of English at Suffolk University in Boston. His work on Updike includes* John Updike and the Cold War. *His most recent books are* A Criminal Power: James Baldwin and the Law *and* The Routledge Introduction to African American Literature. *Forthcoming books are* Understanding John Edgar Wideman, American Literature in Transition 1980–1990, *and* James Baldwin in Context.

48. Richard A. Davison
"Brief Encounters with Updike (2002–2008)"

Although I read John Updike's *Pigeon Feathers* in 1962, first taught "A&P" in 1969 and started collecting his books in 2002, my brief connection with the man began with my daughter Annie's comment: "My friend 'Rick the Poet' asked, 'Why did you fail to mention that your father is John Updike'?"

I met him only six times, talking with him at some length on our first and penultimate meetings. We exchanged only a handful of letters. But John Updike has remained much on my mind as I regularly read and reread his work and still encounter strangers who mistake me for him.

We first met on October 26, 2002, in Rockville, Maryland, where he accepted the annual F. Scott Fitzgerald Award. Awaiting his appearance at the Montgomery College buffet lunch, a group of ladies approached me and asked, "Did you have a good trip, Mr. Updike?" I had hardly finished my denial of what I wasn't when I spotted the genuine Updike just arriving and fled across the large auditorium to greet him: "I'm delighted you're here to take the pressure off—so far five women have mistaken me for you." He smiled that twinkly smile and with his well-known generosity and self-deprecation quipped, "Yes, you're a less flawed version of me."

Some years earlier I was sitting in the huge New York City 92nd Street Y auditorium, at the far end of a long row, half-way from the stage (waiting for a reading by Norman Mailer, Norris Church Mailer, and George Plimpton of Plimpton's play about F. Scott Fitzgerald, Zelda Fitzgerald, and Hemingway), when a middle-aged man came plodding along the long row to my seat and asked, "Mr. Updike, would you autograph my program?" And some years later, while my wife and I were standing in a long line (there were always long lines for Updike), waiting for the doors to open on the north side of the New York Public Library (on F. Scott Fitzgerald's birthday) for the September 2005 interview of Updike, my wife overheard a lady behind us mutter, "Look, even Updike has to wait to get in." These anecdotes are, of course, much less about a superficial resemblance than about the public's demands on a great writer, demands that Updike always handled with grace.

On that autumn day in Rockville, for instance, he chatted with his many admirers, gave radio and newspaper interviews, and then introduced the conference screening of the 1979 television film of his Maple short stories, *Too Far To Go* (with actors Michael Moriarty and Blythe Danner as Richard and Joan Maple). He recalled his mixed reaction twenty-three years before, seeing the film "with bad vibes in the house" and "the usual disturbances that go with watching TV" and liking Danner but not Moriarty. He was visibly moved while viewing the film on the big screen, especially at the conclusion when, at their divorce hearing, Richard gives Joan (now the mother of their four children) the kiss he had forgotten to give her at their wedding so many years before. Wiping away the tears, Updike walked to the podium to answer post-film-discussion questions; he still found Danner "wonderful" but admitted he had been unfair to Moriarty.

His responses during the film discussion and, later, to questions following his acceptance speech, a tribute to Fitzgerald and to good writing, were always clear and on target, whether on literature, art, or politics. Regarding his unpopular support of President Johnson during the Viet Nam war, for example, he talked about writing *Couples* in part from his positive memories of World War II, when, with mutual sacrifice, "the private and the public came together," and there was "true patriotism." Not so in the novel, when the party is not cancelled the day JFK is killed. "Viet Nam was possible" largely "because there were guns and butter."

After only a short break he signed so many books (including three for me)—it was the longest line I have seen at such an event—that he was forty-five minutes late for dinner, at which he continued to charm and enlighten.

Updike's first letter to me, responding to a book of interviews by me and Jackson Bryer that I had given him in Rockville, pursued his observations on actors and acting and people in general. Regarding the Blythe Danner, he noted that Danner's expression with its hint of worry had been inherited by her daughter, Gwyneth Paltrow. He labeled acting an odd profession—like writing on water, in Keats's words.

He recalled that before leaving New York in 1957, his clearest memory of the theatre while he was there was Arthur Miller's *A View from the Bridge* which, like lots of plays, turned into a yelling session and made him even more devoted to the written word which is silent and not histrionic.

Updike's letters always responded to my questions or to items I had sent him. He thanked me for admiring his three *Scarlet Letter* books and said he liked my pairing of Hemingway and Tarzan. (I had sent him my article on Hemingway and Edgar Rice Burroughs.) He wrote of the strong influence that childhood reading has on a writer, that all his [Updike's] fiction basically stems from Walt Disney. He thanked me for a Fitzgerald item, an illustrated article on the Flushing location of "The Valley of Ashes" in *The Great Gatsby*, pleased to have seen vintage Queens and pleased, too, that I still liked *The Centaur*. In his last note to me in answer to my questions about Thornton Wilder's *Our Town*, he allowed that *Our Town* needed no comment from him but cited page 159 (he typically took the time to look it up) of *Due Considerations* for his tribute, in which with nail-on-head precision Updike describes the "brooding sense of cosmic import within ordinary events" in Wilder's great play.

Updike's notes in response to my requests for signatures and/or inscriptions on first editions of his books for my Updike collection were always gracious. (I think he knew I was a devoted reader as well as a collector.) At one signing he laughed when I assured him I was not Marvin Federbush (the dreaded collector in *Bech Is Back*), nor was meant to be. Updike's humor always trumped the sighs beneath.

One time he wrote of coming back from his vacation to a huge pile of books to be signed and that some involved trips to the post office to deal with forms and buy extra stamps. He wished me well in my retirement, wishing that he had that luxury.

We last talked (mostly about the paintings he had chosen to discuss) after his keenly observed May 22, 2008, Jefferson lecture, "The Clarity of Things: What Is American About American Art?" at the Warner Center in Washington, D.C. In the thick of the crowded reception in the Willard International Hotel, tired but full of fun, he (who had greeted me with tongue-in-cheek epithets like "my virtual twin" and "my dashing double") walked with me across the room and introduced me to his wife as his "look-alike." Years before, he had mentioned Martha Updike's reaction to a photo of the two of us side by side. He said that his wife agreed there is a resemblance, but that she said she could tell us apart. She could. She did. We laughed.

Witty and personable, not only a great writer of fiction but a great man of letters, John Updike seemed a man who would never do anything willfully unkind. What a pleasure to know him, albeit in passing. The writing reflected the man, the twinkle at the edges of his poetry and prose. Choosing the best of Updike is a Herculean task. He puts the right word in the right place always.

Who else has so consistently caught the quotidian with such delicacy and resonance, with those pricks and stabs of emotion, with those flickers and flashes of insight. He regularly reminds us of things we have forgotten we experienced, does it so vividly, so precisely, so freshly that we feel more than we remember feeling and learn more than we remember knowing. Alec Guinness, an actor also devoted to the written word, in his memoir, *My Name Escapes Me*, celebrates Updike's "minute observations" that "take one's breath away.... [He] sees the truth of things and expresses the truth brilliantly." Guinness is right on the mark. Over six decades Updike sustained his central goal: "to describe reality ... and to give the mundane its beautiful due."

John Updike's fiction, poetry and essays will continue to sustain long lines of grateful readers, who will make no mistake about the superior quality of what they are reading.

Richard Allan Davison earned his Ph.D. at the University of Wisconsin. He is professor emeritus of English at the University of Delaware. In 1966 he wrote and hosted the series, "Literature and Life," for PBS. Davison has published over eighty articles he has also authored Charles & Kathleen Norris, *and he has edited* The Actor's Art: Conversations with Contemporary Stage Performers *and* The Art of the American Musical: Conversations with the Creators.

49. Robert Wilson
"Updike at Rest"

In all the many elegant tributes to John Updike that appeared in the first days and weeks after his death in late January, I missed any mention of the thing that was troubling me most. Soon after he died, I had said to a friend, half in jest that I felt as if a minor god, who kept careful watch over all our doings, had gone away. That feeling, strange as it is, has only grown. It suggests, perhaps, that the role he played in our culture was not just that of a novelist who was alert to the ways and meanings of our time. Nor was he exactly, as he has been called, a man of letters, some distant figure who loomed above our cultural life, saying once and for all what's what. No, he was someone who simply paid steady attention, and steadily shared the fruits of that attention in his sterling and generally whimsical prose and verse. Novels, yes, short stories, poems, essays, book reviews, art criticism, but also light, hard-to-classify sketches, what might be called *feuilletons*, when he couldn't contain his observations in a more conventional form. One such sketch, published in *The New Yorker* in 1981, called "Invasion of the Book Envelopes," is a small comic meditation on the messy packaging in which books are shipped. The last piece of any sort to appear during his lifetime, which we had the honor to publish in our most recent issue, was another one of these. Called "Nessus at Noon," it is a brief witty dialogue between the owner of a dry cleaners and a customer who has received a puzzling note with an article of returned clothing.

Literary reputations tend to dip for a decade or two after a writer dies, and it is hard to know whether, after that, Updike's mastery of the physical and emotional texture of life in our times will date him (*Rabbit, Run* felt a little faded when I reread it a few years ago) or whether he will emerge as our Anthony Trollope (a wise comparison that Verlyn Klinkenborg made in *The New York Times* recently). For now, it's worth noting that Updike was unusual among our most acclaimed novelists in not retreating from the cultural scene. Name me another major writer who reviews books regularly, writes about new art exhibits, and would lightly turn an Olympian eye to book packaging or the dry cleaners. There was a generosity about this.

It is a joke, of course, to call Updike a minor god ... but the comfort of a steady and attentive gaze is real enough. I've probably read only a million or two of the millions of words Updike wrote during his lifetime, but the stream of words was always there for dipping into or for full immersion. It never occurred to me that it would stop.

Robert Wilson is the editor of The American Scholar. *He has been an editor at* The Washington Post, *book editor of* USA Today, *literary editor of* Civilization, *and editor of* Preservation. *His books include* The Explorer King *(2006) and* Mathew Brady: Portraits of a Nation *(2013). Wilson once asked Updike to write about golfing with Sam Snead on a course using 19th-century equipment, including gutta-percha balls. Updike said he'd always wanted to hit a "gutty," but his answer was a friendly no.*

50. Joyce Carol Oates
"Remembering John Updike"

John was a slightly older classmate in a vast high school populated by not-prosperous rural youths in some nether land of the 1950s. Of course, John was president of this class; no doubt, I was secretary. I've been reading John's work since I became an adult and can only content myself with the prospect of his new, so sadly posthumously published *Endpoint and Other Poems* and *My Father's Tears and Other Stories* and rereading the newly reissued *The Maples Stories* as well as rereading his work through the remainder of my life. I think there must be a story or two, and even one of his more slender novels, which, unaccountably, I have not yet read. My students love "Friends from Philadelphia," which was John's first published story in *The New Yorker*.[45] What a seemingly artless little gem! My students are stunned by it and by the fact that John wrote it when he was hardly older than they are.

We had met a number of times—my (late) husband Raymond Smith and I visited John and Martha in Beverly Farms, Massachusetts on several very nice occasions. John was always gracious, warmly funny, kind, and bemused—and of course very bright, informed, and ardent when it came to literature. When he gave a brilliant talk and reading at Princeton some years [ago,] I was honored to introduce him to a large, packed auditorium [December 6, 1990]. I teach his lovely stories each semester—John's language is luminous, sparkling, and glinting, with a steely sort of humor. Think of an iridescent butterfly of surpassing beauty that yet—if you persist in examining it—will yield a considerable sting. I could never gauge how serious John was about his Christian faith—or, rather, the Christian faith—though some sense of the sacred seems to suffuse his work in its most ordinary, even vulgar moments, at which Updike was a master at transcribing. "Snow makes white shadows, there behind the yews, / dissolving in the sun's slant kiss, and pools / itself across the lawn as if to say / *Give me another hour, then I'll go*." ("Endpoint").[46] I will miss John terribly, as we all will.

Joyce Carol Oates is the author of a number of works of fiction, poetry, and criticism, most recently the novel The Man without a Shadow *and the story collection* The Doll-Master. *She is a recipient of the National Book Award, the PEN/Malamud Award, and the President's Medal in the Humanities. Since 1978, she has been a member of the American Academy of Arts and Letters and is a newly inaugurated member of the American Philosophical Association. Between April 1977 and May 2008, she and John Updike exchanged many letters; at a rough estimate, there must have been hundreds. It is a loss to American letters that, because of a restriction of Updike's estate, this correspondence will never be published.*

PART V:
FAMILY REMEMBRANCES

John Updike and Mary Pennington Updike had two sons and two daughters, Elizabeth (1955), David (1957), Michael (1959), and Miranda (1960). They were sometimes the inspiration for characters in short stories like "Should Wizard Hit Mommy" and the novel *Couples*. They were, of course, witnesses to their father's writing habits and his trips which sometimes combined research resulting in background for *Of the Farm*, the "Rabbit" books, and stories set in foreign locales like Morocco. The children were not concerned with their father as a literary celebrity. For them John Updike was an imaginative, kind father who invented games for them, created bedtime stories, taught them golf, chauffeured them to their sports, and who was concerned with every phase of their education. He remained close to them after his divorce, playing golf with his sons only weeks before his death. But they knew that his "favorite child" was his writing. While that may be true, and though Updike remarked that his children "raised themselves," the reminiscences of his children reveal that he was an indelible presence in their lives.

51. Elizabeth Updike Cobblah
"Remembering Daddy"

I am the same age as my father's career. We got started together in 1955. His books, stacked on top of each other now, would be about my height. Recent photos taken of our father and his four children suggest, given the way we are standing, side by side, a row of books.

So as I try to come to terms with the absence of my father, it helps to think of his body of work as a sort of half sibling, both familiar and strange, a thing to be awed by and annoyed by, a competing force perhaps but ultimately, and especially now, a way of knowing more deeply the man who I've been yearning for since he began slipping away, first to his desk and his muse, then to fame, to the rhythms and lifestyle of his other family while we were preoccupied with ours, and finally to his illness and death in January.

So though he slipped, or so it seemed, he never got very far. In recent years, we would reel him in for graduations, openings, backyard events and such. He would arrange movie outings, July Fourth picnics, golf or tea. Without being overly involved, he remained a positive, supportive presence, a tender father and grandfather but one whose writing, after all, was his favorite child.

I think we're at peace with that. Our father couldn't help it. Becoming a darling of American literature was a natural transition to make after growing up brilliant and good-natured, the only child in a house of four adoring adults. Less natural for him may have been redirecting the flow of attention to his four children, growing up in the turbulent '60s. But he did. And he juggled his gift and his family for the twenty years we shared a threshold. We had a good and memorable childhood spent in parallel play with our father's writing.

My siblings and I like to come across characters and places bearing resemblance to whom and what we know. We like his humor, his familiar slant on things edged with irony or reverence or irritation, his sensitive descriptions of everyday objects or moments that others might dismiss. We liked to see that we share a sensibility with him. In any case, his discipline and focus as a writer have ensured that we will have continuous access to him, to his way of thinking, of noticing, of caring, even when reading him sometimes makes us cringe. We have a powerful line to tug on, again and again, with gratitude, some embarrassment, love, and awe.

Our mother, a painter, who married my father in a huge act of faith before his career path was even clear, together with him gave the four of us the freedom to find our way, to be artistic, to be ourselves. As unwitting apprentices to the ways of our parents, we have become comfortable with the creative process and with our muse. Perhaps we are all, everybody, half siblings to our parents' work. We can take neither credit nor blame, but we can choose a quality of theirs, a way of being in the world, and use it how we see fit, for whatever ails us or heals us, or moves us through our days. In that way, a departed parent, whether leaving behind a body of work—a great body of work—or a pair of shoes, never completely slips away.

Elizabeth Updike Cobblah was born in 1955. She and her husband live in Maynard, Massachusetts. They have two adult sons, both teachers, like their parents. Elizabeth has been a teacher of art at the Fenn School in Concord Massachusetts since 2000. She is active in her Unitarian Universalist church and is committed to social and racial justice. Elizabeth illustrated her grandmother Linda Grace Hoyer's book of short stories The Predator (1990).

52. David H. Updike:
"A Toast to the Visible World: Remembering John Updike"

My father's parents were Wesley Russell Updike, a high school math teacher and coach, and his wife, Linda Grace Hoyer, a bookish farm girl who gave her only child his first inklings of a creative life beyond their small Pennsylvania town. Their son, *Jahnny*, was not famous in 1950—he was a skinny, brainy boy with an abundance of creative energy, an aspiring cartoonist who also had asthma, psoriasis, and a stammer, and in the high school hierarchy felt himself a considerable step down from the athletes and their glamorous girlfriends. Despite being first in his class he was not accepted at Princeton—admissions office take note—and so went to Harvard instead and flourished there, in class and on *The Lampoon*. But an unexpected obstacle remained to his graduation: all Harvard graduates must be able to swim, and he could not. Inhibited as a child by his own imperfect skin, he had shied away from public swimming pools, and never learned. And so he dutifully went to swimming classes and eventually managed two lengths of the pool—an achievement he seemed as proud of later as graduating summa cum laude. But for the rest of his life he swam with what I would describe as a rather studied dog paddle.

In an art history class, he met a smart and beautiful woman two years his senior, wooed her with kindness and wit, and spent his senior year in off-campus housing, a married man. His writing career began, as you know, a few hundred yards from here, but he was not famous yet, then, either, in 1957, and it took a lot of chutzpa to pack his wife and two very small children into a car and drive north to set up shop in the small New England town of Ipswich. He borrowed money from his not wealthy parents to buy a house, and occasionally drove back to New York to write another "Talk" piece, to bolster his income.

Hints of fame began to appear in our small town life: interviewers from New York, articles and photographs in magazines, visiting Russians in fur coats and funny hats. But for someone who was getting famous, my father didn't seem to work overly hard: he was still asleep when we went to school, and was often home already when we got back. When we appeared unannounced, in his office—on the second floor of a building he shared with a dentist, accountants, and the Dolphin Restaurant—he always seemed happy and amused to see us, stopped typing to talk and dole out some money for movies. But as soon as we were out the door, we could hear the typing resume, clattering with us down the stairs.

As it grew, he wore his fame lightly as his due, like one of his own well-worn sweaters, thin at the elbows. He loved public institutions—libraries, schools, the post office—letters arriving and departing, the simple act of completion—dropping it in the slot. I did this for him, this past January, when he couldn't make it downtown himself—a small typed letter, a final correction for an English publisher who was reprinting *The Maple Stories*: he had reread them in proof, he told me, "Not without some pleasure."

He played in the same poker group on Wednesday nights for more than 50 years, along with the local cobbler, a doctor, the owner of the auto supply store. He learned to play golf on a couple of scruffy local courses, and looked most at home there, most himself. Later he joined a fancy old country club,[1] but he always seemed slightly ill at ease there, like someone who had wandered into the wrong cocktail party and was afraid of being found out.

In late October [2008] we played at the same marshy course where he had learned the game, my brother and father and a friend, but he looked a little frail, and had a tough time on a long par four, and I watched from a distance as he topped a couple of fairway woods before he finally caught hold of one. "Come on, Dad," I muttered to myself, "hit the damned ball." But he had a way of feigning disinterest in a match until it really mattered, and by the last hole, the match tied, I noticed in him a gathering concentration, a new-found focus. Politely competitive and gracious in defeat, he much preferred to be gracious in victory. He hit a good drive, and a useful second. Our opponents were up in some apple trees and I had plunked my second into a green side bunker. I watched him as he bounced a low workmanlike chip to 12 feet, and while the rest of us bungled our way to sixes, he two-putted for a five. He walked off the course quickly, and wanted to get home—no soft drink or potato chips today. He was already ill. But I don't think he would mind my telling you that he won the last hole, and match, he ever played.

Among the last books he was reading was *Dreams from My Father*, by Barack Obama. He read it in bed in a sunny room overlooking the ocean, and I believe for him it was especially poignant, trying to catch up on the history he was about to miss, that was about to leave port without him. He was well aware, too, that Mr. Obama shares with his three oldest grandsons a parentage both of America and of Africa, of Kenya and Ghana, and so connected him in a personal, familial way to this transcendent moment in American history.

Through it all, his unkind illness, he remained, in his wife's words, "dignified and noble"—continued to be what his own father called a "gen'leman." And he continued to shave—each day, my sisters noted, even when it was perilous to do so. And as he so often did, he left for us a glimmer, a gift of himself, heart and mind conjoined.

David H. Updike (born 1957) is John Updike's first son. He graduated from Harvard where he earned a B. A. in Art History. He is Professor of English at Roxbury Community College, in Boston. David Updike has published two collections of short stories, one young adult novel, and six children's books. His stories and essays have appeared in The New Yorker, Harpers, The New York Times Magazine, *among others. He lives in Cambridge Massachusetts, with his wife, Wambui, and his son Wesley.*

53. Miranda Updike Freyleue: "Reflections on My Father"

My fondest memories of my father are from the summers in the 60's, when I was small and the days unfolded at a leisurely pace. Relaxed plans had built-in flexibility and were often steered by us four children and our friends, unless we were on the road in our mother's Ford Fairlane station wagon, taking one of our annual pilgrimages. Most summers we took three trips: One to Plowville, Pennsylvania to visit father's parents, another to central Vermont to visit our mother's parents, and a third trip to Martha's Vineyard, that excluded grandparents but included our dogs and cats and bikes and bulky, rubber water accoutrements, along with a barbed jumble of fishing equipment, affixed to the roof of the station wagon. The month-long trip to Martha's Vineyard was more of an island immersion than a family vacation, and required not only the Fairlane, but my father's car too. In those days, he drove used American convertibles.

My father rarely sang, but on route to Plowville there were two tunes he initiated that everyone in the car sang too. Both songs were sung crossing rivers. The first was a song sung crossing the George Washington Bridge, over the Hudson River. The lyrics were a simple refrain that repeated; "George Washington bridge, George Washington Bridge..." and was sung to an old waltz melody, the kind you might hear at a penny arcade or during a trapeze artist's act, swinging high in a circus tent. The second song we sang while crossing the Delaware River and was sung to the tune of, "great-green-globs-of-greasy-grimy-gopher-guts..." although each verse had one of our names in it; " there-goes-Michael-floating-down-the-Delaware, chewing-on-his-underwear, can't-afford-another-pair..." and would repeat for the entire bridge crossing, each time replacing a passenger's name. Our long steaming slippery ride was momentarily made comfortable while focus went to the jingles. With no AC, windows stayed open wide and it was hard to hear anything other than the constant growling traffic before we hit the Pennsylvania turnpike, which makes a different noise. As my sister reminded me recently, "PA turnpike is/was a series of concrete slabs (not tar) so there was a rhythmic budum budum budum as the car drove along it, signaling we were almost there!!"

These large trips stand out in my mind as the American dream which positioned my father as the family head leading the whole unit of smaller members. On those long trips, he was the driving force who symbolized stability and safety. However, it was the short local road trips in my father's convertible, driving back and forth to our own hometown "Crane's Beach" on sunny summer afternoons, where I remember my father's delight and youthful spirit letting loose. With the roof down and a gaggle of children crammed in every which way, he would transform from parent to a moderately reckless teenage babysitter. "Look! No hands!" he would shout, driving the car for several yards, hands-free before jerking the steering wheel back on course. And it would have been normal for a child riding in the front to take the wheel while he adjusted his bucket seat. En route back home, after our hours of sun, sand, and sea, it was easy to convince him we needed ice cream from Robinson's ice cream stand. With melting cones in hand, we would scramble over the hot trunk and perch on the folded roof with our legs dangling down into the seat chamber. Off he would drive, with our oozing cones cascading over our stubby knuckles, and splattering onto his crumpled cloth roof. My fondest memories stem oddly, from the back of my father's head.

Miranda Updike Freyleue (born December 12, 1960) is the fourth child and second daughter of John Updike and Mary Pennington Weatherall. Miranda is a painter and Special Education and Art teacher. She has exhibited her work in many venues in and around the Boston area. Updike wrote a poem to his daughter on her birthday. She appeared as a little girl in the stories "Morocco" and "Plumbing." Miranda Updike married Donald Freyleue; they have two sons, Kai Daniels and Seneca Dunn.

54. Updike Family Panel in Reading, Pennsylvania

This panel was part of the first conference of The John Updike Society (Alvernia University, Reading, Pennsylvania, October 1, 2010). Professor James Plath interviewed the panelists. The panel featured John Updike's first wife, Mary Pennington Weatherall, their daughters, Elizabeth Cobblah and Miranda Updike, and their son, Michael Updike. Absent: David Updike.

54. Updike Family Panel in Reading, Pennsylvania

PLATH: We're especially delighted to have with us Mary Weatherall, who was John Updike's first wife, and three of his four children: Elizabeth Cobblah, Michael Updike, and Miranda Updike. It doesn't get any better ... unless David were here.

MICHAEL: Well ... maybe not.

PLATH: And the first revelation bubbles to the surface! Can each of you talk briefly about your earliest or most prominent memory of your father-slash-former husband, as a writer?

MICHAEL: I remember mostly the wizard stories he told us. They were formulaic, with some little animal having a problem and traveling through the woods, and then it would get participatory.... Even as a child you could tell that sometimes he'd get the plot into a corner and not quite be able to get out of it. And the wizard's solution would be to turn the animal over and there was a switch, indicating skunk smell or porcupine quills, that was set the wrong way. And then he'd call it the end.[2] That's my first memory.

MIRANDA: I'm thinking more about his writing process and where he was—how he had an office at our house and how relaxed he was when writing. There were always lots of us around—four kids, and at any given time there might have been a bunch of our friends there as well. As he was typing away he was very relaxed and didn't get annoyed if interrupted. He was very good at multitasking and was always happy to see us—our little heads poking into his office and stealing rubber bands or sharpening pencils. He was very open to that, incorporating his family life into his work life.

ELIZABETH: As the eldest, even I got wise old wizard stories and they were delightful. But I have a distinct memory—I don't know if it's my earliest—of the sound of his typewriter, lickety-split. He was a very rapid typist, and he had his little office upstairs. Another memory I have is sitting with him in church. He is responsible for my kind of faith, I guess. He got us to Sunday school. Mom, being the minister's daughter, really didn't care about Sunday school much; she didn't emphasize that. But it was his Christian faith that he passed to me, in a way. I remember him jotting notes on his program during services, and you learned that he was always thinking about what he was going to write next. Another image I have is of him sitting around the house with his proofs on his lap—long sheets of proofs—with all the hubbub going on around him, just sitting there working on his proofs in the rocking chair.

MARY: Well, my first memory of John as a writer was in college when we took a fine arts course together and I saw what a good writer he was on a term paper. Later on, he typed up my thesis for me—which I thought was a great act of generosity, since he was also taking many courses and on the *Lampoon* and, at the time, very busy. Then shortly after that in the summer we exchanged letters while he was working at the *Reading Eagle*. He talked a lot about the rejection slips he was getting from the *New Yorker* and how miserable it made him, and how hard he was working. He was thinking about writing every minute of the day. It never stopped, after that. Eventually, he got some positive replies, and it was very exciting for him—for all of us, actually.

PLATH: Mary, do you remember at what point you both realized that he wasn't just a writer, but that he was a writer with a capital "W"?

MARY: I think as soon as he got a book published, that was the first, for him, and having so many stories accepted by the *New Yorker*, also. It was very important to him.

PLATH: Many of us here are familiar with that well-known detail about John writing three pages of polished prose per day. Can you add anything else to that? Anything about his work habits? You said something about him having a home office and being very calm. Is there anything else you can tell us about his work?

ELIZABETH: Well, even though he was very present in our lives growing up, he would often be off in thought, so he would have this distracted response to a simple question like—oh, I don't know, What time are we leaving?—and he would take his time to getting around to the answer because he was deep in thought. I think he was always thinking about the life of his fiction or poetry. Whatever was going on in his office was also going on in his head, all the time.

MIRANDA: About that three pages, I'm not sure if he actually wrote three pages. I know he *said* he did. He definitely had one deep, heavy chunk of hard time that he spent writing, usually in the morning—not early morning, either. He slept late-ish, at least when we were growing up, and he would stop after lunch and take us to the beach or something. So it was a short workday. Yet he was always thinking about writing and had clearly committed himself to a certain period of time during the course of the day for his writing.

MICHAEL: There was always a book in his hand, along with a pencil, and on these trips to the beach he'd be laying there on the sand reading or writing. That was just sort of something he was doing all the time while walking through the rest of his life, attentively or inattentively. It was just there. I don't know where I'm going with this, but he was able to manage all the social niceties while also managing this never-ending job of being a writer.

PLATH: Let's talk about some of those social niceties and diversions. How did he divert himself from the writing regimen and from filling his head so full of ideas? What did he enjoy for recreation? Did you, for example, take family vacations?

MICHAEL: There was the nine-hour trip we made to Pennsylvania every summer, for a week, and the trips to Vermont, where my mother's parents had a house up on a mountain. "Expo 67" I think we did. Then later, when there was a little more money, we'd go to Martha's Vineyard. Ipswich, Massachusetts, is notorious for greenhead flies, which render the outdoors uninhabitable for a month every summer, so we'd go to Martha's Vineyard, usually for July or August, and he'd set up his little writing station in an outbuilding or upstairs in a quiet place in whatever house we rented. He kept his routine pretty much there, but then the beach came, and the cocktail parties, and golf with various writers and friends on the Vineyard. If he did any hobnobbing with fellow writers, it was always on the Vineyard. He'd play poker with Lillian Hellman and saw friends like Robert Crichton.[3]

MIRANDA: He liked to go to movies and to take us bowling, and on rainy days he would often take all of us kids to a greasy clam food place called Woodman's, in Essex, and ... what else?

ELIZABETH: Ski trips in the winter, volleyball on Sunday afternoons with his buddies. He was very active, physically, very socially animated, much loved by his social peers in Ipswich. He played poker a couple times a month.

MARY: He had to learn games. He had to learn to swim in college, and to ski, because our children wanted to ski. He played basketball a bit with his friends in mud season in Ipswich, which was between winter and spring, and touch football. He also learned how to play tennis. What was amazing to me was that, for somebody who hadn't taken sports very seriously at school, he all of a sudden in his early adulthood began pursuing all kinds of physical activities with great enthusiasm and quite a lot of ability too.

MICHAEL: I think the only sport he came into adulthood with was roofball, which I had never heard of but which was learned, apparently, on the streets of Shillington. He taught us all how to play roofball. I don't know if it still exists as a playground game or not.

PLATH: Can you describe it, Michael?

MICHAEL: You have a roof ... and you just line up the kids for a game of elimination. It's played on the low roof of a shed or garage. The kids face the roof and form a line away from it. The first child serves the ball volleyball-style onto the roof and runs to the back of the line. The ball needs to hit the roof at least once. As it descends, the second child hits it volleyball-style back up to the roof, and so it goes like this down the line. Failure to get the ball on the roof means you're eliminated. This continues until there's a single winner.

PLATH: I think the most extreme thing I've done for any of my kids is playing the part of the king in the *Sleeping Beauty* ballet because my daughter was

Little Aurora. Do you remember your father doing anything extreme that way, like you're thinking, Boy, he's really doing this for me?

MIRANDA: Not really, though maybe the wise old wizard stories functioned that way.

MICHAEL: Yeah, and the way he would mow the lawn in circular paths back and forth so we could run across it. But he was more of a home father than not. Most fathers would come home around five-thirty or six, but he was around the house essentially from one in the afternoon until the next morning at nine, when he would get up and go off for his four hours of writing for the day.

ELIZABETH: He took me to my flute lessons, and I think he took our brother David to his guitar lessons. He was available in the afternoon.

MARY: In a nice way.

ELIZABETH: Even though Mom was also available.

MARY: He didn't think of himself as being musical but he learned how to play the recorder, and we both played recorder in a group for several years. He also wrote reviews of the local classical concerts for the town newspaper and was quite good at it.

PLATH: Was he free of household chores, or did you divide up the work? He writes domestic fiction, but how much of a domestic was he?

MARY: He didn't wash dishes. He didn't cook very often.

ELIZABETH: Grocery shop?

MARY: He *would* grocery shop. And the first thing he did when we moved into a new house was not to help unpack the car. Instead, he got out a saw and cut a mailbox in our front door so he could be sure to get his news from *The New Yorker*.

ELIZABETH: He was very handy with little repair jobs around the house. Things like a door not closing properly would bug him enough that he'd get out his plane and make it a good tight fit. He taught me how to glaze windows. He also taught me that if you have a cracked window, how to take it out and replace it, which entailed cleaning the little trough and knowing how to run the putty knife over the corners. Things bugged him about the house, particularly things that didn't work properly, so that was kind of cool.

PLATH: This question is for Mary. This conference celebrates the fiftieth anniversary of the publication of *Rabbit, Run*. John had received a Guggenheim [fellowship] to help him complete the novel, and I was wondering if you could talk about what your life was like as a couple while this second novel was being written. Does anything stand out?

MARY: Well, nothing much changed, except Miranda hadn't been born and Michael was very young, perhaps a year old, I think. The others were also young, maybe five and three. We had our hands full. I think that everything was going smoothly, but we were both very busy.

PLATH: Did he share chapters or drafts in progress?

MARY: Well, not so much with novels, but with short stories. When he finished a short story, I would read it and I would be able to say what I thought about it. Then he would send it to the *New Yorker*. When it came back, if there were editorial changes, he always wanted to know whether they were good or whether the original, his first version, was better. That's the sort of thing I was doing. Also little things ... about whether he was repeating himself, or whether characters were saying appropriate things to each other.

PLATH: Appropriate things meaning, does this character sound like the person upon whom it's based?

MARY: No, not so much that, but the consistent personality of the fictional character.

PLATH: As for the children, I was wondering something about the later writing, particularly *Couples*. When was it that each of you realized your father had written what some people were calling a dirty book? How did you feel about that?

MIRANDA: For starters, it took a long time for me to figure out that he was a famous person. I mean, he was a writer and the next-door neighbor was a lawyer, or something like that, but he was just our father. He did what he did, and that was that. It wasn't important for a long time, and maybe it still isn't. I would have been seven or so when *Couples* appeared, and because of that novel we went to England for a year. We were wealthy enough after *Couples* to go and spend a year abroad, and that was big for us. So I guess it sort of sneaked into my consciousness that it was a racy book, and a lot of the characters were based on people from our community.

MICHAEL: We had to get out of the town we lived in when the book came out. So that was in my fourth grade year, and we stayed in lovely Cumberland Terrace, Regent's Park, and I remember always watching the *New York Times* best-seller list, because *Couples* was second for so many weeks, behind *Airport*. I think he was No. 1 for maybe one or two weeks, so he just made it, but he was No. 2 forever. We came back from England and bought a much bigger house as well, and then a few years later Liz decided she wanted private school, so the rest of us all realized private school was an option. That's when we realized, I *think*, that he was doing all right.

ELIZABETH: I was more concerned with the painting of a nude man in our dining room than I was with his books. When the Girl Scouts were coming for dinner, I asked if that painting could *please* be removed. So when it came to the racy book thing, I was pretty naive and a slow bloomer. I think

I didn't fully grasp that until college, really, and I still have not read *Couples*. Have you guys read *Couples*?

MICHAEL: I did climb that mountain, and it wasn't as bad as I suspected it was going to be. It was nice to have my mother to say, "Oh, that's Mrs. Thompson," or, "That was a rumor." It's always been dismissed as the best seller he had to write to get wealthy, but I thought there's a lot in there that's really good. I enjoyed it more than I thought I would.

MARY: I read it once, and I think I'll not read it again. But there *were* some good parts, and the characters derived from reality but were always mixed up with another character from reality.

PLATH: So they were composites.

MARY: They were very composite, and he worked hard at it. Sometimes it carried the day, and other times people recognized themselves in spite of it. But he did it very well. I don't think anybody was totally offended or surprised.

MICHAEL: As you read, especially the early short stories, you really get a sense for the history of Ipswich and what is happening. For instance, there was an incident where a car smashed into the house across the street, which I barely understood at age four. But then I read about it later [in "The Corner"] and learned that the axle had broken, that the driver was a young guy, and that he had almost run over my sister. When I read that, I read it as all being fact in a way, and I think I'm correct in saying that it is very factually based … but not all of it.

ELIZABETH: When I recognize people I know in his work, it can be a little bit distracting from the main story. Yet I marvel at his ability to really nail a certain character—townspeople, friends included. So yeah, it's both a distraction and a source of awe for me.

MICHAEL: There's a pretty damning account of my grandmother [Linda Grace Hoyer Updike] in *Of the Farm*, and it's just amazing how much he nailed it. He knew exactly her conniving, manipulative ways, and he just lived with it and wrote about it.

PLATH: Have you read *The Centaur*? I remember his father Wesley's remark about that book and how "the kid got me right."

MICHAEL: Yeah, I've never understood why my father didn't respect *his* father more, and I think he got it right in *The Centaur*. We saw our grandfather as just a lovable and gregarious person, and my grandfather always looked at himself as a failure because he ended up as a schoolteacher and barely made a go of it. But I love *The Centaur* and I love the depiction of my grandfather. It really displays his charm and why he was valued in this very community that we're in.

MIRANDA: I agree with Michael. It was the very first book I ever read of my father's, so it was a long time ago, and though it's very fuzzy I remember the car scene well—the car breaking down in the winter, and the main character being very embarrassed by his father. I just don't understand what his problem was with his father.

ELIZABETH: Well, *The Centaur* was the one book of my father's I was ever asked to read by a teacher, and that was in the eleventh grade, I think. I loved it. While I haven't read it since, I do intend to reread it. And yes, we *adored* our grandfather Wesley. He was a saint in our eyes.

PLATH: There's a tour [during the conference] for John Updike Society members to Plowville, and I was wondering if you could talk about your family vacations there and your memories of the farmhouse.

MARY: The house was very small, but they managed to squeeze us in when we arrived. It was wonderful being there. It's a lovely old house. The barn was absolutely beautiful, the landscape lovely, and I missed going there after John and I were separated. The kids loved it too.

MIRANDA: I would like to add that our grandparents would accommodate us, when we came, by sleeping in the barn while we all slept in the house. But all of us kids wanted to be with *them*, so we all piled into the barn to sleep, which meant that my mother and father had the house to themselves. It was a very old-fashioned kind of visit—crickets chirping, fireflies buzzing. We'd catch fireflies at night, and we'd eat corn on the cob and fresh peaches—it was really nice. We'd also take long walks in the early morning with our grandfather and his collies, his dogs.

ELIZABETH: Well, when you come from New England, one thing you notice about this area is the stone, the stone constructions and the use of sandstone in the buildings. We were admiring, yesterday, just driving into Berks County and seeing those familiar sandstone houses. Some of them have become quite decrepit and others abandoned, but the sandstone is what I associate with this area.

MICHAEL: I'm going to "out" you a little bit, Liz, and talk about your early college visit to Mom-mom's farm. Correct me as I go, but you thought you were being helpful by going out and weeding the garden on a Sunday, and my grandmother, being a strict Lutheran, didn't agree with working on the Sabbath. So as punishment, she declined to report that you had been crying the entire time [following a confrontation]. She let you cry while my mother thought that everything was fine. That's the kind of manipulation that you see from the grandmother in *Of the Farm*.

MIRANDA: Yes, our grandmother had a short fuse and was very focused on our father when we went to visit. The rest of us would have to work around that, but she had a sharp tongue and was quick to scold.

ELIZABETH: She also outlived our other three grandparents, so we had, I think, the privilege of knowing her into our adulthood. She mellowed and softened over the years, and it was sad when she died in 1989.

PLATH: Could you talk a bit more about Wesley Updike?

MIRANDA: First of all, he was just so charming. He would meet strangers as we'd go into town or people he knew and he would always compliment them. He would find some way of giving them a compliment, making them feel like a wonderful person, and he did that with us. He gave us all sorts of nicknames, although I'm drawing a blank on them.

MICHAEL: My father drove from Plowville to Shillington with my grandfather every day, and he would sometimes joke, though often at my grandfather's expense. For instance, he would describe, for laughs, lurching the car ahead two feet as his father was getting into the car in front of a group of high school kids. My grandfather was of the personality that he would let it go.

PLATH: What books by your father speak to you most, or which books do you identify with? Any standouts or favorites?

MARY: Well, I'm partial to the early short stories, probably because I know them so well. It was all very exciting as, one by one, they were accepted, and then later collected and reviewed, which verified our feeling about their success.

PLATH: Have any of you seen yourselves in those short stories? If so, what was your reaction?

ELIZABETH: I'm touched but also a little unnerved. His observations are just so keen, and he had a way of being a little harsh while loving at the same time. So it's an awkward thing. But what I love about his writing, really—and I don't have a favorite, I'm not particularly well-read when it comes to his writing—are his observations, and the combination of his playfulness and reverence, which comes through in his poems. So yes, that combination of playfulness and reverence.

MIRANDA: He began giving me the books when I was nineteen or so, and I started most of them. I gravitate toward the thinner books, although I do like *In the Beauty of the Lilies*. *Seek My Face* is a book in which I saw a lot of my grandmother, and the descriptions were just beautiful. There's one description of this older woman who lives alone and makes herself a cup of tea; she reuses the teabag, then puts it on the corner of the sink where it looked like a little purse. That reminded me exactly of my grandmother's purse, and it kept sticking in my head. I would agree with Elizabeth that his descriptions are just wonderful.

MICHAEL: I think the question was about standout novels. *The Poorhouse Fair* I read, and, to be honest, just didn't quite get. There are lovely parts in it, but I think what bothered me is that it's more dialogue, which leads to a discussion Miranda and I have had about his dialogue. Are the people too smart? Is the dialogue too polished? A lot of us say things that go nowhere. We say things that sound flat and silly. When you're writing about fictional people, his dialogue is very crisp and the people are smart, intelligent. But what I think is preferable is the description and the many different details, such as Miranda described, like the purse, and that bit from *Couples* where he's coming down to a house that's being renovated and describes the [unconnected pipes under the] kitchen sink, which [had been left] "open like a cry." That makes perfect sense, I thought, that's wonderful! So it's all peppered with little fine details.

PLATH: Do you recognize yourself or others in the short stories, Michael?

MICHAEL: Yeah. I can read all the short stories and see my siblings in most of them. I'm not in too many of the novels that I know of. In *Marry Me* I think I'm a young child. The family [in the books] ranges from five to three, so I think my brother is the one who [disappears/appears]a lot in these books. I'm sort of the limbo in between, and I think my divorce was informed by his divorce, where I was trying to do something different, such as hold onto my kids more at the time than he did. So there was this commentary in his short stories about that which I don't think he fully understood or appreciated.

ELIZABETH: I was getting ready to marry my husband, a man from Ghana, West Africa, and my dad thought I needed to read *The Coup*. I confess, however, that I have not yet read *The Coup*, but I *will*.

PLATH: All of you turned out to be artistic in some way, whether writing, painting, or sculpting. Could you talk about the influence of your parents?

ELIZABETH: Dad drew—we both drew—you know, cats and little scenes of babies being fed, landscapes and vases with flowers, that sort of thing. Cartoons, birthday cards. Our birthday cards from our father were almost always hand-drawn. Up until he died, he was even giving hand-drawn caricatures of grandchildren in birthday cards, that sort of thing.

MIRANDA: I think our parents' lifestyle encouraged us to become artists just by seeing that we didn't have to go to a real job. You could make a living free-flowing, intertwining with your family life, and I think we all liked that idea.

ELIZABETH: It was a trial-and-error sort of thing. They had expectations but they were not that explicit. They were permissive and inventive and creative, and they had a faith in us, I think, as creative beings. Mom took a leap of faith in marrying my father in the first place when he was only— what?—twenty and still in college, and I think the two of them transferred that faith to us—a faith in life, art, God, everything.

PLATH: We now have time for just a few questions from the audience.

AUDIENCE MEMBER: Well, first of all, thank you for sharing all these personal stories about your father and family. It sounds as if you had such affection for your grandfather, and I'm wondering, did you see your grandparents more than the one week in summer when you came here to visit?

MARY: Oh, yes. They came to visit us in Ipswich several times, and they came to France when we were there in the winter of …

ELIZABETH: '62.

MARY: Yes, '62, and they baby-sat for the children while John and I went to Italy for a week. That was, I thought, very brave and heroic of them. They had to drive a car in France, and they were very good babysitters.

AUDIENCE MEMBER: Can I ask, what was your reaction to *Self-Consciousness*, his memoir?

ELIZABETH: I personally feel it's a gift to his progeny. I've been using it as a resource, and, yes, a love letter, really.

MICHAEL: I loved *Self-Consciousness*. It has so many beautiful descriptions of Shillington and his childhood here.

AUDIENCE MEMBER: Is it true that John Updike did not like Frank Sinatra, and if so, what singers and musicians did he like?

MIRANDA: He liked Bing Crosby.

MICHAEL: Boy, you stumped the panel. I will say, however, that I lived with my father my senior year in high school, which was 1976, I think, and he loved the Captain & Tennille.

MARY: We actually met Frank Sinatra in New York, courtesy of Bennett Cerf, who was entertaining us at dinner at a restaurant, and John seemed very pleased to meet Frank Sinatra, even though *I* never knew that he didn't like him.

AUDIENCE MEMBER: My other question about music, given Rabbit's listening tastes, is whether he liked disco. Did he like Donna Summer?

MIRANDA: I don't think he did, but I could be wrong. He liked the Beatles, jazz, and classical music.… What else?

ELIZABETH: The Supremes.

MIRANDA: Motown! He liked Motown.

PLATH: And on that note, we shall conclude. Thank you to all of our panelists.

Appendix: A Chronology of John Updike's Life and Works[1]

1932   An eleventh-generation American (two Updikes fought in the Civil War on opposite sides),[2] John Hoyer Updike is born March 18 in West Reading Hospital, Reading, Pennsylvania, to Wesley Updike, a mathematics teacher at Shillington High School (1934–72), and Linda Grace Hoyer, a writer. Updike lives with his parents and grandparents, John and Katherine Hoyer, at 117 Philadelphia Avenue, Shillington, a suburb of Reading. Shillington was the locale of the memoir "A Soft Spring Night in Shillington" (*Self-Consciousness* 3–41), fictionalized as Olinger (*Olinger Stories*, v), and used as the subject of the poem "Shillington" (*Collected Poems* 15).

1933   On March 18, to celebrate his first birthday, Updike's parents and maternal grandparents plant a dogwood tree in their front yard. It still stands forty-feet tall. Dr. John Hunter bought the house in 1945 and nurtured the tree.[3]

1937   Enters public school in Shillington. Publishes a collage in *Children's Activities*. Mother arranges art lessons from noted artist Clint Shilling.

1938   Contracts psoriasis and begins stuttering.

1944   As a Christmas present, Updike's paternal aunt Mary gives the Updikes a subscription to *The New Yorker*.

1945   First literary publication, "A Handshake with the Congressman," appears February 16, in *Chatterbox*, the Shillington High School newspaper. On Halloween, his parents and maternal grandparents move eleven miles south to the sandstone farmhouse in Plowville where Linda Updike was born, and where she, her parents, and husband would die.

1946   Enters Shillington High School (now Governor Thomas E. Mifflin Intermediate School). Writes a murder mystery (published 1994), light verse, and prose. Works in a lens factory.

1948   Contributes weekly to *Chatterbox*. The death of his paternal uncle[4]

1949   Publishes a poem, "I Want a Lamp" in the *American Courier* X (July 1): 11. Elected class president. Writes and stars in the junior class play (as he will in the senior play). Since he played the father in both plays, Updike quipped that he "fathered" them.

1950   Graduates co-valedictorian of class of 1950. Updike had contributed over 300 drawings, articles and poems to *Chatterbox*. In the yearbook, *Hi-life*, he authors drawings, a poem, a farewell, and captions for photos of seniors. His caption reads "the sage of Plowville," who "hopes to write for a living." This summer, and for the next two summers, Updike works as a copy boy for the Reading *Eagle*. He publishes poetry in that newspaper. Enters Harvard on a full-tuition scholarship, majoring in English.

1951 "The Different One" is published in *Harvard Lampoon*. More than forty poems and drawings will follow. Discards a novel about two-thirds written called "Willow," about a town like Shillington; it forecasts his stories about Olinger.[5]

1952 Named editor of the *Harvard Lampoon*.

1953 A story (later titled "Ace in the Hole") about "Flick," an ex–basketball player, written for Albert Guerard's creative writing class, receives an "A" and is encouraged to send it to *The New Yorker*, which rejects it.[6] Marries Mary Pennington, a Radcliff Fine Arts senior, on June 26. *The New Yorker* buys a story and a poem. Updike's maternal grandfather, John Franklin Hoyer, dies.

1954 His senior thesis is titled, "Non-Horatian Elements in Robert Herrick's Imitations and Echoes of Horace." Graduates from Harvard *summa cum laude*. Wins a Knox Fellowship to attend the Ruskin School of Drawing and Fine Art, Oxford, England.

1955 While at Oxford he meets E. B. White, and White's wife, Katharine White, fiction editor of *The New Yorker* who offers him a job as a reporter for the "Talk of the Town" column. Beginning a life-long association with *The New Yorker*, Updike publishes "Duet with Muffled Brake Drums" (a poem) and "Friends from Philadelphia" (short fiction) and begins work as a staff writer. Updike's maternal grandmother, Katherine Kramer Hoyer, dies. Daughter Elizabeth is born April 1.

1957 Leaves *The New Yorker* and New York in April for Ipswich, Massachusetts. Leases "Little Violet" house in Ipswich. Completes "Home," an unpublished novel which is rejected by Harper & Bros., though they accept a sheaf of poems for publication. Son David is born January 19. Takes up the recorder and golf.

1958 Publishes his first of numerous books, *The Carpentered Hen and Other Tame Creatures*, a gathering of fifty-five poems originally published in *The New Yorker*. Buys a seventeenth-century home at 26 East Street, Ipswich, living there until 1970. (It would later be purchased by Martha Bernhard the woman who would become his second wife.)

1959 Publishes with Alfred Knopf (his life-long publisher) *The Poorhouse Fair*, his first novel, and *The Same Door* (stories). *The Best American Short Stories 1959* selects "A Gift from the City." Winning a Guggenheim Fellowship enables him to write *Rabbit, Run*. Michael, his third child, is born May 14.

1960 Publishes *Rabbit, Run* (novel). The family vacations in Anguilla for five weeks. *The Poorhouse Fair* wins the Rosenthal Award of the National Institute of Arts and Letters. *The New Yorker* publishes "Hub Fans Bid Kid Adieu," among the greatest sport stories ever written. Miranda, his fourth child, is born December 15.

1961 *Prize Stories 1961* includes "Wife-Wooing." Visits Puerto Rico, St. John and St. Croix alone.

1962 Publishes *Pigeon Feathers* (stories) and *Rabbit, Run* in England, including "emendations and restorations" made while in Antibes, France. Adapts Mozart's *The Magic Flute*. *Prize Stories 1962* includes "The Doctor's Wife." *Best American Short*

Stories 1962 includes "Pigeon Feathers." Teaches a summer creative writing course at Harvard.

1963 Publishes *The Centaur* (novel) and *Telephone Poles and Other Poems*.

1964 Publishes *Olinger Stories*. Adapts Richard Wagner's "Ring Cycle" operas, and contributes the memoir, "The Dogwood Tree" to *Five Boyhoods*. *The Centaur* wins the National Book Award. National Institute of Arts and Letters elects Updike, the youngest member ever so honored. Visits the USSR and Eastern Europe under the auspices of State Department. Ursinus College awards Updike an honorary degree. Leaves temporarily unpublished *Marry Me* (novel).

1965 Publishes *Of the Farm* (novel), *Assorted Prose*, *A Child's Calendar* (poetry); and *Verse* (a coupling of *The Carpentered Hen* and *Telephone Poles*). Wins *Le prix du meilleur livre étranger* for *The Centaur*.

1966 Publishes *The Music School* (stories). "The Bulgarian Poetess" wins the First O. Henry Prize and appears in *Prize Stories 1966*.

1967 *Prize Stories 1967* includes "Marching through Boston." Writes "Three Texts from Early Ipswich" and appears in Ipswich's Seventeenth Century pageant. Moravian College awards him a Doctor of Letters degree.

1968 Publishes *Couples* (novel); it makes the best-seller list for 36 weeks. *Prize Stories 1968* includes "Your Lover Just Called." Relocates his family to London, 1968–69. Goes to Egypt alone.

1969 Publishes *Midpoint and Other Poems* and adapts Shakespeare's *A Midsummer Night's Dream* as *Bottom's Dream*. With his family goes to Morocco.

1970 Publishes *Bech: A Book* (stories). "Bech Takes Pot Luck" chosen for *Prize Stories 1970*. *The Fisherman's Wife*, an opera for which Updike writes the libretto, is produced in May. Travels with daughter Elizabeth to Japan and Korea to give a paper. The family moves to 50 Labor-in-Vain Road, Ipswich, Massachusetts.

1971 Publishes *Rabbit Redux* (novel). Receives the Signet Society Medal for Achievement in the Arts.

1972 Publishes *Seventy Poems* and also *Museums and Women and Other Stories*. Appointed Honorary Consultant in American Letters to the Library of Congress (1972–75). Visits Venezuela. Updike's father, Wesley Russell Updike, dies April 16.

1973 At Harvard Updike reads the Phi Beta Kappa Poem, "Apologies to Harvard." With his wife visits Africa on a Fulbright grant. Later travels to Canada.

1974 Publishes *Buchanan Dying*, his only play. *Prize Stories 1974* includes "Son." Pending his divorce, Updike moves in September to 151 Beacon Street, Boston. In Australia gives talk, "Why Write." Lafayette College awards Updike a Doctor of Letters degree.

1975 Publishes *A Month of Sundays* (novel) and *Picked-Up Pieces*. *Prize Stories 1975* includes "Nakedness." Wins the Lotus Club Award of Merit.

1976 Publishes *Marry Me: A Romance* (novel). *Best American Short Stories 1976* includes "The Man Who Loved Extinct Mammals." "Separating" is selected for *Prize Stories 1976*, which gives Updike the "Special Award for Continuing Achievement." *Buchanan Dying* premiers at Franklin and Marshall College. Elected to the American Academy of Arts and Letters. Grand Marshall of the Shillington Fourth of July parade. Moves to 58 West Main Street, Georgetown, near Ipswich. He and Mary divorce.

1977 Publishes *Tossing and Turning* (poems) and *The Poorhouse Fair*, revised edition, with a Foreword by Updike. Marries Martha Ruggles Bernhard September 30. Spends April in Spain with mother and Miranda, then travels to Denmark, Sweden, and Norway with his wife.

1978 Publishes *The Coup* (novel). Travels to Israel and Greece with his wife.

1979 Publishes *Problems and Other Stories* and *Too Far to Go: The Maples Stories*.

1980 *Best American Short Stories 1980* chooses "Gesturing."

1981 Publishes *Rabbit Is Rich* (novel). *Best American Short Stories 1981* selects "Still of Some Use." *Prize Stories of the Seventies* includes "Separating." Awarded the Edward MacDowell Medal.

1982 Publishes *Bech Is Back* (stories), and Knopf issues the revised *The Carpentered Hen* originally published by Harper's. *Rabbit Is Rich* wins the Pulitzer Prize, the National Book Critics Circle Award, and the American Book Award. Updike receives the Pennsylvania Distinguished Artist Award in May. Awarded an honorary degree from Albright College, Reading, Pennsylvania. Moves to Beverly Farms.

1983 Publishes *Hugging the Shore: Essays and Criticism*. *Best American Short Stories 1983* includes "Deaths of Distant Friends." *Prize Stories 1983* includes "The City."

1984 Publishes *The Witches of Eastwick* (novel). Edits and introduces *The Best American Short Stories 1984*. Publishes *Jester's Dozen*, pieces from the Harvard *Lampoon*. *Hugging the Shore* wins the National Book Critics Circle Award for Criticism. Publishes "A Soft Spring Night in Shillington." Awarded the National Arts Club Medal of Honor.

1985 Publishes *Facing Nature* (poems). *Prize Stories 1985* includes "The Other."

1986 Publishes *Roger's Version* (novel).

1987 Publishes *Trust Me* (stories). *Best American Short Stories* includes "The Afterlife." Awarded the Elmer Holmes Bobst Award for fiction.

1988 Publishes *S.* (novel). *Prize Stories 1988* includes "Leaf Season." Awarded Brandeis University's Life Achievement Award. In April visits the Wilson Sporting Goods Factory in Ada, Ohio.

1989 Publishes the memoir *Self-Consciousness* and *Just Looking* (art essays). President George H. W. Bush confers on Updike the National Medal of Arts. His mother, Linda Grace Updike dies October 10.

1990 Publishes *Rabbit at Rest* (novel). *Best American Short Stories of the Eighties* includes "Deaths of Distant Friends."

1991 Publishes *Odd Jobs: Essays and Criticism*. *Best American Essays 1991* includes "The Female Body." Wins the "First O. Henry Prize" for "A Sandstone Farmhouse"; it is selected for *Prize Stories 1991* and *Best American Short Stories 1991*. *Rabbit at Rest* wins the Pulitzer Prize and the National Critics Circle Award.

1992 Publishes *Memories of the Ford Administration* (novel). *Best American Essays 1992* includes "First Things First." Awarded a Doctor of Letters degree from Harvard.

1993 Publishes *Collected Poems 1953–1993*. *Best American Short Stories 1993* includes "Playing with Dynamite."

1994 Publishes *Brazil* (novel) and *The Afterlife and Other Stories*. *Best American Essays 1994* includes "The Disposable Rocket."

1995 Publishes *Rabbit Angstrom: A Tetralogy* (novels) and *A Helpful Alphabet of Friendly Objects* (poems). *Prize Stories 1995* includes "The Black Room." Awarded the Howells Medal from the American Academy of Arts and Letters. Awarded the French rank of *Commandeur de l'Ordre des Arts et des Lettres*.

1996 Publishes *Golf Dreams* and *In the Beauty of the Lilies* (novel). Revises the "Rabbit" novels for the Fawcett Columbine edition.

1997 Publishes *Toward the End of Time* (novel). Awarded the Campion Award as "a distinguished Christian writer."

1998 Publishes *Bech at Bay* (stories). *Best American Short Stories 1998* includes "My Father on the Verge of Disgrace." *Best American Essays 1998* includes "Lost Art." Edits *The Best American Short Stories of the Century* which includes his "Gesturing." Edits *A Century of Arts and Letters*, contributing the "Foreword" and the chapter, "1938–47: Decade of The Row." Awarded the National Book Foundation Medal for Distinguished Contribution to American Letters.

1999 Publishes *More Matter: Essays and Criticism*.

2000 Publishes *Gertrude and Claudius* (novel). *Licks of Love* (stories) includes "Rabbit Remembered," the final installment of the "Rabbit" saga. *The Best American Essays of the Century* includes "The Disposable Rocket."

2001 Publishes *Americana and Other Poems* and *The Complete Henry Bech*. *Best American Short Stories 2001* includes "Personal Archaeology."

2002 Publishes *Seek My Face* (novel).

2003 Publishes *The Early Stories 1953–1975*. President George W. Bush awards Updike the National Medal for the Humanities.

2004 Publishes *Villages* (novel). *Best American Short Stories 2004* includes "The Walk with Elizanne." *The Early Stories 1953–1975* wins the PEN/Faulkner Award in Fiction.

2005 Publishes *Still Looking: Essays on American Art*.

2006 Publishes *Terrorist* (novel). Awarded the Rea Award for lifetime contribution to the art of the short story.

2007 Publishes *Due Considerations: Essays and Criticism*. Awarded the Gold Medal in Fiction from the American Academy of Arts and Letters.

2008 Publishes *The Widows of Eastwick* (novel). *Best American Spiritual Writing 2008* includes the poem "Madurai." *Best American Essays 2008* includes "Extreme Dinosaurs." Begins "The Last Epistle," a novel about St. Paul. National Endowment of the Humanities lecture, "The Clarity of Things: What Is American in American Art?"

2009 *Endpoint and Other Poems* and *My Father's Tears* (stories) are published. *The Maples Stories* is re-issued. Dies January 27. Some of his ashes are buried in his parents' plot in Plow Cemetery. "The John Updike Society" is launched.

Posthumous Publications

2010 *Hub Fans Bid Kid Adieu* re-issued with a revised introduction.

2011 *Higher Gossip: Essays and Criticism*, ed. Christopher Carduff, is published

2012 *Always Looking: Essays in Art*, ed. Christopher Carduff, is published

2013 *John Updike: The Collected Stories*, ed. Christopher Carduff, is published

2015 *John Updike: Selected Poems*, ed. Christopher Carduff, is published

Chapter Notes

Preface

1. Though he gave hundreds of interviews, Updike resisted personal questions. In an early interview Updike declared, "My life ... is only that of which the residue is my writing." His training at Harvard taught him to approach literary works without recourse to biographical information, and he must have desired the same approach to his own work. So it is no surprise that when his own creation, Henry Bech, interviewed him (!) he received this response:
Q (*getting down to business*): Now, I have here a number of more specific and personal questions which—
Tape Recorder: Click.
2. Despite this, Updike reviewed several biographies for *The New Yorker*, Dreiser and Katharine White among them.
3. Updike thought my *John Updike Encyclopedia* could proceed because "it seems harmless, though an awful lot of work for you, poor devil." Letter from Updike to De Bellis, July 15, 1997.
4. Yet, as Martin Amis remarked, Updike is the most autobiographical author. For example, Updike stated in his "Foreword" to *Olinger Stories* that although his stories were not an autobiography, *Olinger Stories* "made one impossible." Clearly, Updike resented anyone but him drawing connections between himself and his fictional characters. Making such links, he wrote, was "morbid." Although he wished to protect real persons about whom he made what he called "composites," Mary did identify some persons described in *Couples*. Recent commentators on the stories "The Bulgarian Poetess" and "Walter Briggs" have discovered real persons behind the "composite." The creation of the John Updike Society and *The John Updike Review* could be realized only after his passing. See also my discussion of the relation of Nancy Wolf to Updike's work in *John Updike's Early Years*, 89–99.

Introduction

1. The novel was a perfect fit for my freshman literature course, and Updike was a perfect fit for me. After all, I had been born in Philadelphia three years after Updike. When I began teaching, Updike starred in all my courses—literature, film, composition, and, naturally, creative writing. When I began a book on the Rabbit novels, I realized a bibliography was needed, so I supplied one and he signed it. Then I compiled an encyclopedia and a biography, while contributing essays and speaking at conferences. Driving this fixation was my thirty-year correspondence with Updike. He generously supported my projects.
2. The only years in which Updike published no books were: 1961, 1967, 1973, and 1980. The following books have been published since his death: *Endpoint and Other Poems, My Father's Tears, The Maples Stories, Hub Fans Bid Kid Adieu, Higher Gossip: Essays and Criticism*, and *Always Looking: Essays in Art*.
3. Although he reviewed biographies of Theodore Dreiser, Edith Wharton, Katharine S. White and others, Updike asserted that such interest in the writer's life was "morbid"

(Plath, 27). The serious reader apparently makes the biographer unnecessary, as he suggested in "On Literary Biography": "When an author has devoted his life to expressing himself, and, if a poet or a writer of fiction, has used the sensations and critical events of his life as his basic material, what of significance can a biographer add to the record?" *Due Considerations:* [3].

    4. Linda Updike wrote an autobiographical novel, *Enchantment*, and a collection of stories, *Predator*, treating Updike's "destiny." The fictionalized mother in "Flight" is described by Allen Dow, Updike's fictionalized stand-in, as having a "genius" for giving "people closest to her mythic immensity. I was the phoenix." *The Early Stories*, 57.

    5. See my *John Updike's Early Years*, 109–112. As president of his class, Updike attended every reunion. His love of what he called his "Pennsylvania thing" is amply described in: Dorothy Lehman Hoerr, "Shillington Native, World-renown Author John Updike." *Berks County Living* May-June 2005:48; Dusty Kreider, "The Class of 1950 at Shillington High School Remembers John Updike and He Remembers Them." *Susquehanna Magazine* 3 (Jan. 1978):18; and Ellen Sulkis, "Berks County Game: Find Yourself in John Updike's Books." *The Sunday Bulletin* [Philadelphia] 21 Nov. 1965. 10.

    6. For a fictionalized description of his high school experiences see "A Sense of Shelter" and "Flight." *The Early Stories*, 41–66, esp. 63–64.

    7. "Seniors." *Hi-Life*. Shillington, Pennsylvania: Senior Class of Shillington High School 1950. 31.

    8. As late as 1969 in his poem "Midpoint" Updike wrote:
        Praise *Disney* for dissolving *Goofy's* stride
        Into successive stills our eyes elide.
Since this couplet is sandwiched between remarks about two artists he loved, Henry Green and Jan Vermeer, these lines are all the more significant.

    9. Updike's children and their birthdates are: Elizabeth (April 1, 1955), David (January 19, 1957), Michael (May 14, 1959), and Miranda (December 12, 1960).

    10. Eventually he would publish 750 pieces in *The New Yorker*, about 300 poems and stories, and more than 300 reviews.

    11. James Plath, *Conversations with John Updike* (Jackson, Mississippi: University Press of Mississippi, 1994), 25.

    12. General comment on the progress of *Rabbit, Run.*

    13. Updike's daughter Elizabeth married a doctor from Ghana, and his son David married a teacher from Kenya.

    14. A *Bildungsroman* is a novel that dramatizes a large portion of a person's life, especially how it is linked to his family. Though the traditional hero grows to accept society's values, Updike shows the weakness of such values, in charting the life of Essie Wilmot/Alma DeMott.

    15. Plath, *Conversations with John Updike*, 25.

    16. Randall Jarrell, *Poetry and the Age* (New York: Vintage, 1955), 112.

Part I

    1. Updike said in an interview: "Having had a mother who did go to such lengths to reclaim a piece of Pennsylvania soil ... I think that women do get more out of a sense of ownership and land than men do. To men, at least my men, as they seem to emerge in the books, the property is often an encumbrance, it's a ball and chain around your feet, it keeps you from flying." David Cheshire, "John Updike: A Small-Town Boy Who Tried To Make The Most Of What He Had." *The Listener.* 28 Jan. 1982: 4–6.

    2. Joan Youngerman recalled that she and Updike wrote the captions. Updike must have written his own at least; the caption refers to him as "the Sage of Plowville."

    3. *Self-Consciousness*, 41.

    4. *Endpoint*, 26.

    5. Albright College is in Reading, Pennsylvania.

    6. Wolfgang Amadeus Mozart (1756–1791) is declared by some as the greatest composer of classical music.

7. Fred Muth was one of Updike's closest friends. He became a lawyer. He is mentioned in Updike's poem, "Peggy Lutz, Fred Muth 12/13/08."

8. Mrs. Thelma Kutch Lewis taught German and was advisor to *Chatterbox* at Shillington High School. She also supervised the nearby playground where Updike played roofball and other games.

9. Robert Arndt graduated in 1947 from Shillington High School, where he starred in basketball. Updike watched him during the season of 1946-47 and noted, "there was something very pale and rabbity about him" (Plath xvi). How did Updike come to know Bob Arndt so well? As Harlan Boyer explained, in 1947-48, Updike's father Wesley was allowed two tickets to all the basketball games in the Berks County, and Boyer accompanied Updike to every game. The star of the team was Bob Arndt, and Updike said "I used him as a model of the super athlete." De Bellis, *John Updike's Early Years*. 93.

10. "While Updike was still in Kindergarten, his mother persuaded artist Clint Shilling, grandson of the town's founder, Samuel Shilling, to provide painting lessons. A painter and sculptor, Shilling specialized in mural painting. He had done drawings based on his experiences in the Mexican border campaign of 1916-1917 against Pancho Villa, and during World War I. Shilling had earned an international reputation as an art restorer, and he worked on the renewal of the Reading Museum (*SC* 21). Since Clint Shilling lived across Philadelphia Avenue from the Updikes, they must have met informally many times. Updike honored him by describing one of his lessons to his "Kindergarten eyes" in his memoir and by noting the importance to his development in his philosophical poem "Midpoint."" (De Bellis, *John Updike's Early Years*. 26; John Updike, *Self-Consciousness*, n21; and John Updike, *Collected Poems* 66).

11. Charles J. "Jack" Hemmig (Jan. 1, 1893-June 22, 1989) became Supervising Principal of Shillington High School. He hired Updike's parents and recommended John Updike for a full scholarship to Harvard (*Story* 70-71, 95, 99-100).

12. "By her senior year she [Peggy Lutz] was dating exclusively Tjaden ("Jady") Roberts, a 1948 graduate of Shillington High School, whom she later married. Her death came six weeks before Updike's. De Bellis, *John Updike's Early Years*. 70.

13. Estelle Pennypacker taught French at Shillington High School.

14. Tootie was a character played by Margaret O'Brien in the film *Meet Me in St. Louis*.

15. Wernher von Braun was a German engineer instrumental in developing rocket technology for Germany and then the United States during and following World War II.

16. Updike's essay on Ted Williams, "Hub Fans Bid Kid Adieu," *The New Yorker* 36 (22 Oct. 1960): 109-31 is often considered the finest piece of sports journalism, and it capped Updike's life-time devotion to the Boston Red Sox Hall of Fame slugger. No doubt he was unaware that when he was five years old Reading's Dom Dallessandro was traded from the Red Sox to San Diego of the Pacific Coast League to acquire Ted Williams. Also, in the 1946 World Series Williams played against Reading's Whitey Kurowski, St. Louis Cardinals third baseman from 1952 to 59. Williams played alongside first baseman/outfielder Dick Gernert, also a Reading native. Updike thanked Williams in a letter "for enhancing his life and all he had done to give him 'some notion of excellence to shoot for.'" (Brian Smith, "Sportswriters' Notebook." Reading *Eagle* 12 June, 2016.)

17. *Meet Me in St. Louis* by Sally Benson. See footnote 29.

18. A card game.

19. After graduating from Muhlenberg College and Lehigh University, Russell Kistler taught social science at Shillington High School.

20. *Villages*. New York: Knopf, 2004. This novel depicts multiple affairs.

21. Boscov's Department Store is primarily located in Pennsylvania.

22. Updike was a guest in the 1976 parade celebrating the 175th anniversary of Shillington's founding. Updike's story, "The Parade" (1976), concerns a celebrity returning to his hometown, a town similar to Shillington. (See, "The Parade." *John Updike: Collected Early Stories*. Christopher Carduff, ed. [New York]: The Library of America, [2013]. 47-52.)

23. John Updike, "The Alligators" in *John Updike: Collected Early Stories*. Christopher Carduff. [New York]: The Library of America, [2013]. 164-70.

24. *The Alligators*. Mankato, Minnesota: Creative Education, 1990. This is a special edition.

25. Mary Pennington, a Radcliffe art student. She married Updike in 1954.

26. Jack and Patricia De Bellis attended the program and, asking three women how they knew Updike, were delighted to hear them chorus, "We dated him!"

27. Bruce R. Posten. "Berks-born Author John Updike Dies." Reading *Eagle* 28 Jan. 2009: A2.

28. A fishing resort in Berks County north of Reading.

29. Originally a series of *New Yorker* short stories by Sally Benson, *Meet Me in St. Louis* was adapted for the movies by Irving Brecher and Fred F. Finklehoffe in 1944. The movie starring Judy Garland and Margaret O'Brien was a huge success.

30. "East on Philadelphia Avenue was the Poorhouse, the setting for Updike's first novel, *The Poorhouse Fair*. The Poorhouse was authorized in 1824 and situated on the former property of Thomas Mifflin along the Old Lancaster Road. It contained 417 acres, and was purchased for $16,690. On October 21, 1825, the first poor people were admitted, octogenarians William Hydecam, and his wife Dorothea. Normally the institution housed about 350 people prior to 1885. Other important buildings on the property were the Insane Building (1837) and the Hospital (1871–1874)." De Bellis, *John Updike's Early Years*. 26.

31. Beth E. Trapani, "Pastor Revs up Fun." Reading *Eagle* 23 July 1994: B1, B4.

32. Probably the baby was Elizabeth who was born April 1, 1955.

33. In an apparently apologetic poem, the first letters of each line, read vertically, spell "Nuts." Updike added a self-mocking note to two poems in *Chatterbox*.

34. Franklin and Marshall College is in Lancaster, Pennsylvania, about 30 miles from Shillington. Updike went to Lancaster when researching James Buchanan who had lived nearby.

35. Nickname of the Brooklyn Dodgers' outfielder Edwin Donald "Duke" Snider (1926–2011).

36. In John D. Forester, Jr.'s "Berks-born Updike Ignores Hometown" the reporter accused Updike of shunning Shillington. Reading *Eagle* 13 Feb. 2005: 15.

37. Tommy Dorsey (1905–1956) was a bandleader noted for his smooth trombone playing. Among his most popular songs were: "Song of India," "Marie," and "You."

38. This was a common misconception among classmates. Although Updike sent his cartoons to many magazines, no cartoons have yet been discovered in them. He did, however, publish a political cartoon in the Amesbury *Daily News*, July 22, 1958.

39. Math teacher Paul F. Freed.

40. A poem by James Whitcomb Riley, 1853–1916.

Part II

1. Whit Burnett, *This Is My Best*. Dial Press, 1942. Ninety-three living American authors selected their best poetry, essays, drama and stories, and defended their choice.

2. See, for example: *Buchanan Dying, The Coup, Roger's Version, Brazil, S., Seek My Face*, and *The Witches of Eastwick*. He also used his research for many stories and poems.

3. In 1973 Updike acknowledged in his "Phi Beta Kappa" poem (published privately by Harvard) the continuing impact of Harvard since it "hatched" him, took him in raw, then "spit him out a gentleman." If he had "no regrets" he also felt "little gratitude."

4. The futuristic comic strip was drawn by Alex Raymond. It began publication January 7, 1934.

5. De Bellis adds: Austin Briggs's Note: "For more of my impressions of Haven Hill, see Begley, 404–5. John's friend Joyce Carol Oates was on the mark, I think, when she wrote to him that the house reminded her of the East Egg mansion of Tom and Daisy Buchanan that Jay Gatsby gazed at longingly across the bay from West Egg (Begley 404)."

6. Austin Briggs's Note: "Concerning the illustration he was working on for John's 'The Lucid Eye in Silver Town' that would appear in the May 23, 1964, issue of the *Saturday Evening Post*, Dad wrote to his art director reporting that John was 'very pleased' that he had been given the assignment. John had confirmed over the phone, Dad said, his suspicion that the story was at least in part autobiographical, supporting his plan to portray the thirteen-year-old boy from the story after what he imagined John would have looked like at that age."

7. Austin Briggs's note: "I replied that the gift was John's to do with what he wished, and the sketch duly appeared on the dust cover of Knopf's new edition in 1977. My first wife Margaret added a long postscript to my reply to John that included the following, which I think worth preserving: Explaining that in the last few years of his life, Edmund Wilson used to visit us in nearby Clinton from his up-state New York home in Talcottville, she said that she had mentioned to him John's essay about recalling reading *Memoirs of Hecate County* at age fourteen. When she had asked Wilson what he thought of *Couples*, she told John, the answer was on the order of, 'Oh, my dear, I can't read that. I can't make love now.' Margaret added that she wondered whether Wilson 'would have recognized himself as one of the parents of *Couples*.'"

8. John Updike, "One of My Generation," *The New Yorker* (November 15, 1969): 57–58.

9. Sam Tanenhaus, who was granted special access to the Updike archives when it was being processed at Harvard, described the relationship between the roommates as "reciprocal." Sam Tanenhaus, "The Roommates: Updike and Christopher Lasch," The *New York Times* 20 June 2010.

10. CL to Parents, 19 September 1950, CLP, b0, f2.

11. Plath, *Conversations with John Updike*, 23; John Updike, "The Christian Roommates" in *The Early Stories, 1953–1975* (New York, 2003), 174; and Updike, "Apologies to Harvard" in *Collected Poems, 1953–1993* (New York, 1993), 120–125.

12. CL to Parents, 19 September 1952, CLP, b0, f8; CL to Naomi Dagen, 15 February 1954, CLP, b0, f34; CL to Parents 6 May 1954, CLP, b0, f12.

13. CL to Parents, 19 September 1950, CLP, b0, f2. According to Jack De Bellis, Updike chose Harvard over Cornell precisely because the former boasted *The Lampoon*. "He considered himself a cartoonist when he entered Harvard, not a writer." Jack De Bellis to author, 1 July 2011, letter in possession of author.

14. Updike, "One of My Generation," *Museums & Women and Other Stories* (New York, 1972), 178. Updike reprinted a modified version of this short story in his collection *Museums & Women and Other Stories* (New York, 1972), 175–180.

15. CL to Parents, 19 September 1950, CLP, b0, f2; Updike, "The Christian Roommates" in *The Early Stories*, 168.

16. CL to Parents, 9 April 1951, CLP, b0, f5. Interestingly, during this trip, Lasch visited Reading, Pennsylvania, as well as Shillington.

17. CL to Parents, 1 October 1950, CLP, b0, f2; CL to Parents, 23 October 1950, CLP, b0, f2.

18. CL to Parents, 26 September 1950, CLP, b0, f2.

19. CL to Parents, 7 February 1951, CLP, b0, f5; CL to Parents, 15 February 1953, CLP, b0, f10. While he failed to get his material published by any renowned national magazines, Lasch did have one success with the college's literary magazine, *The Harvard Advocate*. The story, "Christmas 1853" was about a young family that lived in a house in which the previous owner hung himself in the attic and remained there for seven days. The main character, a little girl, "could smell it at night." This same little girl, who for many Christmases prayed to receive a horse for her present, finally gets it at age 13. "Christmas 1853" in CLP, b58, f1.

20. For quotes on the exchange between Updike and Lasch as writers, see Tanenhaus, "The Roommates: Updike and Christopher Lasch"; Lasch, "Imperialism and the Independents," CLP, b58, f30, 60.

21. CL to Parents, 15 February 1953, CLP, b0, f10; CL to Parents, 22 September 1952, CLP, b0, f8.

22. CL to Parents, 26 September 1950, CLP, b0, f2; CL to Parents, 6 November 1950, CLP, b0, f2; CL to Parents, 12 April 1953, CLP, b0, f10. "The spectacle of Updike's easy schedule constantly calls attention to my own," Lasch moaned to his parents, "None of his courses seem to demand any work, and all he does is write his novel." CL to Parents, 9 October 1951, CLP, b0, f5.

23. Updike, "The Christian Roommates" in *The Early Stories*, 167–168, 170; Updike, "One of My Generation," in *Museums and Women*, 175. Ludwig commented about the latter

story: Perhaps in a gesture of goodwill—as we shall see, there are some hard words about "Popper" in the story—Updike sent Lasch a copy of *Museums & Women* with a long inscription. The note directed Lasch to a different story, "The Invention of the Horse Collar," which Updike suggested was inspired by a Harvard political science course that they had taken together. Interestingly, in pointing out "The Invention of the Horse Collar," Updike skirted around drawing attention to the unflattering depiction of Lasch in "One of My Generation" which ends with Popper growing "eccentric and fat" after college. But Lasch could doubtless have missed the point, and indeed he returned the favor in private correspondence, issuing cutting jibes about Updike's pretentiousness while also mocking his former roommate's "beaked" nose. In his more vindictive moments, Lasch took pleasure in the occasional hiccup in Updike's rise to literary fame. "I saw the Updikes last night," he wrote in the fall of 1955, making no attempt to cover his delight. "They don't like New York. Updike seems a little disillusioned with *The New Yorker*—it isn't as much like *The Lampoon* as he had expected. Their baby is fat and doesn't say a hell of a lot. Babies sure are stupid." CL to Paula Budlong, 29 September 1955, CLP, b0, f28c.

As of February 2014, the inscribed copy is available for sale on AbeBooks.com, and was called to my attention by Jack De Bellis, for which I am grateful. Finally, I should note that while "Popper" has many Laschian characteristics, it is possible that he is a composite sketch of Lasch and their freshmen year hall-mate, Edward French. Further, in their sophomore and junior years Updike and Lasch lived in a dormitory triple with a young man named Reginald Hannaford, who might also have factored into Updike's semi-fictionalized accounts.

I hasten to also add that in correspondence with me, Adam Begley, currently at work on a biography of Updike has suggested that he believes "Popper" is a combination of two of Updike's friends from his later years in college, English-majors Charles Neuhauser and David Chandler. While he has evidence to support this claim—Chandler identified himself as "Popper" to Begley—I find compelling linkages to Lasch in the character: the Nebraskan roots, the fact that "Popper" was a roommate of the Updike-based narrator, the over-wrought writing style Updike describes, etc. In short, though I concede that "Popper" may not be purely derived from Lasch, I believe he strongly informs the character. Adam Begley to author, 4 July 2011, letter in possession of author.

24. Robert Herrick (1591–1674) was an English lyric poet. Horace (65 BC–8 BC) was a Roman lyric poet and satirist whose *Odes* treat love, friendship, philosophy, and the art of poetry.

25. Lasch, "Imperialism and the Independents," CLP, b58, f30; Tanenhaus, "The Roommates: Updike and Christopher Lasch"; Ward W. Briggs, Jr., "One Writer's Classics: John Updike's Harvard," *Amphora* 1.2 (Fall 2002): 6–8, 14–15. Ludwig comments: "While I have not seen any sources to confirm this, Adam Begley has suggested to me that placing second to Lasch rankled Updike deeply. The evidence of the tensions underlying this friendship gives me no pause to think otherwise." Adam Begley to author, 20 November 2010, telephone interview.

26. Fox, "An Interview with Christopher Lasch," 3. As Lasch told Fox: "I was reading everything he [Updike] wrote almost, for the *Advocate* and the *Lampoon*, and I think it must have been getting through to me that he was a lot better at this than I was."

27. Honoré Daumier (1808–1879) was a French artist famous for his satirical engravings and drawings.

28. Manfred Karnovsky (1918–1999) was a molecular biologist who became Harvard's Harold T. White Professor of Biological Chemistry. He was the husband of Anna Rosenblum.

29. Hyman Bloom (1913–2009) was called the first Abstract Expressionist in America. He depicts grim subjects.

30. Updike published over 700 works in *The New Yorker*. See Jack De Bellis and Michael Broomfield, *John Updike: A Bibliography of Primary and Secondary Materials, 1948,-2007*. Oak Knoll Press, 2008.

31. William Maxwell, Jr. (1908–2000) was *The New Yorker* fiction editor (1936–1975). Maxwell's thirteen books include novels and story collections.

Part III

1. Henry Green was the pen name of Henry Vincent Yorke (1905-1973). Updike cited the English novelist as an influence on him, particularly for his style.
2. In Henry James' *The Ambassadors,* Lambert Stretcher makes a similar remark to Little Bilham.
3. David Levine (1926-2009) was a caricaturist who drew Updike many times from photos, especially for *The New York Review of Books.*
4. Tarbox is the locale of *Couples.*

Part IV

1. The title *Endpoint* (2009) was chosen to echo the poetry collection *Midpoint* (1969), in which Updike explored his life at the half-way point.
2. The American Academy of Arts and Letters awards membership to the greatest writers, artists and composers in America. Updike was its President (1987-1990), and received its W. D. Howells Medal in 1995. Updike edited the history of the academy, *A Century of Arts and Letters,* and provided a "Foreword" and a chapter, "1938-1947: Decade of the Row."
3. In 1967 John Barth sent a typescript of his review of Jorge Luis Borges's books ("The Author as Librarian.") *The New Yorker* 30 Oct. 1965: 223-24, 226-28, 231-36, 238, 241-46. [Reviews *Other Inquisitions, 1937-1952* and *Dreamtigers,* by Jorge Luis Borges; and *Borges the Labyrinth Maker,* by Ana Maria Barrenechea.])
4. PEN is a society of writers which strives "to ensure that people everywhere have the freedom to create literature, to convey information and ideas, to express their views, and to make it possible for everyone to access the views, ideas, and literatures of others."
5. Robie Mayhew Macauley (1919-1995) was an American editor, novelist and critic. Pamela Painter is the author of several story collections.
6. Alan Lelchuk is a professor, editor, and the author of eight novels.
7. Maureen Howard (born 1930) is an American writer, editor, and lecturer known for her autobiography *Facts of Life* which won a National Book Critics Circle Award. She received the Literary Lion Award from the New York Public Library.
8. Gericault's *Raft of the Medusa* (1819).
9. *The Faerie Queene* is an English epic-allegorical poem of Edmund Spenser (1552 /1553-1599). Published in 1590 and 1596, it praises Queen Elizabeth I, who granted Spenser a pension for life.
10. Norman Podhoretz (born 1930) is an American neoconservative writer for *Commentary* magazine. He was often critical of Updike.
11. Vidiadhar Naipaul (born 1932), is a Trinidadian Nobel Prize-winning British writer who has published more than 30 books, fiction and nonfiction. Naipaul was knighted in 1989.
12. Anthony Hecht (1923-2004) was an American poet who wrote of his Second World War experiences and the Holocaust.
13. Randall Jarrell (1914-1965) was an American poet, novelist, and critic. He served as Poet Laureate in 1956.
14. "The Speaker's Millennium Lecture Series" was established in 2000 by the late Speaker of the House Matthew J. Ryan. The event was designed to be a gift to the millions of Pennsylvanians who enjoy and appreciate the arts and humanities, especially Pennsylvania history." (*The Speaker's Millennium Lecture 2007,* vi). Presented by the Pennsylvania Humanities Council in partnership with Speaker of the House Dennis M. O'Brien. April 23, 2007.
15. James Buchanan, the 15th president of the United States, appears in two Updike works—the closet drama *Buchanan Dying* and the novel *Memories of the Ford Administration.*
16. Erskine Caldwell (1903-1987) was an American Southern writer. In *Tobacco Road, God's Little Acre* and other novels he depicted and condemned poverty, racism and social injustice.

17. Glenway Wescott (1901–1987) was a Wisconsin writer whose protagonist of *The Grandmothers* reflects on his family history dating to the Civil War.
18. *The United Methodist Hymnal Number 144.* Text: Maltbie D. Babcock. Music: Traditional. English Melody; adapted by Franklin L. Sheppard.
19. Karl Barth (1886–1968) was considered the greatest Protestant theologian of the twentieth century, and Paul Tillich (1886–1965), the greatest Christian existentialist philosopher and Lutheran theologian.
20. Gilbert Keith Chesterton (1874–1936) was an English man of letters famous for his fictional priest-detective, Father Brown.
21. Søren Kierkegaard (1813–1855) was a Danish philosopher and theologian, generally recognized as the first modern existentialist philosopher.
22. Rudolf Otto (1869–1937) was a German theologian and comparative religion scholar.
23. David Silcox's correction: "The shop was owned by my godparents. They wanted to give it to him but he declined as he was only eight years from being 65 and didn't want the responsibility of running a small business." Silcox, e-mail 5/25/16.
24. John O'Hara (1905–1970) was an American fiction writer whose work examines society and class distinctions. He is perhaps best known for *Appointment in Samarra* (1934) and *Butterfield 8* (1935).
25. Conrad Richter (1890–1968) was an American novelist whose Ohio frontier novel *The Town* won the 1951 Pulitzer Prize.
26. Anton Chekov (1860–1908), dramatist and short fiction writer, was born in a city in southern Russia. He became a doctor and contracted tuberculosis while publishing stories in local newspapers. His plays include: *The Seagull, Uncle Vanya, Three Sisters* and *The Cherry Orchard*. When translated into English he became an influence on Vladimir Nabokov and James Joyce, writers who made major impacts on Updike.
27. Possibly *A Glimpse of Scarlet* (1991).
28. Count Leo Tolstoy (1828–1910) was the foremost Russian novelist and essayist. His *War and Peace* is often hailed as the greatest novel of modern times. He also wrote the story "The Death of Ivan Ilyich" and the novel *Anna Karenina*.
29. Virginia Woolf (1882–1941) was an important modernist novelist of the twentieth century. A leader of the intellectuals comprising the Bloomsbury Group, she wrote *Mrs. Dalloway* (1925) and *To the Lighthouse* (1927).
30. *Bech: A Book,* p. 134.
31. Sir Henry Maximilian "Max" Beerbohm (1872–1956) was an English writer and artist. *Zuleika Dobson*, his sole novel (1911) and his caricatures are his best-known work.
32. Jane Smiley was Professor of English at Iowa State University, 1981 to 1996. Among her two-dozen books is her novel *A Thousand Acres* which won the 1992 Pulitzer Prize, the National Book Critics Circle Award for fiction, and was made into a 1997 film.
33. "Wife-wooing." *The Early Stories.* New York: Knopf, 2003. 350–53.
34. Jay Gatsby, the tragic hero of F. Scott Fitzgerald's *The Great Gatsby*.
35. "Many Bens." *Odd Jobs.* New York: Knopf, 1991. 240–61, with notes, 252, 253 and 256.
36. "Grandparenting." *Afterlife*, New York: Knopf, 1994. 298–316.
37. "At War with the Eskimos." J. D. Salinger's *Nine Stories,* published in 1953.
38. John Hawkes (1925–1998), an American post-modern writer, had taught English at Brown University (1958–1988).
39. Frederick Busch (1941–2006) was a short story writer who won the American Academy of Arts and Letters Fiction Award in 1986.
40. *Olinger Stories* was re-issued on the fiftieth anniversary of its original publication. New York: Knopf/Everyman's Pocket Classics, 2014.
41. After his death, many of Updike's stories were published in two volumes as a boxed set: *Collected Early Stories* and *Collected Later Stories*. Ed. Christopher Carduff. [New York]: The Library of America, [2013].
42. Andrei Sinyavsky (pseudonym, Abram Tertz; 1925–1997) was a Russian dissident writer and political prisoner.
43. Updike had written "Sinyavski" rather than "Sinyavsky."

44. "The American Scholar" was a speech given by Ralph Waldo Emerson about creating an American identity.
45. "Friends from Philadelphia." *The New Yorker* 30 Oct. 1954: 29–32.
46. *Endpoint*, p. 3.

Part V

1. The Myopia Country Club.
2. John Updike answered a question about the relation of a cartoon wizard [*The Wizard of Id*] to the wizard in his story, "Should Wizard Hit Mommy?" this way: "The wizard story came about because I used to tell my children, when they were little, wise old wizard stories. I would make them up, and the first couple were pretty good, I thought, but after a while these nights keep coming around and they deteriorated in quality, I thought. But my youngest child, my daughter, really became hooked on these wise old wizard stories.... Roughly, an animal of some kind was in some sort of fix and needed a cure. And the wizard came and, instead of making it better, made it worse. That is, he was an inept and very irascible wizard. But I don't know how this relates to your wizard or the cartoon wizard." James Plath, *John Updike's Pennsylvania Interviews*. Question and Answer session following a reading at Moravian College, March 12, 1982. Bethlehem, Pennsylvania: Lehigh University, 2016.
3. Lillian Hellman (1905–1984), an American dramatist (*The Little Foxes*, 1939) who was famously blacklisted by the House Committee on Un-American Activities. Robert Crichton (1925–1993) was the American author of the acclaimed *The Secret of Santa Vittoria*.

Appendix

1. This is a selective chronology. More details can be found in my *John Updike Encyclopedia*, xxv–xxxiii; and the following works edited by Christopher Carduff: *The Collected Stories: Collected Early Stories*, pp. 879–909, *Collected Later Stories*, pp. 917–47, and *Selected Poems*, 279–84.
2. *Assorted Prose*. 211n.
3. The Shillington home was sold by Dr. Hunter in 2008 to the Niemczyk Hoffman Advertising Agency. The Agency sold it to the John Updike Society in 2012.
4. See, "My Uncle's Death," collected in *Assorted Prose* 200–09.
5. James Plath, *Conversations with John Updike*, 165–66.
6. *Early Stories* [ix]. See Begley, 94.

An Updike Bibliography

Novels

The Poorhouse Fair. New York: Knopf, 1959.
Rabbit, Run. New York: Knopf, 1960.
The Centaur. New York: Knopf, 1963.
Of the Farm. New York: Knopf, 1965.
Couples. New York: Knopf, 1968.
Rabbit Redux. New York: Knopf, 1970.
A Month of Sundays. New York: Knopf, 1975.
Marry Me: A Romance. New York: Knopf, 1976.
The Coup. New York: Knopf, 1978.
Rabbit Is Rich. New York: Knopf, 1981.
The Witches of Eastwick. New York: Knopf, 1984.
Roger's Version. New York: Knopf, 1986.
S. New York: Knopf, 1988.
Rabbit at Rest. New York: Knopf, 1990.
Memories of The Ford Administration. New York: Knopf, 1992.
Brazil. New York: Knopf, 1994.
Rabbit Angstrom: A Tetralogy. New York: Knopf, 1995. No. 214 in Everyman's Library.
In the Beauty of the Lilies. New York: Knopf, 1996.
Toward the End of Time. New York: Knopf, 1997.
Gertrude and Claudius. New York: Knopf, 2000.
Seek My Face. New York: Knopf, 2002.
Villages. New York: Knopf, 2004.
Terrorist.New York: Knopf, 2006.
The Widows of Eastwick. New York: Knopf, 2008.

Short Fiction

The Same Door. New York: Knopf, 1959.
Pigeon Feathers. New York: Knopf, 1962.
Olinger Stories. New York: Fawcett, 1964. (Reissued, NY: Knopf/Everyman's Pocket Classics, 2014.)
The Music School. New York: Knopf, 1966.
Bech: A Book. New York: Knopf, 1970.
Museums and Women and Other Stories. New York: Knopf, 1972.
Problems and Other Stories. New York: Knopf, 1979.
Too Far To Go: The Maples Stories. Greenwich, Connecticut: Fawcett, 1979. (Reissued as *The Maples Stories*. New York: Knopf/Everyman's Pocket Classics, 2009.)
Bech Is Back. New York: Knopf, 1982.
Trust Me. New York: Knopf, 1987.
The Afterlife. New York: Knopf, 1994.

Bech at Bay. New York: Knopf, 1998.
Licks of Love: Stories and a Sequel, "Rabbit Remembered." New York: Knopf, 2000.
The Complete Henry Bech. New York: Knopf/Everyman, 2001.
The Early Stories 1953–1975. New York: Knopf, 2003.
My Father's Tears. New York: Knopf, 2009.
Collected Early Stories. New York: The Library of America, 2013.
Collected Later Stories. New York: The Library of America, 2013.

Poetry

The Carpentered Hen. New York: Harper's, 1958.
Telephone Poles. New York: Knopf, 1963.
Verse. New York: Fawcett, 1965.
Midpoint. New York: Knopf, 1965.
Tossing and Turning. New York: Knopf, 1977.
Facing Nature. New York: Knopf, 1985.
Collected Poems, 1953–1993. New York: Knopf, 1993.
Americana and Other Poems. New York: Knopf, 2002.
Not Cancelled Yet. Boise, Idaho: Limberlost, 2003.
Endpoint. New York: Knopf, 2009.
Selected Poems. New York: Knopf, 2015.

Literary Essays and Criticism

Assorted Prose. New York: Knopf, 1965.
Picked-up Pieces. New York: Knopf, 1975.
Hugging The Shore. New York: Knopf, 1983.
Odd Jobs: Essays and Criticism. New York: Knopf, 1991.
More Matter. New York: Knopf, 1998.
Due Considerations. New York: Knopf, 2007.
Higher Gossip. New York: Knopf, 2011.

Memoir

Self-Consciousness. New York: Knopf, 1989.

Other Collections

Just Looking. New York: Knopf, 1989.
Golf Dreams. New York: Knopf, 2000.
Still Looking. New York: Knopf, 2005.
Always Looking. New York: Knopf, 2012.

General Bibliography

Baker, Nicholson. *U and I*. New York: Random House, 1991.
Begley, Adam. *Updike*. [New York]: HarperCollins, 2014.
Bloom, Harold, ed. *Modern Critical Views: John Updike*. New York: Chelsea House, 1987.
Boswell, Marshall. *John Updike's Rabbit Tetralogy: Mastered Irony in Motion*. Colombia: University of Missouri Press, 2001.
Broer, Lawrence R, ed. *Rabbit Tales*. Tuscaloosa: University of Alabama Press, 1998.
Bruccoli, Mary, ed. *The Dictionary of Literary Biography Documentary Series*. Vol. 3. Detroit, Michigan: Gale, 1983. 251–320.
Campbell, Jeff H. *Updike's Novels*. Wichita Falls: Midwestern State University Press, 1987.
Cheshire, David. "'A Small-Town Boy Who Tried to Make the Most of What He Had.'" *The Listener* 28 Jan. 1982: 6.
Cobblah, Elizabeth Updike. "Remembering Daddy." John F. Kennedy Library Tribute to John Updike. 7 June 2009.
Corbett, Burl N. "Lightning Bolt Led to Author Updike." *Country Shoppers News* 3 Feb. 1987: 35.
De Bellis, Jack. *The John Updike Encyclopedia*. Westport, Connecticut: Greenwood Publishing Group, 2000.
_____. *John Updike, 1967–1993: A Bibliography of Primary and Secondary Sources*. Foreword by John Updike. Westport, Connecticut: Greenwood Publishing Group, 1994.
_____, and David R. Silcox. *John Updike's Early Years*. Bethlehem, Pennsylvania: Lehigh University Press, 2013.
DeBellis, Jack, and Michael Broomfield. *John Updike: A Bibliography, 1947–2007*. Foreword by John Updike. Newcastle, Delaware: Oak Knoll, 2007/2008.
De Bellis, Jack, ed. *Critical Responses to John Updike's "Rabbit" Saga*. Westport, Connecticut: Praeger, 2004.
Detweiler, Robert. *John Updike*. New York: Twayne, 1972. Revised, 1984.
Greiner, Donald J. "John Updike." *Dictionary of Literary Biography Yearbook: 1980*. Detroit: Gale, 1981. 107–16.
_____. "John Updike." *Broadening Views, 1968–88: Concise Dictionary of American Literature Biography*. Detroit: Gale, 1989. 276–297.
_____. "John Updike." *Dictionary of Literary Biography*: Ed. Mary Bruccoli. *Documentary Series: An Illustrated Chronicle*. Volume 3. Detroit: Gale, 1983. 251–320.
_____. "John Updike" in *American Novelists since World War II*, ed. James R. Giles and Wanda H. Giles. Volume 143. 250–276. Dictionary of Literary Biography, Third Series. Detroit: Gale Research, Inc., 1994.
_____. *John Updike's Novels*. Athens: Ohio University Press, 1984.
_____. *The Other John Updike*. Athens: Ohio University Press, 1981.
Hamilton, Alice, and Kenneth Hamilton. *The Elements of John Updike*. Grand Rapids: Eerdmans, 1970.
Hartman, Susan Beth. "The Role of the Berks County Setting in the Novels of John Updike." Diss. U of Pittsburgh. 1987.
Hunt, George. *John Updike and the Three Great Secret Things*. Grand Rapids: Eerdmans, 1980.
Kreider, Dusty. "The Class of 1950 at Shillington High School Remembers John Updike and He Remembers Them." *Susquehanna Magazine* 3 (Jan. 1978):18.

Luscher, Robert M. *John Updike: A Study of the Short Fiction*. Boston: Hall, 1992.
Macnaughton, William R, ed. *Critical Essays on John Updike*. Boston: Hall, 1982.
McEwan, Ian. "On John Updike." *New York Review of Books* 12 March, 2009: 4, 6.
McGrath, Charles. "Farewell: John Updike." *Time* 28 Dec 2009–4 Jan. 2010: 164–65.
McTavish, John. *Myth and Gospel in the Fiction of John Updike*. Eugene, Oregon: Cascade Books, 2016.
Markle, Joyce B. *Fighters and Lovers*. New York: New York University Press, 1973.
_____, Anthony Olivas, and Herb Yellin, et al., eds. *The John Updike Newsletter*. n. p. 1975–1981.
Miller, D. Quentin. *John Updike and the Cold War*. Columbia: University of Missouri Press, 2001.
Neary, John M. *Something and Nothingness*. Carbondale: Southern Illinois University Press, 1991.
Nelson, Barry. "The House on Philadelphia Avenue." Unpublished typescript. Fourteen pages, plus two pages of deeds and one page of photos. April 1999.
_____. Interview, May, 2009.
_____. "John Updike at Shillington High School." No date. Unpublished typescript. October, 2002.
_____. "The Updike Terrain." Reading, Pennsylvania. Typescript. Eleven pages. 1996.
_____. *Updike's Pennsylvania Interviews*. Bethlehem, Pennsylvania: Lehigh University Press, 2016.
Newman, Judie. *John Updike*. New York: St. Martin's, 1988.
O'Connell, Mary. *Updike and the Patriarchal Dilemma*. Carbondale: University of Southern Illinois, 1996.
Perkins, Wendy, ed. "A & P." New York: Harcourt Brace College Publishers, 1998.
Plath, James. *Conversations with John Updike*. Jackson: University Press of Mississippi, 1994.
Pritchard, William H. *Updike*. South Royalton, Vermont: Steerforth Press, [2000].
Ristoff, Dilvo. *John Updike's Rabbit at Rest*. New York: Lang, 1998.
_____. *Updike's America*. New York: Lang, 1988.
Schiff, James A. *Updike's Version*. Columbia: University of Missouri, 1992.
_____. *John Updike Revisited*. Boston: Twayne, 1998.
_____, ed. *The John Updike Review*. Fall, 2011–present.
Searles, George J. *The Fiction of Philip Roth and John Updike*. Carbondale: Illinois University Press, 1985.
Stafford, William T., ed. *Modern Fiction Studies* (John Updike Number) 20 (Spring 1974).
Sulkis, Ellen "Berks County Game: Find Yourself in John Updike's Books." *The Sunday Bulletin* [Philadelphia] 21 Nov. 1965. 10.
Tallent, Elizabeth. *Married Men and Magic Tricks*. Berkeley: Creative Arts, 1982.
Taylor, Larry E. *Pastoral and Anti-Pastoral Patterns in John Updike's Fiction*. Carbondale: Southern Illinois University Press, 1971.
Thorburn, David, and Howard Eiland, eds. *John Updike: A Collection of Critical Essays*. Englewood Cliffs: Prentice, 1979.
Trachtenberg, Stanley, ed. *New Essays on Rabbit, Run*. New York: Cambridge University Press, 1993.
Updike, David. "A Toast to the Visible World: Remembering John Updike." *Eulogy read at the New York Public Library's* Tribute to Updike. March 19, 2009.
Uphaus, Suzanne Henning. *John Updike*. New York: Ungar, 1980.
Vargo, Edward P. *Rainstorms and Fire*. Port Washington, New York: Kennikat Press, 1973.
Vaughan, Philip H. *John Updike's Images of America*. Reseda: Mojave, 1981.
"View from the Catacombs." *Time* 26 Apr. 1968: 66–68, 73–75.
Yerkes, James, ed. *John Updike and Religion*. Grand Rapids, Michigan: W.B. Eerdmans, 1999.

Index

"Ace in the Hole" 73
Adam and Eve Sleeping 77
Adams, Betty 34
Adultery in the American Novel: Updike, James, Hawthorne 155, 156
The Afterlife 2, 158
Albee, Edward 128
Albright College 10, 15, 16, 64
"The Alligators" 33
Alvernia University 106, 121–126, 178–188
Always Looking 77, 96
America (magazine) 7
"American Century" 79
American Motorcycle Association 48
"The American Scholar" 163
American Short Story Writers Since World War II 161
American Telecommunications Diversified 40
"America's Man of Letters" 5
Ames Library 144
Amherst College 101–102
And Then there Were None 31
Anderson, Sherwood 82
Angell, Roger 74
Angstrom, Harry 19
"A&P" 115, 117, 160, 167
"Apologies to Harvard" 79
Arlen, Michael 74
Arndt, Bob 19, 44, 56
art and artists: Benarda Palm 69–72; Carlton Boyer 45, 54, 61–63, 69; Clint Shilling 20, 53–54, 61; as "great secret thing" 6, 139; in *Hi-Life* 4; in high school newspaper *see Chatterbox*; Joan Conrad 62–63; Reading Museum 56; reviews 77, 90
The Art of Youth: Crane, Carrington, Gershwin 90
Asian woman 26, 32
Associated Writing Programs, Boston 116
Astra-Zeneca 10
At the Heart of the Universe 101
The Atlantic 119
Atlas Powder Co. 10

Backhander, Richard W. 35–37
Bague Bindery 38

Baker, Nicholson 2, 118–121, 161
Ballentine edition 154
bandage wrapping 29
baptism, John 48
Barth, John 2, 97–98
Barth, Karl 113
Barth, Shelly 97
Barthold, Richard 30, 56
The Bartlet's Tale 89
baseball 38, 111–112
basketball 18, 37–38, 44, 57–58
Baxter, Charles 137
Bech, Henry 7, 88, 146, 159, 163
Bech: A Book 7
Bech at Bay 7
Bech Is Back 7, 156, 169
Becker's Garage 122
Beerbohm, Max 144
Begley, Adam 2, 145–147
Behney, Barbara Hartz 12–13, 29, 53–56
Bell, Madison Smartt 137
Bell Telephone 61
Bellow, Saul 7, 151
Benchley, Robert 73
Benjamin's Crossing 114
Berger, Shirley F. Smith 24–27, 29–30
Bergman, Stephen 98–101
Bergman, Toby 99–100
Beverly Farms (1976–2009) 95–172
Big Little Books 9, 13, 54, 57, 60
Bill W. and Dr. Bob 101
birth: John 1, 4, 42–43; Linda 1
Black Forest Park 58
Blackwell Companion to the American Short Story 161
Blake, William 156
Bloom, Hyman 84
Blotner, Joseph 151
Bobbie, Yogi 19
book reviews 5
book signings: Barbara Behney 55; enjoyment 8; Guerin 52; Luscher 160; Moravian College 105; Youngerman family 28–29, 31
Borgman, Jim 2, 128
Bowdoin Prize 82
Bowers, Fredson 151–153

box hockey 17
Boyer, Carlton 45, 54, 61–63, 69
Boyer, Harlan L. 42–48
Brazil 96
Briggs, Austin 2, 76–78
Broomfield, Michael 153
Brown University 92, 94
Bruccoli, Matthew J. 154, 155
Bryer, Jackson 168
Bryn Mawr College 121
Buchanan Dying 15, 87–88, 93–94, 152
bullying 21
Burt, DeVere 127–128
Busch, Frederick 154
Bush, George W. 147
By Its Cover: Modern American Book Cover Design 77

Caldwell, Erskine 46, 108
Calvin College 149–150
Cambridge University 15
Camp David, New York 21
Carduff, Christopher (editor of posthumous books) 96
Carnegie-Mellon 116
carnival 23
The Carpentered Hen 5, 13, 77, 89, 153
cartoons, in *Chatterbox* see *Chatterbox*
Cassar, Ann Weik 10–14, 59, 64
Catawba College 158
The Catcher in the Rye 151
Caulfield, Holden 151
The Centaur 60; awards 93; Caldwell in 46; characters 45; Corbett influenced by 107–112; Council opinion 67; Dr. Rothermel in 24, 26; familiar characters 13; Hemmig in 21–23.52; as introduction to John's work 22; local people's opinion 33; Michael's thoughts on 184–185; mythical theme 6; real persons traceable to 38; recorded version 128; for student instruction 115; Wesley featured 87–88; written at young age 89
Chatterbox 73, 155; advisor for 39; as alumni newsletter 66; Benny Palm on 70–71; class president and 17; editorial page 59; Jim Trexler cartoon 15; staff members 12, 30, 33–34, 37–38; works published 4, 9, 62, 63, 68
Chavetz, Hope 164–167
Cheever, John 8, 145
children: John and Mary 2, 50, 96, 98, 100, 112, 173–188; Plath 140
children's books (Plath) 141
children's books (Smith) 116–117
children's books (Updike) 52, 88, 116–117
Chillingworth, Roger 6, 95
"The Christian Roommates" 80, 82
chronology, of life and works 189–193
The Clarity of Things: What Is American About American Art 169

class president 14, 17, 29–30, 37
class reunions *see* reunions
classmates, interviews with 9–72
Clayton, Alfred 95
Clockwatch Review 139
Cobblah, Elizabeth Updike 2, 171–174, 178–188
Coetzee, J. M. 147
Cold War, impact on fiction 161–167
Collected Poems 96
collections 206
Collier's 61, 73
Columbia University 82
Columbian Cutlery, Inc. 15
Columbus Museum of Art 118
Conch Republic Prize for Literature 141
Conlan, Maureen 127
Conrad, Allyson 61
Conrad, Harlan 61–63
Conrad, Joan Borner 61–63
Conrad, Michael 61
Conversations with John Updike 140–141, 143, 145
Coon Tales 112
Corbett, Amber 107–112
Corbett, Burl N. 1, 2, 107–112
Cornell University 73
correspondence 8, 14; Gerry Potts 17; James Schiff 131–136; Jay Parini 113; Joan Venne 28; Joyce Carol Oates 172; parents 84; Robert Rhoads family 19–20; routine with 92; Silcox 126
Council, Myrtle 66–68
The Coup 7, 95, 155
Couples 157; art work for 77; Asian woman and 32; family moving after 183–184; financial benefit 88, 93; John wishes in 47; from memories 168; real persons in 26, 51, 142; sex in 6, 13, 156
Cozzens, James Gould 154
Crab Barn 16
Crane's Beach 178
Crews, Frederick 102
Crichton, Robert 181
A Criminal Power: James Baldwin and the Law 167
Crosscurrents 110

dancer, John as 62–63
Daniel Boone High School 108
Danner, Blythe 168
Daubert, Bobby 54
Daubert, Richard 54
Daumier, Honoré 83–84
Davidson, David Austin 78
Davidson, Richard A. 167–170
Davis, Lynne 147–148
"Dawson" 82
Dear Madeline: Letters to the Daughter I Never Had 138

death: John 3, 9, 20; Linda 20, 96, 111–112, 123; Wesley 20, 21, 88
De Bellis, Jack 104–106, 124–125, 153
De Bellis, Patty 104–106
"Deceptively Conceptual" 77
Delbanco, Nicholas 88–90
DeLong sisters 30
Descartes, René 79
Dickey, James 141
Dickinson, Charles 150
Dickinson, Raymond 11
Dimmesdale, Arthur 6, 88, 95
Disney, Walt 4, 57, 169
divorce 32, 94
Do Not Enter: The Visa War Against Ideas 94
"The Dogwood Tree: A Boyhood" 88, 162
The Doll-Master 172
Double Fold: Libraries and the Assault on Paper 120
Dreams from My Father (Obama) 176
Drew, Ned 77
Duke University 158
dust jackets, design 77

The Early Stories 1953–1975 113–114, 159–160
Eaton Literary Agency Short Fiction Contest 112
"Ed Popper" 80, 82
Edgeworth, Maria 162
Edmund Campion award 7
Eifert, Jouette 54
Eliot, T.S. 9, 84, 151
Emerson, Ralph Waldo 163
Empire State Building 144
Enchantment 148
Endpoint 5, 17, 34, 68, 96, 97, 114, 164, 172
English Papers 104
Ephrata whitewash incident 43, 54, 71
Essick, Larry 13
Evening Bulletin, Philadelphia 9
"Evening with a Great Teacher" 128
The Explorer King 171

F. Scott Fitzgerald Award 167
family *see* children
farm *see* Plowville
Faulkner, William 108, 151–152
The Fermata 120
Festival of Faith and Writing 149–150
feuilletons 170–171
Fiedler, Leslie 129
Fitzgerald, F. Scott 154
Five Boyhoods 16
Flannery O'Connor in the Age of Terrorism 150
Flash Gordon 76
Flickinger's ice house 17
Flood, C. B. 74
Fogg Museum 80, 83
Fool's Hill 30

"The Football Factory" 114–118
Forry, William 25, 35–36, 43, 60
Four Witches 77
Fox, William Price 116
Frank A. Franco Library 122
Frankhauser, Mahlon 35, 54
Franklin, Ben 150
Franklin and Marshall College 55
Frederick, Dolores 59
Freed, Paul 11
Fresh Air 138–139
Freyleue, Miranda Updike 177–188
"Friends from Philadelphia" 28, 172
Frost, Robert 84, 151–152, 158

Gallen, Jim 32
"gangs," high school and neighborhood 4, 17, 35–36, 54, 65
The Geek's Guide to the Writing Life 138
Gelnett, Francis 30, 32
George Mason University 137
Georgetown University 115–116
Gertrude and Claudius 7, 95, 155
"Getting the Words Out" 7, 160
Gifford, Lew 74
Giles Goat-Boy 98
Girls of '51 get together 62
Glass Family stories 151
The Golden Bowl 155
Goldstein, Ann 2
golf 98–101, 176
Governor Mifflin school district 16–18, 37–39, 112
Grace Lutheran Church 48–49
Grand Valley State University 150
grandchildren, John and Mary 96, 173–188
The Grandmothers 108
The Great Gatsby 169
"great secret things" 6, 139
Green, Henry 89
Green Hill Lake summer stock 40–41
Greiner, Donald 2, 104, 135, 151–156
The Gritzer 30–31
Gross, Terry 2, 138–139
Guerard, Albert 73
Guerin, Jack E. 49–53
Guerin, Roger 51
Guiness, Alec 170
Gundy, Emerson 39–42, 43, 125
Gundy, Marlene 41, 125
Gwynne, Fred 74

Hamilton College 77, 78
Hamlet 7, 95
Hammett, Dashiell 76
"The Hamsters" 35–36
Hanema, Piet 6
"The Happiest I've Been" 36
Hartz, Clare 55
Harvard Faculty Club 100

Harvard Summer School 89
Harvard University 9, 125; *Lampoon* 4, 71–77, 118, 155; visits 36–37, 40; years at 73–85
A Haven from Violence 112
Hawkes, John 154
Hawthorne, Nathaniel 114
Hecht, Anthony 104
Heister, Richard, "Rabbit" 19, 44, 53–56
Heizmann Tool Makers 15
Hellman, Lillian 181
Hemingway, Edward 141–143
Hemingway, Ernest 82, 108, 151–152
Hemingway Days Writers' Workshop & Conference 141
Hemmig, C.J. 21, 25, 52
Henry Bech stories 155
Herrick, Robert 82
Hewitt, Avis Grey 149–150
Hi-Life (year book) 4, 9, 24, 30, 38, 53; biographies 10, 15, 24, 28, 33, 35, 37, 39, 42, 49, 53, 56, 64, 69
Higher Gossip 96
Hiller, Catherine 91–94
"His Finest Hour" 113
Hoffenstock restaurant 21
Hollis Hall 76, 79
"Home" 87
Hook, John 77–78, 87
Houghton Library 90, 100, 162–163
Houghton Mifflin Publishing Company 148
The House of God 99, 101
Howard, Maureen 102
Hoyer, John 1, 9, 10, 78
Hoyer, Katherine Kramer 1, 9, 10
"Hub Fans Bid Kid Adieu" 88
Hubbard, John 74–76
Huffington Post 138
Hunter College 131

Illinois Wesleyan University 143–145
Immanuel United Church of Christ 18–19
immortality 150
"Imperialism and the Independents" 81–82
"In Search of the 'Common Life': The Intellectual Orbit of Christopher Lasch" 82
In the Beauty of the Lilies 7, 96
"In the Cemetery High Above Shillington" 124
interviews 8
"Invasion of the Book Envelopes" 171
Ipswich, Massachusetts (1957–1975) 87–94

James, Henry 8, 150, 155, 162
Japanese woman 26, 32
Jarrell, Randall 8
John Updike: A Bibliography of Primary and Secondary Materials, 1948–2007 106
John Updike: A Study of the Short Fiction 156–157
The John Updike Encyclopedia 1, 106, 124

John Updike Revisited 136
John Updike Society 106, 144–145; family panel (October 2010) 178–188; first conference 121–126
"John Updike Week": Ohio Northern University 116; Virginia Tech 116
John Updike's Early Years 106, 124
John Updike's Novels 154, 156
Johns Hopkins 97
Jones, Judith 5
Joyce, James 9, 78, 89
"Junior Commandos" 29
"Just Before War with the Eskimos" 152
Just Looking 77, 90

Kadaba, Lini S. 121–126
Kafka, Franz 89
Karnovsky, Manfred 84
Kathryn (fictional interviewer) 164–167
Kendall, Carl 33–35
Kendall, Jacqueline J. Hirneisen 20, 26, 33–35, 54
Kistler, Russell 31
Klinkenborg, Verlyn 171
Knopf 74, 77, 88, 96
Knox fellowship 73, 85
Kohler, Dale 6, 120
Kroninger, Rev. Victor 48–49
Kurowski, George "Whitey" 24
Kutztown University 69

Labor-in-Vain Road 91
Lambert, Roger 6, 95, 165
Lampoon 4, 71–77, 118, 155
Larue's hardware store 43, 46
Lasch, Christopher 78–83
The Last Crossing 114
"The Last Epistle" 7
The Last Station 114
Lastingness: The Art of Old Age 90
Lawrence, H. 13
Lawrence University 145
"Leaf Season" 157
learning, John continuing 70
Leggert, John 116
Lehigh University 3, 104–106, 124
Lelchuk, Alan 102
"The Lens Factory" 115–118
LeVan, Jackie 54
LeVan, Nancy March 29, 64–66
LeVan, William 64
Levine, David 92
Lewis, Edmund 63
Lewis, Sinclair 157
Lewis, Thelma Kutch 19, 22, 39, 123–124
Licks of Love 96
"The Lifeguard" 152
literary essays and criticisms 206
"The Literature of Exhaustion" 98
"Little Golden Book" 116–117

Little Magazine 119
The Little Shilling 13, 33–34, 45
Look Homeward, Angel 154
Love Factories 117–118
Lowell, Robert 80
Lowell House 75, 83
Lucky Street Gallery 142
Ludwig, Jeffrey 79–83
Luscher Robert M. 156–161
Lutheran Theological Seminary 48

Macauley, Robin 98
MacLeish, Archibald 73
"Made in Ada: The NFL Football" 117–118
Mailer, Norman 7–8, 94, 146, 151, 167
Mailer, Norris Church 167
Main Street 157
The Man Without a Shadow 172
Mandrake store 84
"Many Bens" 150
The Maples Stories 96, 150, 168, 172, 176
Marry Me 88, 137, 143–144, 155
Marshfield, Tom 6, 88, 95, 165
Martha's Vineyard trips 181
Marx, Karl 79
Matthew Brady: Portraits of a Nation 171
Maxwell, William 5, 74
McComsey, Charles 12, 16, 24–25, 63
McCoy, Skip 23
"Me and My Shadow" 30
Meditations After the Bear Feast: The Poetic Decalogue of N. Scott Monday and Yuri Vella 118
Meet Me in St. Louis 33, 36, 40–41
Melville, Herman 5
Memories of the Ford Administration 7, 95, 132–133
memory 151–156
Metropolitan Museum of Art 90
Middlebury College 114
Midpoint 5
Miller, Arthur 169
Miller, D. Quentin 161–167
Millersville State College 42
Milton, John 79, 84
Mirren, Helen 114
Mitchell, Gene 126
Modern Book Collecting 152
Montgomery College 167
A Month of Sundays 6, 22, 88, 95, 105
Moravian College 105
More Matter 99, 117
Morgantown Library 108
Moriarty, Michael 168
mortality 164
Moskowitz, Faye 137
motorcycles 48
"Movie House" 12
movies 24, 63, 71
Moyer, Mary Ann Stanley 19, 43, 50, 54, 55

Mozart, Wolfgang Amadeus 13
Muhlenberg College 48
Museums and Women 101
"The Music School" 148, 155
music trio 64
musical abilities 12–13
musical shows, at Harvard 81–82
Muth, Fred: Big Little Book readings 13; card games 25; *Chatterbox* "feud" 36–37; chess games 51; country club membership 26; in gang 50; Gundy and 40; in handwriting class 30–31; as John's best friend 43, 59; from lawyer's family 24; play written by 65
My Father's Tears 22, 96, 172
My Name Escapes Me 170
Myopia Hunt Club 100

Naipaul, V.S. 104
narcissism 79
Nash, Ogden 73
Native Son: John Updike's Pennsylvania Interviews 145
Nature 113
Nature of First Acts 90
Nelson, Barry R. 37–39; as class president candidate 29–30; at dance 70; on John's books 44; at Pulitzer prize program 46–47; on sports teams 45; at Stephen's 65; strokes in 124
"Nessus at Noon" 171
New and Collected Poems: 1975–2015 114
New York, years in 73–85
New York Public Library 168
The New York Review of Books 102
The New Yorker 69, 115, 137; cartoons 9; poetry 5; years at 73–85
newspapers, read to grandfather 54
Niehoff, H.C. Buck 127–128
Niehoff, H.C. Patti 127–128
Niehoff, Peter 127
Nixon, Pres. Richard 53
"Non-Horatian Elements in Herrick's Echoes of Horace" 82
Novak, Peter 30
numinous writing and literature 112–114

Oates, Joyce Carol 7, 128, 171–172
Ocean Key House 142
Odd Jobs 73
Of the Farm: background 173; editions 153–154; familiar characters 13, 87; impression by 112; as Linda's favorite 111; for student instruction 115
O'Hara, John 125, 154
Ohio Northern University 116, 118
Old Girlfriends 50
Olinger Stories 159–160
Oliva, Michael 153
"On Being a Self Forever" 7, 150
"On Not Being a Dove" 7

"One of My Generation" 80, 82
Orff, Mary 71; mother 29
Ostrich 27
The Other John Updike 154
Otto, Rudolf 114
Our Town 169
Oxford University 5, 50, 73

"Packed Dirt, Churchgoing, a Dying Cat, a Traded Car" 134, 152
Painter, Pam 98
The Painterly Aspects of John Updike's Fiction 139
Palm, Benarda 69–72
Paltrow, Gwyneth 168
"The Parade" 128
parades 32
Parini, Jay 112–114
"Part of the Process" 115–118
"party of inspection" 115–118
The Passages of H.M. 114
Paul, Saint 7
Paul Bowles 94
Pennsylvania Speaker's Millennium Lecture 106
Pennsylvania State University 35, 97, 125, 126
"Pennsylvania thing" 6
Penny (*Centaur* character) 38
Pennypacker, Estelle 23
Phi Beta Kappa 73, 82
PhotoHut 91
Picked-up Pieces 162
Pienta, Edward 16
Pigeon Feathers (entire volume of stories) and "Pigeon Feathers" (single story) 115, 152, 155; fame from 89; impression 112; mortality 165–167; popularity 115–116; as Rev. Rhoads' favorite 22; rifle used in 126
Plath, James 1, 139–145, 178–188
Plath, Zarina 143–144
play productions: *And Then There Were None* 59; at Harvard 81–82; *Meet Me in St. Louis* 33, 36, 40–41
playground activities 17, 30, 53
Plimpton, George 74, 167–168
"The Plot Against Myself" 87
Plow Church 20, 111
Plowville 20; changes after 17; complaints 38; influence 4; interviews 9–72; move to 57; parties 15; renovations 42; selling farm to cousin 40; tavern incident 1; visits 6, 28, 31
Plummer, Christopher 114
Podhoretz, Norman 104
Poe, Edgar Allan 151
poetry: exhibit 3; John 5, 66, 88, 96, 206; memorizing in school 71–72; Nancy LeVan 64
Pomeroy department store 28
poorhouse: fair 23–24; fire 23; visits to 49
The Poorhouse Fair 5–6, 152; for book report 115; fame 89; impression 112; as prize winner 88
popularity, of John 29
posthumous publications 96, 136, 172, 193
Potts, Gerry 16–19, 23, 44, 56, 59
The Predators 174
Princeton University 172
Pritchard, Eddie 27
Pritchard, William H. 2, 5, 101–104, 155
Prynne, Hester 6, 95
psoriasis 24, 25, 29, 45, 50, 55, 125
Pulitzer prizes 6, 46–47, 95, 128

Rabbit, Run: as best Updike novel 5–6; carnival in 23; in college courses 3; fame from 89; fiftieth anniversary of publications 182; germ of 73; grant making possible 87; Lutheran minister in 49; movie made from 18, 60; rereading after several years 171; as research subject 152; for student book reports 115; written before age 40 93
Rabbit, Run (movie) 18, 60
Rabbit at Rest 5–6, 95, 99, 105, 127
"Rabbit" books 22, 68, 137
Rabbit Is Rich 5–6, 95, 101–102
Rabbit Redux 5–6, 88, 93
Rabbit Remembered 5–6, 8, 96
rabbits on stationery 19
Radcliffe College 4–5, 73, 83
Reading Eagle 56–60, 85, 107, 123, 180
Reading Museum 56, 61
Reading Public Library 52, 108
readings, public 97
"The Real Story" 115–118
recreation 8
religion 65; as "great secret thing" 6, 139; problems 39
Rethinking Creative Writing 138
retirement, thoughts of 145–146
reunions (Harvard) 78
reunions (high-school) 17–18, 26–27, 32, 52, 107
Rhoads, Rev. Dr. Robert I., Sr. 18–24
Rhode Island School of Design 142
Richards, Allen, Jr. 11
Richards, Allen, Sr. 11
Richter, Conrad 125
Ritter, Warren 10
Roberts, Jady 22
Roberts, Peggy Lutz: in gang 65; John's interest 17, 22, 25, 27, 54; obituary 59; at party 30, 32; as student council candidate 29–30; Wesley disciplining 50
Robinson, Roxana 129–131
Roger's Version 6–7, 95, 120, 131–136
roofball 15, 17, 18–19, 30, 57–58, 181
roommate, Harvard 79–83
Rose, Charlie 134
Rosenblum, Ann 84
Rosenthal award 87

Roth, Philip 7, 103, 146
Rothermel, Dr. Ernest 24, 26
Rougemont, Suki 6-7
The Routledge Introduction to African American Literature 167
Roxbury Community College 177
Ruskin School of Drawing and Fine Arts 73, 76-77

S. 6, 7, 52
"Sage of Plowville" 30
Salinger, J.D. 73, 151-152
The Same Door 89, 152
Sanders Theater 84
"A Sandstone Farmhouse" 124
Saturday Evening Post 20, 54, 61
Saville Book Shoppe 115
savings stamps 29
The Scarlet Letter 88, 114, 131-132, 155; trilogy 95, 169
Schiff, James 127, 131-136, 155, 158, 160
Schneider, Kenneth 97
Schoenhof store 84
scholarly abilities 38-39
Schrack, Florence 34, 52
Schrack, John 34
Schwartz, Donald 29-30
Second Street Gang 28
Secret Agent X-9 76
"secret things" 6, 139
Seek My Face 96, 164-167
Selected Poems 96
Self-Consciousness 7, 150; descriptors 149; as gift to Rev. Rhoads 20, 22; as memoir in place of biography 96; physical ailments 138-139; Trexler in 16
self teaching 73
"Seniors Stink" poem 50
sex, as "great secret thing" 6, 139
Shawn, William 5
Shem, Samuel (Stephen Bergman) 98-101
Shilling, Clint 20, 53-54, 61
Shillington, Pennsylvania, interviews in 9-72
Shillington High School 4; conversion into Governor Mifflin High School 16-17; mementos 16-18
Shillington Women's Club 68
Shivera, Joseph 63
"Should John Updike Receive the Nobel Prize?" (seminar) 106
"Should the Wizard Hit Mommy" 173
Showalter, Kathryn, classroom incidents and respect for 23, 30-31, 46, 52, 58-59, 63-65
Sideways, Irene 59
Silcox, Bradley 122
Silcox, David 121-126
Sinyavsky, Andrei 163
Skin: Sensual Tales 94
Slate Hill, games played on 56

Smart, Jane 6-7, 13
Smiley, Jane 146
Smith, Claude Clayton 114-118
Smith, Lee 137
Smith, Raymond 172
smoking 27, 43-44, 50-51
A Soft Spring Night in Shillington 7, 34, 47-48, 67
Solomon, Mr. 84
South Carolina University 156
Southern Illinois University Carbondale 148
Soviet hostility, impact on fiction 161-167
Sparta 131
The Spirit of the Place 99, 101
Spofford, Alexandra 6-7
Stamm, Margaret 11
Starbuck, George 116
Steger, Joel 128
Steinbeck, John 151
Stephen's Luncheonette 27, 38, 43-44, 55, 65, 122
Stephen's Sweet Shop 53
Sternberger, Paul 77
Stevens, Harry 21
Stevens, Wallace 84
Still Looking 90
Stork Club 76
Stovall, Floyd 151
Stover, Marty 71
stress, in New York 87
student council, campaigning for 29-30
A Study of Short Fiction 161
stuttering 20, 24, 25, 29, 36, 44-45, 50, 55, 76, 89, 125, 138-139
"Styles of Bloom" 106
Substitute: Going to School with a Thousand Kids 120
Suffolk University 163, 167
summer stock 40-41
"The Swimmer" 145
swimming hole 49

"A Tea and a Dance" 62-63
Terrorist 7, 22, 28-29, 96
Tessie (dog) 110
theologic nature, of writings 112-114
"This Is My Father's World" 111
Thomas, Timothy 158
Thorne, Freddy 142-143
Thurber, James 73
Thurlow, Brad 75
Tillich, Paul 113
Time magazine 73, 93
"To Martha, on Her Birthday, After Her Cataract Operation" 97
"To the Juniors from the Seniors" 65
Too Far to Go 7, 103, 168
Toward the End of Time 96
Train, John 74
translations 8

travel 96
Trexler, James "Jim" 15–16, 29, 32
"Tribute to John Updike" 100
"Tristan and Iseult" 158
Trollope, Anthony 171
Troy, Betty 35
Trust Me 137
"Turgid Thirties" 29
Turkish Bath 77

U and I: A True Story 120
Understanding Reynolds Price 136
Unitarian views 22
University of California Los Angeles 3
University of Cincinnati 127–128, 136, 155, 158
University of Delaware 170
University of Iowa 116
University of Maryland Overseas Program 15
University of Michigan 90
University of Michigan–Milwaukee 139
University of Nebraska 161
University of Pennsylvania 11
University of Virginia 151
University Press of Mississippi 140
Upchurch nickname 75
Updike, David 2, 50, 98, 100
Updike, Linda Grace Hoyer 1, 10–11, 14, 34; attitude toward Shillington 52; Barbara Behney and 54–55; Corbett visit to 107–112; death 96, 111–112, 123; education 16; Harvard selection 73; Jack Guerin and 51–52; Joan Venne and 31–32; John relationship with 38; move from farm 41; move to farm 4; Nancy Wolf and 26, 47; at Pomeroy department store 28; at Pulitzer program 45–46; Rhoads family and 21; Silcox visits 125; spoiling John 49; typing 45; VanLiew and 57–58; visits to 184–185; wartime work 9; writings 20, 27, 52, 68, 71, 148, 174
Updike, Martha Bernhard 14, 26–27, 58, 169, 172; Christmas card 42; final poem to 97; Linda and 42; move to Beverly Farms 88; on reunions 14; visit from Joyce Carol Oates 172
Updike, Michael 2, 178–188
Updike, Toby 99–100
Updike, Wambui 177
Updike, Wesley 1, 4, 31, 34; Barbara Behney and 54–55; as basketball ticket collector 44; in *The Centaur* 87; classroom mementos 16–18; as coach 15, 21; death 6, 88; driving habits 40; at Grace Lutheran Church 48–49; grandchildren's view of 186; John embarrassed by 25; marriage 9; Plymouth of 28; sense of humor 39; as teacher 11–14, 24–27, 30, 36, 46–50, 57–58, 62, 64, 67, 69, 108

Updike, Wesley (grandson) 177
Updike, America's Man of Letters 104
Updike and the Cold War 167
Updike in Cincinnati 136
"Upon Coming a Senior Citizen" 42
Ursinus College 16

"The Valley of Ashes" 169
Vanderslice, Stephanie 137–138
Van Horne, Darryl 7
VanLiew, Tony 56–60
Venne, Mark 28–29
A View from the Bridge 169
Villa, Pancho 61
Villages 77, 96, 156
Virginia Tech 116
"Visual Poetry" exhibit 3
von Braun, Werner 25
Vonnegut, Kurt 7
Vox 120

Walker, Dennis "Wildman" 135
Wallace, John Foster 8
Wanamaker's Department Store 61–63
"At War with My Skin" 7
Weatherall, Mary Pennington Updike 11, 14; children 2, 98, 100, 111–112, 173–178, 250; correspondence 67; divorce 32, 88; at family panel (October 2010) 178–188; father 22; golf friends 91; at Harvard lecture 89; Harvard years 73, 83–85; interviews for book 2; marriage during Harvard years 4–5; Rhoads family visiting 21
Weaver's Orchards 107–109
Weik, Luther 11–13, 43
Weik, Martha 11–13
Welch, Carey 74
Wescott, Glenway 108
Wesley Updike Field 111–112
Wesleyan University 115
Western Electric 35
White, E.B. 73
White, Katherine 73, 121
Whitman, Foxy 26–27
Whitman, Walt 8, 151
Whitner's Tea Room 35
Widener Library 83
The Widows of Eastwick 6–7, 50, 96, 155
"Wife Wooing" 148, 152, 156
Wilder, Thornton 169
Williams, Ted 29, 57–58
"Willow" 87
Wilson, Robert 152, 170–171
Wilson Sporting Goods factory 117–118
Windmill Restaurant 21
The Witches of Eastwick 6–7, 13, 65, 77, 96, 106, 154
Wolf, Chaplain 21
Wolf, Nancy 21, 25–27, 31–32, 39, 50, 62–63, 66, 70

Wolfe, Thomas 154
Women's Club of Shillington 68
work ethic 93
World War II: activities during 29; effects on Shillington 23; *Lampoon* during 74–75; Myrtle Council in 66
Worth, Sarah 6, 95
Writers' Workshop 116
writing marathons 81

Writing Seminars I 97
Wyomissing Polytechnic Institute 35

Yale University 115
Youngerman, Joan Venne 14, 26, 43, 55–56, 65, 71
Youngerman, Mark 28–29

Zug, Joan George 29, 31–32, 43, 50, 65

www.ingramcontent.com/pod-product-compliance
Ingram Content Group UK Ltd.
Pitfield, Milton Keynes, MK11 3LW, UK
UKHW041953140426
5217IPUK00015B/773